PERSON-ENVIRONMENT PRACTICE

MODERN APPLICATIONS OF SOCIAL WORK

An Aldine de Gruyter Series of Texts and Monographs

SERIES EDITOR

James K. Whittaker

Paul Adams and Kristine E. Nelson (eds.), **Reinventing Human Services: Community and Family Centered Practice**

Ralph E. Anderson and Irl Carter, **Human Behavior in the Social Environment: A Social Systems Approach** (Fourth Edition)

Richard P. Barth, Mark Courtney, Jill Duerr Berrick, and Vicky Albert, **From Child Abuse to Permanency Planning: Child Welfare Services Pathways and Placements**

Kathleen Ell and Helen Northen, **Families and Health Care: Psychosocial Practice**

Marian Fatout, **Models for Change in Social Group Work**

Mark W. Fraser, Peter J. Pecora, and David A. Haapala, **Families in Crisis: The Impact of Intensive Family Preservation Services**

James Garbarino, **Children and Families in the Social Environment** (Second Edition)

James Garbarino, and Associates, **Special Children—Special Risks: The Maltreatment of Children with Disabilities**

James Garbarino, and Associates, **Troubled Youth, Troubled Families: Understanding Families At-Risk for Adolescent Maltreatment**

Roberta R. Greene, **Social Work with the Aged and Their Families**

Roberta R. Greene, **Human Behavior Theory: A Diversity Framework**

Roberta R. Greene and Paul H. Ephross, **Human Behavior Theory and Social Work Practice**

André Ivanoff, Betty J. Blythe, and Tony Tripodi, **Involuntary Clients in Social Work Practice: A Research-Based Approach**

Susan P. Kemp, James K. Whittaker, and Elizabeth M. Tracy, **Person-Environment Practice: The Social Ecology of Interpersonal Helping**

Paul K. H. Kim (ed.), **Serving the Elderly: Skills for Practice**

Jill Kinney, David A. Haapala, and Charlotte Booth, **Keeping Families Together: The Homebuilders Model**

Robert M. Moroney, **Social Policy and Social Work: Critical Essays on the Welfare State**

Peter J. Pecora, Mark W. Fraser, Kristine Nelson, Jacqueline McCroskey, and William Meezan, **Evaluating Family-Based Services**

Peter J. Pecora, James K. Whittaker, Anthony N. Maluccio, Richard P. Barth, and Robert D. Plotnick, **The Child Welfare Challenge: Policy, Practice, and Research**

John R. Schuerman, Tina L. Rzepnicki, and Julia H. Littell, **Putting Families First: An Experiment in Family Preservation**

Madeline R. Stoner, **The Civil Rights of Homeless People: Law, Social Policy, and Social Work Practice**

Betsy S. Vourlekis and Roberta R. Greene (eds). **Social Work Case Management**

James K. Whittaker, and Associates, **Reaching High-Risk Families: Intensive Family Preservation in Human Services**

PERSON-ENVIRONMENT PRACTICE
The Social Ecology of Interpersonal Helping

Susan P. Kemp, James K. Whittaker,
and Elizabeth M. Tracy

ALDINE DE GRUYTER
New York

About the Authors

Susan P. Kemp is Assistant Professor, School of Social Work, The University of Washington, Seattle.

James K. Whittaker is Professor, School of Social Work, The University of Washington, Seattle.

Elizabeth M. Tracy is Associate Professor, Mandel School of Applied Social Sciences, Case Western Reserve University, Cleveland, Ohio

ALDINE DE GRUYTER
A division of Walter de Gruyter, Inc.
200 Saw Mill River Road
Hawthorne, New York 10532

This publication is printed on acid free paper ∞

Library of Congress Cataloging-in-Publication Data
Kemp, Susan P., 1953–
    Person-environment practice : the social ecology of interpersonal
helping / Susan P. Kemp, James K. Whittaker, and Elizabeth M. Tracy.
        p. cm. — (Modern applications of social work)
    Includes bibliographical references and index.
    ISBN 0-202-36102-0 (cloth : alk. paper). — ISBN 0-202-36103-9
(paper : alk. paper)
    1. Person-in-environment system.   2. Social case work—Evaluation.
3. Social service—Research.   4. Needs assessment.   5. Evaluation
research (Social action programs)   I. Whittaker, James K.
II. Tracy, Elizabeth M.   III. Title.   IV. Series.
HV43.5.K395   1997
361.3'2—dc21   97-7417
                                                                          CIP

Manufactured in the United States of America
10 9 8 7 6 5 4 3 2 1

In Memory of

Carol H. Meyer (1924–1996)
Ruth Harris Ottman Professor of Child & Family Welfare
School of Social Work
Columbia University
New York

Valued professional colleague to all social work practitioners and practice teachers. Her richly detailed view of practice and sense of context inform the spirit and content of our present work.

Contents

Foreword

Social work practice is prey to the vagaries of fashion. New approaches are adopted and applied with uncritical enthusiasm until they in turn are succeeded by a more novel approach. The pendulum in the UK has swung from specialist work to generalist and back to specialist again, but the swing has invariably been accompanied by what marketing people would call repackaging of the product as generic social work, patch, or community social work. The quest for an all encompassing approach is, however, illusory for what above all social workers should recognise is the uniqueness of each individual's human experience and the futility of applying a single approach.

Despite sharing common theoretical approaches in social work education, the development of social work practice in the UK has proceeded upon different lines from the USA. This reflects the still dominant role of the public sector in Britain providing employment for social workers, their location in multipurpose social services departments, and the focus of those departments on the delivery of services rather than individual counseling. With the exception of child and family work where skills in careful and detailed work with individuals remain the primary tool in the kitbag of the social worker, the role of social workers is focused on the organisation of services to support vulnerable individuals.

The need to secure a more holistic approach to practice is, however, as acute in Britain as in the United States. The shared context of cutbacks in welfare provision and the level of cash benefits payable to those in need, accentuates the urgency for social work better to integrate its tradition of work with individuals and families but in their social context. This task requires us to re-engage with the social policy issues at a macro level by demonstrating the consequences of the retreat from collective social responsibility. But, social workers are not politicians and their professional role may not extend beyond documenting and mapping the human and financial costs of reductions. Where, however, they have a clear professional role is in working with those who bear the brunt of these changes, helping them to articulate their needs, and to develop their own skills and resources.

Kemp, Whittaker and Tracy use the themes of empowerment and a focus on strengths to inform practice with clients, in particular those with limited financial resources, in ways that give voice to individual and collective concerns and provide a platform for action.

While the rhetoric of partnership is much used by social workers, the reality is often very different. The inevitable imbalance in the power relationship between worker and client has to be acknowledged and discussed if partnership is to be translated into action. The worker's role becomes then one in which the development of the client's skills and capacities becomes a legitimate area for joint working. Both in the UK and the USA, coercive approaches are increasingly in vogue as public authorities attempt to deal with escalating reports of child maltreatment, or seek to reduce numbers on public assistance through a variety of welfare-to-work schemes. *Person-Environment Practice*, which attends carefully both to the client's immediate context and to wider environmental realities, offers the potential for constructive partnerships even in such involuntary situations.

The long debate in Britain about specialist versus generalist practice has concentrated too much on settings for social work and too little on practice itself. Of course the complexity of human behaviour and the contemporary legislative framework are too great for omniscience from any individual. What really matters, however, is the ability of social workers to address the interaction between the client and the environment and to use that positively to develop the strengths in the situation. That is equally applicable in specialist roles as in generalist. Kemp, Whittaker and Tracy offer a valuable starting point in the task of building a holistic practice equipped to meet the challenges of the twenty-first century.

Terry Bamford
Executive Director
Housing and Social Services
The Royal Borough of Kensington & Chelsea
London, U.K.

Introduction

This book addresses a core but long-neglected dimension in social work and human services practice: accurate environmental assessment and strategic environmental intervention. Despite the centrality of "person-in-environment" as a key construct in direct practice, the domain of environmental assessment/intervention has received relatively little systematic attention in the practice literature. For a variety of reasons, the core focus of direct practice assessment and change strategies has centered more on "person" than "environment." This book seeks to redress that imbalance.

Ironically, the relative lack of attention to environmentally oriented practice persists even as current demands of practice fall increasingly under the rubric of what we here call "environmental intervention," defined as both *action in the environment and the process of transforming individual and collective perspectives through critical analysis of the impact of environmental conditions*. Indeed, we will argue in the chapters to follow that the ability to understand "environment" from the client's perspective and to function effectively in the environmental domain is central to many emergent areas of practice, such as practice with extended families and personal networks, practice from a "strengths" perspective, and culturally competent practice. In *Person-Environment Practice*, we offer a coherent critique and overview of environmental assessment and intervention congruent with the demands of both newly emerging and established interpersonal helping approaches within social work's domain.

We intend this book as both an affirmation and a challenge to direct practice in social work. We write out of the conviction that direct social work practitioners make an important personal difference in the lives of people in distress—a contribution that will never be entirely replaced by macrolevel interventions, however powerful, encompassing, or elegant. We consider, as did Mary Richmond, that the "retail" part of social services is a needed and valuable societal resource. By the same token, we are convinced that interpersonal practice—if it is to remain relevant—must reflect more accurately and respond more effectively to the complex interrelationships between clients and their proximate and distal environments. We believe strongly that the central features of environmental practice described in this book lie at the very core of what we consider to be direct practice in social work and sister human service disciplines. We define direct practice as encompassing work with individuals, families, small groups, and neighborhoods. Many important aspects of direct practice, such as fostering supportive helping networks, involve activities at the local community level as well as actions on behalf of individual clients (such as facilitating access to resources and services). The broader view enables us to address this reality. Our decision to focus this text on an expanded view of direct practice is made in full knowledge of the centrality of environment to macropractice approaches such as community organization, social planning, policy practice, and social action. The environmental dimension of these and other spheres of human service activity await further work. They lie beyond the boundaries of this present effort. We are encouraged by the recent work of scholars of practice such as Bernard Neugeboren (1996), which approaches the topic of environment from the rich and detailed knowledge base of macropractice (see Chapter 7). Similarly, even though we present environmental intervention from the perspective of multiple and interlocking systems levels, ours is not a generalist text in the commonly understood sense. We believe, nonetheless, that there is much in this present volume to enrich and enhance generalist practice as well as the major interpersonal practice approaches (e.g., task-centered, psychosocial, and cognitive-behavioral) that make up direct practice in contemporary social work. Finally, we write from the perspective of interpersonal or direct practice, but we do not attempt to cover all that is central to that domain. We have omitted, for example, core practice components such as interviewing and communication skills and specialized person-centered assessment protocols, in part because they are well documented elsewhere, but primarily because we wish to focus full attention on what we consider the neglected dimension in direct practice: environmental assessment and intervention.

We intend the primary audience for *Person-Environment Practice* to be the great majority of social workers whose helping efforts extend to individuals, families, groups, and neighborhoods. The book's primary aim is to examine each of these levels critically through the prism of environment and offer practical suggestions for both assessment and intervention. We offer a conceptual framework for understanding environmentally oriented practice; we explore its theoretical, historical, and empirical underpinnings; and we provide extensive information on environmental assessment and intervention, including assessment and intervention with personal social networks. The book is organized as follows:

Chapter 1 defines an approach to environmentally oriented direct practice that we term *person-environment practice* (P.E.P.). Key building blocks (values and principles), practice features, and challenges are identified.

Chapter 2 explores the historical legacy of "environment" in the social work practice tradition from the Progressive era to the present, with particular emphasis on the contributions of such early major architects of practice as Mary Richmond and Bertha Reynolds, as well as lesser known contributors, such as Ada Sheffield. The struggle in contemporary practice to balance person and environment is captured in the work of such scholars as Carel Germain, Alex Gitterman, Carol Meyer, and Anthony Maluccio.

Chapter 3 provides a critical perspective on the knowledge base for environmentally oriented direct practice. Critical and constructivist views of environment are explored from a wide variety of sources, including social and feminist geography. The relationship of the "strengths," "empowerment," and "ecological-systems" perspectives to environmental practice is explored. Key definitions for "environment," "environmental assessment," and "environmental intervention" are offered.

Chapter 4 provides a detailed examination of environmental assessment at five key levels: perceived environment, physical environment, social/interactional environment, institutional/organizational environment, and sociocultural environment. Central to this chapter is a detailed treatment of social support and personal network assessment using the social network map (Tracy & Whittaker 1990), viewed in the overall context of environmental assessment. General guidelines for environmental assessment are provided.

Chapter 5 focuses on environmental intervention in direct social work practice. A wide variety of intervention approaches are identified and general guidelines for environmental intervention are provided. Detailed information is provided for a number of social network interventions: utilizing "natural helpers," facilitating personal networks, working with mutual aid and self-help groups, and training clients in social network skills.

Chapter 6 deals with the diversity of environmental experience including such topics as race, class, and environment; women and environment; sexuality and space; the contexts of physical and developmental disability; and environments at the beginning and end of life.

Chapter 7 concludes the book with an analysis of future challenges for environmentally oriented direct practice in social work. These include the challenge of knowledge development (research), the challenge of knowledge dissemination (professional education and training), and professional, organizational, and political challenges and strategies for dealing with them.

Person-Environment Practice is in many ways an unfinished work. We view it as a small step in the direction of a revitalized direct service focus in social work: one that will take us back to our roots in contextually grounded, situated practice. As we will argue in the chapters to follow, an honest and critical appraisal of the place of environment in direct social work practice will lead us "back to the future": to the activities, values, and principles that are distinctive features of social work's practice heritage.

We are deeply indebted to a wide range of practice theorists, researchers, and scholars—past and contemporary—from our primary profession, social work, and from related social science fields. Their sheer numbers and the subtlety of their influences on our own views of practice preclude individual recognition here. The substance and significance of their contributions will be abundantly evident in the chapters to follow. We wish to thank our faculty colleagues and our many present and former students at the Schools of Social Work, University of Washington and Columbia University, and the Mandel School of Applied Social Sciences, Case Western Reserve University, for their substantive contributions and their critical reflections on our work at various stages of its development. We thank, as well, the numerous practitioners whose generous participation in a variety of workshops, action research projects, and consultations have sharpened our understanding of environmental assessment and intervention. We are greatly in debt to our immediate families for continuing emotional support and encouragement, as well as to our more extended kin, "fictive kin," and friendship networks for contributing so greatly to our individual sense of space and place.

Susan P. Kemp
James K. Whittaker
Elizabeth M. Tracy

1

An Introduction to Person-Environment Practice

At its heart, this is a book about what Mary Richmond ([1906] 1930) ninety years ago referred to as social work at the "retail" level. We write in the spirit of direct practice, in its broadest traditional formulation. Our primary audience is the very great majority of practitioners whose helping efforts extend to individuals, families, groups, and neighborhoods. *Our primary aim is to examine assessment and intervention activities critically at each of these levels through the prism of environment.* For a variety of reasons, we believe this examination is long overdue. Chief among these is social work's preoccupation with person-centered, overly individualistic assessment, often undertaken out of context and without regard for the complex web of environments—proximate and distal— that define and influence behavior. Systematic, critical examination of this environmental context leads us to a reformulation of direct practice that we call here *person-environment practice* (P.E.P.).

This initial chapter explores the critical features of P.E.P. as an emergent approach to social work intervention with individuals, families, small groups, and neighborhoods. Drawing on past work as well as work in progress, we will selectively explore the theory, research, value bases, and critical features of this practice approach and identify challenges for intervention design, implementation, and practice research.

We will argue that person-environment practice offers a positive social work response to the many external challenges that confront us as we attempt to meet human needs at the dawn of what promises to be a very different century for social welfare. Paradoxically, P.E.P. allows us to move forward into the next century by taking us back to some of the seminal ideas that informed our profession's infancy at the beginning of this nearly completed century. The two chapters immediately following examine this legacy in detail. In its most essential form, our message is

1

that social work practice intervention needs to return to its original conception, which placed assessment and intervention with the environment on an equal footing with assessment and intervention with the person.

This initial chapter sketches the skeletal features of person-environment practice, with greater elaboration provided in the chapters to follow. Specifically, we

1.   offer a brief definition of P.E.P. and the building blocks or principles on which it rests;
2.   briefly explore three historical practice themes that have significantly affected the development of P.E.P.;
3.   advance several compelling reasons why P.E.P. meets critical needs for renewal in social work practice;
4.   identify some of the key features of P.E.P. and briefly contrast these with selected alternative practice formulations;
5.   conclude by briefly identifying emergent challenges for P.E.P. as well as some issues posed by P.E.P. for future practice research and theory development.

We undertake these tasks in full knowledge that those practitioners and students of social work whom we seek to reach are increasingly pressed by the demands of clients as well as by the expanding prescriptiveness of the settings and systems in which they practice. We believe, with the late social psychologist Kurt Lewin, that "[t]here is nothing as practical as a good theory" (quoted in Marrow 1969, 128). Our conviction is that the ideas, practice conceptions, and strategies in the chapters that follow can inform and alter practice in ways that are helpful in both the long and short term. We write from the continuing conviction that social work practice, skillfully and compassionately delivered, has a critical impact on the lives of individual people, as well as on communities and society as a whole.

DEFINITION OF PERSON-ENVIRONMENT PRACTICE

What is person-environment practice and what are its defining features and boundaries?

Person-environment practice is an emergent model of direct practice that makes strategic use of time to accomplish three things:

1. *Improving a client's sense of mastery in dealing with stressful life situations, meeting environmental challenges, and making full use of environmental resources.*

2. *Achieving this end through active assessment, engagement, and intervention in the environment, considered multidimensionally, with particular emphasis on mobilization of the personal social network.*

3. *Linking individual concerns in ways that promote social empowerment through collective action.*

As a strategy of intervention, P.E.P. draws from such rich, diverse sources as Kurt Lewin's notion of "life-space" (1931, 1936, 1951), Bronfenbrenner's "ecology of human development" (1979, 1995), Riessman's "helper principle" (1990), and Maluccio's competency-oriented model of practice (1981) as well as a growing body of empirical research on risk and resilience that points to the power of proximate and distal environments to influence human behavior for good or for ill. P.E.P. looks to the critical function of personal ties and social support in coping and adaptation.[1]

Several aspects of the definition of P.E.P. are worthy of note. First, a clear emphasis on mastery of both environmental challenges and resources reflects a strong commitment to nurturing and supporting an active client role in both assessment and intervention, with the goal of ever-increasing levels of environmental competence. We take this view for individual clients, as well as for families, small groups, and neighborhoods. Second, our basic frame for environmental assessment and intervention for all clients is multidimensional, that is, it extends from the objective-concrete to the subjective-personal and from the proximate and familiar to the more distal and foreign. Continuing critical analysis furthers the client's developing sense of context: viewing concerns at the individual, family, group, and neighborhood level against their fullest and richest environmental backdrop. We make a particularly strong and systematic effort to understand personal social networks, both as a source of social support and challenge and also for their potential power as collectivities. Third, in our view, P.E.P. seeks to foster social as well as individual empowerment by maintaining a constant vigilance for ways to create a seamless path between individual concerns and shared actions. Our goal is an informed client able to act effectively in the many contexts of his or her life.

Most important, P.E.P. refocuses attention on *environmental intervention*, a critical and historically significant, but long-neglected construct in social work practice theory and research. The next chapter offers a detailed examination of direct social work's legacy of environmentally oriented practice, and Chapter 3 provides working definitions for environment as a multidimensional concept and environmental intervention as a core practice activity. Suffice it to say here that while we hope to break new ground and offer fresh insights in our approach to practice, we are mindful that this enterprise has roots deep in the earliest history of social work.

THE BUILDING BLOCKS OF PERSON-ENVIRONMENT PRACTICE

Person-environment practice proceeds from a value base concerning human behavior that underpins and transcends the particular interventions we discuss. Its building blocks are illustrated in Figure 1.1. We describe them as follows:

Partnership

We meet as clients and professionals on common ground and as a unified team.

Mutuality

We create an atmosphere where clients and professionals communicate openly about their most sensitive concerns in a relationship built on openness, mutual respect, and trust.

Reciprocity

We operate on what Riessman (1990) calls the "helper principle," where giving and receiving help go both ways among all of the key players: professional to client, client to professional, and client to client.

Social Assets

Our assessment begins not by looking at what is going wrong in clients (deficits), but at what is going right (strengths).

Resilience

We are always alert for those protective factors and mechanisms that blunt and divert the effects of known risk factors and permit individuals families, and groups to overcome extraordinarily difficult life situations.

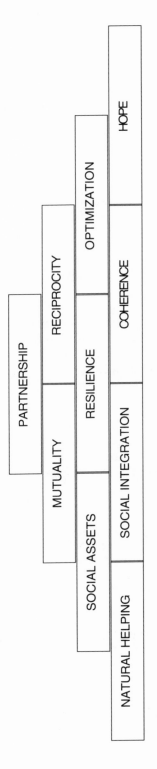

Figure 1.1. Building blocks of person-environment practice.

Optimization

Our goal is always to create conditions within which each individual, each client family, group, and neighborhood reaches the upper limit of its developmental potential.

Natural Helping

Our search is for those approaches to change that draw fully on the ability of clients and communities to aid themselves through ritual, spiritual practice, celebration, and reflection.

Social Integration

We work with the "private troubles" of individual clients in the context of raising public concern about the critical integrating function of individuals, families, small groups, and neighborhoods in maintaining social order and promoting public safety. We believe this function is often best realized after external social/environmental change has occurred. Imparting skills to cope with harmful and dangerous environments is often an important proximate goal but cannot, in our view, define the real objective of practice: to remove risk and change the environment.

Coherence

We use this term in the sense intended by the Israeli sociologist Antonovsky (1979, 1994) to describe processes through which individuals, families, and groups discern a sense of meaning beyond the struggles of day-to-day existence.

Hope

Finally, P.E.P. is about fostering a sense of hope: hope that things can change for the better, that the power for change resides within, that someone is listening . . . and cares.

SOME KEY HISTORICAL IDEAS THAT INFLUENCE PERSON-ENVIRONMENT PRACTICE

As noted, much of we offer here as a "new" practice formulation, person-environment practice, draws on many ideas that have long been at the core of social work theory and practice. We briefly identify three of these here and explore them and related ideas more fully in the next two chapters. The first notion, that of *understanding behavior in context* appears in the earliest work of the pioneer theorist of social casework, Mary Richmond, in her selection of sources for her classic texts. For example, in the introduction to her seminal casework text, *Social Diagnosis* (1917), Richmond quotes a leading physician of the day, James Jackson Putnam, on the importance of understanding the social context of individual problems:

> One of the most striking features with regard to the conscious life of any human being is that it is interwoven with the lives of others. It is in each man's social relations that his mental history is mainly written and it is in his social relations likewise that the causes of the disorders that threaten his happiness and his effectiveness and the means for securing his recovery are to be mainly sought. (p. 4)

This person-environment focus is also apparent in the origins of medical social work at the turn of the century, with its strong emphasis on the critical function of social factors in determining the outcome of physical illness. It is present in the core of settlement work, which sought to provide help in a context familiar to clients, one that celebrated cultural heritage and neighborhood diversity. We believe calls for the contextualization of social work practice require a careful examination of the roots of the person-environment nexus and the ways in which its interpretation was transformed over time. Chapter 2 tells this story in the rich detail it deserves.

A particular variant of this first theme of understanding behavior in context is the concept of "situated" practice (Haraway 1988; Kemp 1994), which we take here to mean the delivery of professional helping in the familiar environment of the client's home and neighborhood, as opposed to the often foreign and sterile environment of the clinic or agency. Social work's practice history provides a few stellar examples, such as the pioneering St. Paul family work project (Birt 1956) in the early 1950s and the more recent family support and family preservation initiatives. The family support movement, in particular, offers many recent examples of situated, multiservice practice in nonthreatening, inviting, community settings (Dunst, Trivette, & Deal 1988; Halpern 1995b; Larner, Halpern, & Harkavy 1992). Efforts at service "normalization" in such fields as developmental disabilities and mental illness provide additional examples of policies, procedures, and practices that bridge the gap between professional and client cultures (Wolfensberger 1972; Vandenberg 1993).

A second idea from the earliest of social work practice formulations concerns the *blending of concrete and clinical services*. The former refers to services such as transportation, domestic assistance (housekeeping), and respite care; the latter to interventions such as marital counseling, life skills teaching, family therapy, and group work. Again, it is Mary Richmond who provides us with an early view of the critical interplay of both types of helping. "Friendly visiting", she said in 1899,

> is not wise measures of relief; it is not finding employment; it is not getting the children to school or training them for work; it is not improving sanitary arrangements and caring for the sick; it is not teaching cleanliness, or economical cooking or buying; it is not encouraging habits of thrift or encouraging healthful recreations. It may be a few of these things, or all of them, but it is always something more. Friendly visiting means intimate and continuous knowledge of and sympathy with a poor family's joys, sorrows, opinions, feelings and entire outlook on life. (p. 180)

Recent research from what we call *intensive family preservation* services, which are designed to prevent the unnecessary placement of children into foster care, provides empirical evidence of the wisdom of Richmond's admonition, that is, the desirability of combining the concrete and the clinical (Fraser, Pecora, & Haapala 1991). For many clients, particularly those tangled in a web of interpersonal and social systemic problems, a critical first step in helping often involves restoring a simple level of dignity: helping to clean up a cluttered and chaotic apartment, restoring basic services such as electricity and telephone, providing emergency cash assistance for food. These often provide the platform for effective clinical intervention and skills teaching. Such shared activities can reduce the status differences between helpers and helped and offer hope that things can change for the better.

A third idea influencing P.E.P. that has deep roots in social work's history concerns what Richmond (1917) called "individual and mass betterment", and what the late sociologist C. Wright Mills (1959) referred to as the raising of "private troubles" to "public issues". Historically a source of contention in social work, the joining of the private/personal with the public/social has always had strong adherents among architects of practice theory. For example, within the group work tradition, Grace Coyle (1947) and others stressed the power of group efforts to achieve social goals. Person-environment practice stresses, as does feminist practice, that the personal is political and that it ought to be the aim of practice to link clients with similar problems and life circumstances so that they might find power in one another. These and many other "new/old" ideas influenced the formulation we here call person-environment practice.

SOME SPECIFIC RATIONALES FOR
PERSON-ENVIRONMENT PRACTICE

"Practice," for the individual social worker or the profession as a whole, is not a static entity. New inputs from emergent theory, current research, and—equally importantly—direct experience with clients continually shape and mold the contours of the practice repertoire. This is true at the level of interventive strategies and techniques, as well as in the conceptual models we use both to order and to explain discrete practice activities. We believe P.E.P. offers a useful framework for thinking about present, day-to-day practice with individuals, families, groups, and neighborhoods, as well as for generating fruitful hypotheses for future practice innovation and experimentation. Specifically, PEP:

- Redresses the loss of focus on environment and environmental intervention and the accompanying overemphasis on the individual in much of what constitutes direct, interpersonal, micro-level practice.
- Allows for the incorporation of empowerment at the very heart of practice activity, which we define as the "empowerment-environment" nexus.
- More fully reflects the critical importance of understanding the social construction or perception of environments, large and small, proximate and distal, as rich sources of information for client assessment.
- Actively reestablishes the boundaries of direct or interpersonal practice by extending them beyond individual, family, and group to the local neighborhood level.
- Provides a receptive and fertile practice base for such key and emergent concepts as: partnership, strengths, resiliency, and cultural competence in assessment and in intervention.
- Provides a useful, integrative framework for practice activity that is consistent with the core values of social work and serves to mitigate against the fragmentation of practice technique from its conceptual/valuative foundation. As expressed in the earlier "social treatment" formulation of two of the present authors (Whittaker & Tracy 1989), we believe that appropriate frameworks for social work practice should be: (a) clearly reflective of the values that have informed the profession since its origins; (b) broadly gauged so as to subsume differential practice methods and strategies—in our present formulation spanning client sys-

tems ranging from individuals, through families, small groups, and neighborhoods; (c) eclectic with respect to knowledge orientation; (d) contextually grounded by providing a clear and continuing focus on environments both proximate and distal; and (e) capable of producing assessment/intervention protocolsamenable to evaluation. We believe the present P.E.P. frame-work meets these criteria and substantially improves upon the earlier social treatment formulation, primarily by providing a more systematic and richly detailed view of person-in-environment.

- Finally, P.E.P. helps us to anticipate and to respond to such external practice realities as managed care, with its emphasis on goal and procedural specificity, by identifying contextually grounded practice activity and by more accurately assessing environmental risks and assets.

In sum, we believe P.E.P. offers a useful framework for practice activity that redresses the personalistic bias present in many existing modalities by providing a richer, more detailed picture of the social surround of clients, as well as concrete strategies for environmental assessment and intervention.

SOME KEY FEATURES OF PERSON-ENVIRONMENT PRACTICE

As noted above, person-environment practice draws on several interrelated historically relevant practice ideas and comprises basic building blocks reflecting values and principles consistent with social work's core mission. In our view, P.E.P. emphasizes several other features that, taken together, constitute its signature as a practice approach:

1. Strategic and Multidimensional Environmental Assessment. Despite Bronfenbrenner's (1979) early exhortation to think of environment as a set of nested structures with differing features, much of practice thinking about environment has been unidimensional. For us, accurate and complete environmental assessment means looking not simply at the *physical environment* of the individual client, family, group, or neighborhood, but also at the *perceived environment* as constructed by the client. Also important is the *social/interactional environment* including, for example, the client's personal social network as a source of both support and demand, and extending also to group associations and neighborhood networks and collectivities. Key for many clients is the *institutional/organizational environment*, including, for example, the web of health, welfare, and social service agencies with which they must deal. Finally, the *social/political/cultural environment*—what Bronfenbrenner calls the "macro system" of a society, consisting of political, cultural, and social values and beliefs as well as laws and traditions—shapes attitudes toward social problems and defines preferred solutions. Figure 1.2 illustrates the multiple levels of environment and indicates some potential directions for both multilevel environmental assessment and intervention. Chapters 4 and 5 explore these ideas in greater detail. Valid and reliable multidimensional assessment is a key feature of P.E.P.

  2. Dual Focus on Individual and Environmental Change. In our view, P.E.P helps individuals gain skills to obtain what they need from their proximate and distal environments and, simultaneously, works to alter those environments to make them more supportive of human functioning.

  3. The Critical Importance of the Client's Personal Social Network. The web of individual relationships surrounding a client includes nuclear and extended family, friends, work mates, members of formal helping services such as social workers and physicians, and members of informal helping organizations such as self-help or mutual aid groups. We envision the personal network as a source of both help and demand, and it is central to our view of person-environment assessment. Our prior work on the development and refinement of a personal network mapping tool (Tracy & Whittaker 1990) is discussed in detail in Chapter 4. We will argue that a personal network assessment ought to be seen as routine practice with the great majority of social work clients.

  4. Equal Emphasis on Concrete, Informational, and Emotional Helping. P.E.P. asks what type of help is provided and by whom. Who will care for the ill child when the parent must be at work? Who offers solace and support to the family that grieves the loss of a loved one? Who provides critical information on employment skills to the teenager about to enter the world of work? The social network map (Tracy & Whittaker 1990) assumes that all of these types of helping (concrete, emotional, and informational) are critical social life supports for individuals and should be monitored in the manner in which vital signs such as pulse and heart rate are measured in a hospital. The social network map provides a tool for continuously assessing these vital elements. It yields a series of data points that lend themselves easily to routine monitoring and are amenable to the kinds of management/practice information systems becoming more commonplace in our social agencies (Grasso & Epstein 1992).

	PERCEIVED ENVIRONMENT	PHYSICAL ENVIRONMENT	SOCIAL/INTERACTIONAL	INSTITUTIONAL/ ORGANIZATIONAL	SOCIAL/POLITICAL/ CULTURAL ENVIRONMENT
INDIVIDUAL					
FAMILY					
GROUP					
NEIGHBORHOOD					

Figure 1.2. Levels of environment × levels of client system.

5. *Personal and Social Empowerment.*   To be committed to an empowerment agenda, suggests Julian Rappaport (1990), "is to be committed
to identify, facilitate, or create contexts in which heretofore silent and
isolated people, those who are 'outsiders' in various settings, organizations and communities gain understanding, voice and influence over
decisions that affect their lives" (quoted in Saleebey 1992, 8). We believe
both individual and collective empowerment needs to be at the core of
direct practice (see Chapters 3 and 5). Various strategies for enhancing
empowerment are discussed in Chapter 5 on person-environment
intervention.

6. *Person-Centered, Yet Transcends Individual and Family Systems to
Include Group and Neighborhood Level Situated Practice.*   P.E.P. extends
the familiar framework of individual/family/group to the neighborhood level—a long-neglected and critical focus of direct social work
intervention—and places a premium on what we have earlier identified
as situated practice. This practice occurs primarily in the everyday
spaces and places our clients inhabit. Our interest is not in community
organization per se, but rather in the immediate neighborhood where
our clients reside as both foci and loci of intervention. We include here as
well the myriad informal mutual aid, social, spiritual, and indigenous
cultural groups in which our clients are imbedded.

7. *Professional Role of Network Consultant.*   In addition to the conventional social work roles of providing treatment, teaching skills, advocating, offering concrete services, and brokering social services (Whittaker
& Tracy 1989), P.E.P. includes active consultation with existing personal
networks as well as the creation of linkages between clients who share
common challenges, so that they might find strength in their collectivity.
We believe the network consultation role is a key component of P.E.P.
Also critical is flexibility for practitioners as they perform multiple roles
with shifting emphases and work across differing client/system levels in
collaboration with other professionals and lay helpers. We are convinced, finally, given our experiences in the family preservation and
family support initiatives, of the wisdom of blending concrete and clinical tasks in a single worker: We begin with client's basic needs and
assume no hierarchy of helping.

8. *Clear Value on the Power of Peer Helping, the Potential for Personal
Change and Social Advocacy, and the Importance of Client-Consumer Feedback.*   From the beginning of intervention, P.E.P. asks what each client
can contribute as well as receive: to other clients, to the social worker,
and to the collective effort in which the particular intervention is
imbedded.

9. *Participatory-Action Research.* Our view is that P.E.P. requires continuous feedback from clients for its improvement and refinement, and that consumers themselves need to be involved in the design, implementation, and dissemination of practice evaluation. For us, this goes beyond the provision of simple feedback on research generated outside the client's life web and goes to the core issues involved in defining, generating, and disseminating knowledge about the most intimate details of clients' lives. In our final chapter, we deal with knowledge development challenges posed by P.E.P.

10. *Flexible and Strategic Use of Time.* We believe that, in social work intervention, longer does not (necessarily) mean better: that brief, strategic, focused, intensive interventions buttressed by periodic "booster shots" of social support can often be more effective than long-term, open-ended intervention. We are thus interested in assessment protocols and intervention strategies that lend themselves to rapid execution in our clients' real-life environments. We are also mindful that many clients have continuing service needs because of chronic conditions, developmental trajectories that trigger new needs for helping, and changing environmental conditions. In our view, P.E.P. includes brief intensive interventions with varying levels of booster shots and follow-up, as well as longer-term helping. We view time as a critical element in strategic case planning.

11. *Reflective Practice.* P.E.P. involves neither prescription nor panacea. It presumes an active, critically thinking practitioner ever on the alert for the meanings of newly garnered assessment information, vigilant for contradictory interpretations of client behavior, and actively formulating clinical "hunches," testing them against the realities of direct client experience and against new insights from theory and empirical research.

12. *A Strong Value on Diversity.* Diversity, in all of its many forms (race, gender, class, sexual orientation, etc.) lies at the core of P.E.P. This reflects, among other things, the importance of "ecological validity," that is, understanding the environment as experienced by the client and using that understanding as a basis for intervention. It also reinforces the fact that in environmentally oriented practice there is not one modal pathway to adaptation, but many, reflecting particular niches of shared experience. Our underlying vision of the strengths of individuals, families, groups, and neighborhoods is predicated on the notion that they represent a mosaic of many different textures, shapes, and hues rather than a tightly woven tapestry.

Taken alone or in combination with other strategies of intervention, we believe P.E.P. is appropriate for a wide range of clients including, in particular, persons in transition, socially isolated clients, rural clients, clients in conflict with members of their personal network, clients living at or near poverty levels, clients whose personal networks increase the risk of physical danger and violence such as addicts or gang members, and clients in need of community integration such as those returning from institutional or group home settings. Throughout the chapters to follow, we suggest applications in such diverse fields of practice as child welfare and child mental health, family services, adolescent services, services for women in transition, substance abuse, adult mental health and developmental disabilities, health care and health promotion services, and services for the elderly.

P.E.P. AND RELATED PRACTICE APPROACHES

Person-environment practice shares similarities with several other current practice approaches, as well as differing from them in significant ways. Briefly, we illustrate this by looking at similarities and differences between P.E.P. and social treatment, the life model, and the generalist model of practice.

As noted earlier, the social treatment formulation (Whittaker 1974; Whittaker & Tracy 1989) anticipated P.E.P. with its emphasis on values, diverse knowledge sources, and the practitioner's many roles in providing help to individuals, families, and small groups—either through direct intervention or through indirect helping such as advocacy and social brokering. Five key roles of the practitioner were identified: therapist/counselor, skills teacher, social broker, advocate, and personal network/system consultant. Drawing on the earlier work of Siporin (1970, 1972) and others, the social treatment approach was meant to serve as a integrative conceptual framework for diverse practice strategies and methods with a clear emphasis on restoring a social-environmental focus in direct practice intervention.

Person-environment practice builds on and greatly expands this earlier formulation. Key additions include:

- An expanded definition of environmental assessment/intervention.
- A more explicit tie to collective social action as an integral part of direct social work practice.
- A view of intervention extended to the neighborhood level.
- More explicit emphasis on the value of critical reflection in practice, including use of narrative approaches to understand the direct impact of environments on clients' lives.

- A more central focus on social network assessment and intervention.

While building on and enhancing the earlier social treatment formulation, we also view that work as a useful complement to P.E.P., particularly regarding knowledge for practice and the overall sequence of helping activities.

P.E.P. bears many similarities to the life model of social work practice. This pioneering work developed by Alex Gitterman and the late Carel Germain (1980, 1996) provided a significant stimulus to our current work with its focus on ecology as a practice metaphor, life transitions, environmental pressures, and interpersonal processes. Differences include P.E.P.'s more detailed and explicit view of environment as a multilevel concept, greater reliance on and specification of processes for assessing social support and personal network resources, and greater emphasis on a critical view of environmental contexts. With the Life Model, P.E.P. shares a strong bias towards bridging individually-focussed interventions and collective action.

Generalist approaches to practice (Kirst-Ashman & Hull 1996; Pincus & Minahan 1973), with their emphases on multiple system levels for assessment and intervention, continue to provide us with useful insights and challenge us, as direct practitioners, to think beyond the immediate client context. For the immediate future, however, we are impressed enough with the complexities involved in specifying environmentally oriented assessment/intervention procedures for the client levels of individual, family, group, and neighborhood and communicating these to practitioners. More ambitious frameworks that seek to cover all levels of potential social work intervention are clearly beyond the scope of P.E.P. and, save at the most basic introductory level, we would argue are not particularly helpful to the development of practice knowledge or practitioner preparation, since they often yield overly general practice instructions.

CHALLENGES TO PERSON-ENVIRONMENT PRACTICE

When we speak of future challenges for the P.E.P. formulation, there are three levels at which we need to be concerned: the professional level, the client/community level, and the organizational/system level. While we will further explore these and others in the final chapter, we introduce them here to illustrate that adopting P.E.P. as an approach to practice will not be a simple matter.

At the professional level, barriers to incorporating P.E.P. include negative attitudes toward self-help and mutual aid and a value hierarchy that exalts therapeutic interventions and looks down on concrete services. For example, when we tell our students we are going to study "family therapy," their eyes light up. When we tell them we are going to study concrete helping for low-income families, their eyes glaze over! This resistance has several sources: (a) a very limited and mistakenly traditional view of what it is that "professional" social workers are supposed to do; (b) a lack of expertise in engaging clients other than in the safety of the social agency; (c) concerns about personal safety while working in high-risk neighborhoods, a legitimate issue in many of our inner-city urban areas; and (d) a sense of vulnerability in letting go of the professional need always to be "the expert." In addition to teaching new techniques of environmental assessment and intervention, we believe the social work profession has much to do in altering basic conceptions of what a social worker is and does if we are to successfully incorporate person-environment practice. Similarly, the kind of practice we envision does not fit neatly into preconceptions of what BSWs and MSWs do and, we hope, will stimulate healthy debate about what is generic and what is specialized practice knowledge in the preparation of practitioners.

At a client-community level, multiple challenges to P.E.P. exist within each of the many subgroups of clients who are high on our inventory of those with special need. These include, but are not limited to substance-abusing clients, families in crisis, frail homebound elderly clients, socially isolated clients, those living in high-risk inner-city neighborhoods, recently arrived immigrants, and chronically mentally ill clients. Many come from communities with extremely limited economic, social, and cultural resources and many will require multidisciplinary team intervention for maximum effects. Often these client groups have been approached from a deficit or problem orientation; overcoming this orientation and moving toward a strengths perspective will require shifts in practice skill and service delivery. Within each of these client groupings, we now see practitioners and clients alike developing models of effective partnership and collaboration, and this gives us hope. Our task in social work education is to translate that information from the front line of practice to the classroom.

Finally, at the level of organization and institution, we see multiple barriers to incorporating a person-environment approach to practice. One of our great epiphanies as direct social work practice teachers has been realizing the critical importance of organizational supports within the agency necessary to sustain high-quality, effective practice with individual clients. Some notable barriers in current services include restrictive agency policies that constrain the creativity of workers and limit the role of clients; liability concerns that flow from an expanded role of clients as helpers; "turf" issues between clients and workers and between different fields of social work practice about "who owns the territory." Privacy concerns, always an issue in our culture, come to the fore around access to case information and the client's right to privileged communication. Finally, in the critical area of funding, services have yet to reorient their accounting systems to pay for many of the things we will argue for in this book. We are still, by and large, oriented to paying for traditionally delivered one-on-one or group therapy and counseling services in an agency context. Work with extended family, social support network, and neighborhood remains as much a challenge for the accountants of social work as for its practitioners.

CONCLUDING COMMENT

Person-environment practice is an unfinished work. Our hope is that, beginning with this rough topography of its main features and in the more detailed chapters to follow, we offer sufficient information to stimulate further model development, empirical testing of practice strategies, and development of practice theory consistent with the revived and renewed, environmentally focused practice orientation described in this book. We like to think of P.E.P. as "practice with an attitude." We believe P.E.P. requires individuals with strong commitment and a passion for helping, who are comfortable doing situated practice, i.e., "social work without walls."

The great British social welfare theorist Richard Titmuss (1974) long ago spoke of social policy implementation as "detailed acts of imagination and tolerance." We think this is an apt description of the social work practice task: with and for individuals and families, groups, and neighborhoods; in its whole, as well as in its parts. If we are successful, this work will support and honor all citizens in society.

In the final analysis, a vibrant and flourishing social service system—comprising competent professionals in partnership with lay helpers and situated in people's real-life environments—echoes for each individual client in pain or despair the hope, comfort, and shared strength of others not presently afflicted. We begin each foray into the practice arena recalling that, save for the vagaries of birth, errant biology, class, and status, or simply circumstance, we are all but half a step away from the "other" human beings who are our "needy" or "at-risk" clients. In the final analysis, it is not "us" and "them." It is all of us together.

NOTE

1.   Although our main task in this volume is to define and elaborate an environmental perspective in direct practice, we proceed in the belief that a great many streams of research and theory development in what typically falls under the heading of "human behavior and social environment" support our emphases in assessment and intervention. Indeed, advances in these areas of knowledge development often served as stimuli to our work. As an example, the rich and growing literature on risk and resilience anchored by such classic studies as those of Werner and Smith (1982) illustrates the power of environmental supports such as the presence of adult, nonfamilial associates to mediate the harmful effects of known risk factors for adolescent delinquency and mental health problems. See also the work of Sameroff and Seifer (1995) on risk accumulation, as well as Rutter (1995), Rutter, Champion, Quinton, Maughan, and Pickles (1995), and Brewer, Hawkins, Catalano, and Neckerman (1995). An additional discussion of risk and resilience is presented in Chapter 3

The research on risk and resilience flows from an orientation to human development research typically referred to as an "ecological" or person-environment perspective. Building on Lewin's pioneering (1935, 1936) conception of the lifespace, this approach is most associated with Urie Bronfenbrenner, whose now classic work, *The Ecology of Human Development: Experiments by Nature and Design* (1979) has had a powerful effect in shaping both classic child development and family functioning research (Moen, Elder, & Lüscher 1995), as well as research and theory development in such important social problem areas as child maltreatment (Garbarino, Kostelny, & Dubrow 1991; Gaudin & Polansky 1986) and child and youth services (Whittaker, Schinke, & Gilchrist 1986). Chapter 3 provides a fuller explication of the ecological perspective.

Similarly, while we do not wish to repeat their work here, we are in the debt of the many scholars of practice who have enriched and broadened our thinking about strengths-based and competency-oriented approaches to practice. Chief among these is the work of Saleebey (1992) and colleagues from the University of Kansas and the rich and varied contributions of Anthony Maluccio (1981), who introduced many of us to competency-oriented practice and who continues to provide richly detailed work exemplifying competency approaches and "partnership" with families in permanency planning and reunification (Pine, Warsh, & Maluccio 1993). We are similarly in debt to scholars of intervention such as Robert Halpern (1995a, 1995b, 1995c), who have refocused attention on neighborhood-based initiatives for helping vulnerable families.

Finally, while we do not agree with all facets of Etzioni's (1993) conception of communitarianism, we do find helpful the notion of responsibility to community. Similarly, we find useful the notion of reciprocity embedded in Riessman's work—particularly his concept of the "prosumer" (as distinct from "client") who, from the very beginning of the helping encounter is expected to contribute not only to resolution of his/her own problems, but to those of others as well. This idea flows from what we view as a particularly useful insight on "helping" in our culture: namely, that it is a good deal easier (and more satisfying) to be a help-giver than a help-receiver.

2

The Idea of Environment in Social Work Practice

Throughout its history, the social work profession has struggled to develop practice frameworks that fully realize its foundational commitment to a balanced focus on both person and environment. This struggle is most clearly evident in direct practice, where, despite claims to an integrated focus on person and environment, there has been a persistent tendency to elevate person-centered knowledge and interventions. For a variety of reasons, environmental practice languishes on the margins of direct practice, routinely invoked but accorded relatively little meaningful attention. This lack of balance has been troublesome at least since the 1920s, when social casework adopted psychodynamic theory as its primary knowledge base. Truly, as social work theorist Carol Meyer has said, the vexed issue of environmental practice is the "historical gnat" of the American social work profession (Meyer 1989).[1]

For all this, social work has a rich history of environmental practice, and as contemporary practitioners we have much to learn from past efforts to conceptualize the environment and environmental helping. Though social workers look most often to the profession's reform and community-organizing traditions for exemplars of environmental intervention, in every period there have been theorists and practitioners in direct practice concerned to maintain the centrality of environment in professional social work. It is to this tradition, in particular the history of social casework, that we turn in this chapter. In the relatively brief overview that follows, our aims are twofold: We wish to identify issues that, over time, have placed limits on the profession's view of the environment and have constrained its commitment to environmental intervention. At the same time, we hope to bring to the surface and revive the contributions of past generations of direct practitioners to current thinking on the environment and environmental practice.[2]

In keeping with the focus of the book, we are concerned primarily with thinking about the environment in direct social work practice. Our story begins with the Progressive era and the emergence of a dual concern with person and environment as a primary mission of the profession. In the long view, to borrow a phrase from Mary Richmond (1930), it becomes clear both that the issues shaping the profession's response to environment have remained rather constant over time, and that many of them continue into the present. Key among these are the internal preoccupations and insecurities of a developing profession, related struggles over professional identity and purpose, the difficulties inherent in conceptualizing and codifying the complexity of the environment for practice, and the tendency, reflecting that in the wider society, to associate environmental issues with poverty and thus, inherently, with marginality. These constitute, in effect, the "environmental context" of attempts to promote a more vigorous commitment to environmental intervention in social work practice—a set of checks and balances that have profoundly influenced the impact and reach of efforts within the profession to develop knowledge and skill in environmental practice.[3]

ENVIRONMENTAL INTERVENTION
IN HISTORICAL PERSPECTIVE

Since its earliest beginnings in the settlement houses and charity organization societies of the late nineteenth century, the social work profession has been concerned with providing services that span the relationship between people and their environmental contexts. The relative degree of attention accorded to environment or to person has varied, however, with the social preoccupations of the times and with factors internal to the profession, such as its degree of professionalization and the availability and scope of knowledge for practice. Table 2.1 summarizes the complex relationships between different social periods and social work theory development. We examine each of these key periods in more detail in this section.

From Charity to Social Work:
The Progressive Era

In the Progressive era, which is usually considered to span the period from the late 1890s until the entry of the United States into World War I in 1917, the new profession of social work established an identity and jurisdiction that rested on a concern with people in the context of their environments (Leiby 1978; Lubove 1965). This dual focus emerged from the experiences, separate and shared, of the early social caseworkers (based in the charity organizations and the emerging family agencies) and workers in the social settlements. Interactively (if at times acrimoniously, for there were many differences between them), these two groups shaped the emerging purposes of the profession.

The development of a focus on environment as well as person in the early years of the profession reflected in large part the mood and interests of the times. Rising concern about the effects on American society of the linked forces of industrialization, urbanization, and mass immigration found expression in the Progressive era in a wave of social reforms. The reformist ethic was fueled by anxiety about deteriorating social conditions: evidence of the impact of the environment on human well-being was all too obvious, especially in the inner cities. Central also to the Progressive impulse was a growing belief in the possibility of social change through personal effort, the application of science, and government intervention (Bannister 1987; Ross 1991).

Many of the early social workers were deeply involved in the reform efforts of the Progressive era. Their awareness of environmental conditions was sharper than most, for, as neighborhood-based caseworkers and settlement house workers, they had firsthand knowledge of everyday conditions in urban neighborhoods. Unlike the morality-based charity of earlier decades, the "new view" of charity that emerged in the early 1900s (Devine 1910) was centrally concerned with environmental realities and their impact. No longer were the poor held entirely responsible for their circumstances; indeed, all were expected to share in efforts to improve social conditions (Boyer 1978).

The Settlement House Movement

The Progressive era settlement houses provide the most vivid example of the environmentalist practice of the early social workers. The settlements—residential houses located in the urban slums of America's northern industrial cities—provided a setting for socially concerned members of the middle and upper classes to work directly with the poor (Davis 1967; Leiby 1978; Sklar 1985). Unlike organized charity, which was concerned primarily with the individual needs of the poor, the neighborhood-based settlements focused their attention on the social and environmental conditions of urban poverty. At the broadest level, this approach was realized in the active involvement of settlement workers in the social reform movements of the day, including, for example,

Table 2.1. People and Events in Direct Social Work Practice

Period	U.S. Society	Social Work	Key Figures	Intellectual Influences
1890s	Depression	Charity Organization Societies (COS) Settlement Houses	Mary Richmond Jane Addams	Social Darwinism Scientific philanthropy
1900–1920	Progressive era World War I	COS/Settlements 1915 Flexner speech 1917 "Social Diagnosis" (Mary Richmond) Professionalization	Mary Richmond Jane Addams	Social sciences Law Medicine
1920s	Red Scare "Roaring Twenties" Prohibition	Mental hygiene movement Casework "above the poverty line" 1929 Milford Conference	Mary Richmond Annette Garrett Ada Sheffield	Psychodynamic theory (Freud)
1930s	Great Depression New Deal	Pubic relief & agencies Specification of casework method Functional & diagnostic schools	Bertha Reynolds Virginia Robinson Jessie Taft	Psychodynamic theory (Freud & Rank) Ego psychology
1940s	World War II	Functional/diagnostic debate Psychosocial approach	Gordon Hamilton Lucille Austin Ruth Smalley	Psychodynamic theory Ego psychology
1950s	Cold War McCarthyism Korean War Family treatment	1955 National Association of Social Workers 1956 Commission on Social Work Practice Psychosocial treatment	Gordon Hamilton Florence Hollis	Ego psychology Social sciences (e.g., role theory, family theory)

1960s	Vietnam War War on Poverty Civil rights movement Nixon	Radical and empirical critique Psychosocial therapy Problem-solving model Group work methods Family therapy	Florence Hollis Helen Harris Perlman Helen Northen Frances Scherz Scott Briar	Learning theory Behavioral theory
1970s	Women's movement	Integrative practice models Clinical and private practice Task-centered practice Crisis intervention Empirical clinical practice	Carol Meyer Carel Germain Reid and Epstein Pincus and Minahan Anthony Maluccio Ann Hartman Joel Fischer	Systems theory Ecological theory Feminist theory
1980s	Reaganomics Privatization	Ecosystems perspective Cognitive & cognitive-behavioral methods Managed care	Carol Meyer Carel Germain Alex Gitterman Sharon Berlin	Cognitive behavioral theory Cognitive theory
1990s	Clinton administration Welfare reform	Empowerment Strengths perspective Multiculturalism Interventive eclecticism	Lorraine Guttiérez Dennis Saleebey Elaine Pinderhughes Joan Laird	Critical social theory Feminist theory Humanism/existentialism Postmodernism Constructivism

tuberculosis prevention, enactment of child labor laws, advocacy for public health provisions, establishment of housing codes, and development of outdoor playgrounds. Closer to home, the "settlers" developed a host of classes, clubs, and neighborhood groups catering to the many needs of immigrant families in the urban environment. Unlike the charities, the settlement house programs were targeted to all local residents, not just those identified as unable to cope, and were concerned as much with building community and connections between the social classes as with serving the poor.

Charity Organization Societies

The Charity Organization Societies (COS), which proliferated in the United States at the end of the nineteenth century, aimed at developing a systematic approach to the provision of relief to the poor, through coordination of information, registration of applicants, and the outreach of volunteer "friendly visitors" (Boyer 1978; Leiby 1978; Lubove 1965). Underlying this "scientific" approach to charity (Germain 1971), however, was the hardy belief, derived from the Elizabethan Poor Laws, in the moral responsibility of the poor for their own circumstances. The early leaders of the COS transformed the problem of poverty into one of dependency, related it thus to defects in individual character, and considered it most appropriately ameliorated through the personal rehabilitation of the poor. Charitable relief was to be given only when absolutely necessary and, where possible, the poor were encouraged to take responsibility for changing their own circumstances. At the heart of this effort were the friendly visitors: middle- or upper-class volunteers (mostly women) whose role was "not alms but a friend," and who were expected to investigate, advise, educate, and, through the transforming power of friendship and moral persuasion, improve the conditions and character of the poor.

The friendly visiting model, with its moralistic overtones, waned in popularity after 1900, as social work became a profession and as awareness grew that poverty was deeply linked to social and environmental conditions (Stadum 1991). In the decade from 1910 to 1920, a new casework model, implemented by trained, paid workers, supplanted the friendly visitors. Yet the legacy of the friendly visitors endured in the new social casework, with mixed consequences for the environmental domain of practice. On one hand, the practical, everyday involvement of the friendly visitors with poor families and neighborhoods established an environmentally oriented template for the social casework that followed. At the same time, the friendly visiting model framed social casework as an individualizing approach to those in need. Social caseworkers thus inherited from the COS and the friendly visitors the perception that their most significant and valuable work would come, case by case, through the influence of one person on another. Environmental issues were filtered largely through the lens of individual character, a focus that constrained the social casework response to the environmental dimensions of practice, and laid the foundations for the later tendency to elevate personal helping over environmental intervention.

Mary Richmond

A central figure in the transformation of charity into social work was Mary Richmond (1861–1928), a distinguished practitioner, leader in the COS movement, and, as author of *Social Diagnosis* (1917), social casework's first theoretician. Richmond, a prolific writer and speaker, insisted that a dual concern with person and environment was the hallmark of the new profession. Of social casework, she said that "the distinctive approach of the case worker is back to the individual by way of his [sic] social environment, and wherever adjustment must be effected in this manner . . . there some form of case work is and will continue to be needed" (1922, 98). Unimpressed with "solitary horseman" views of the individual, she insisted that the proper focus of social work was the complexity of variables in both person and situation.

Richmond organized the methods she considered relevant to this holistic view of social casework into a simple, four-part interventive system (ibid., 101–102):

1. insight into individuality and personal characteristics,
2. insight into the resources, dangers, and influences of the social environment,
3. direct action of mind upon mind,
4. indirect action through the social environment.

Although in the hands of others priority came to be given to the personal and interpersonal dimensions of Richmond's framework, to her all were of equal importance. Indeed, she considered indirect action through the environment to be "particularly well-adapted to the end which social casework has in view" (ibid., 111). In this "comprehensive, many-sided approach" (ibid.) she included mobilization of existing material resources; work with other relevant people, institutions, and agencies; the development of new environmental resources; change in the environment (e.g., placement in foster care or an institution); and work with the environmental challenges facing new immigrants.

Frances Perkins, a settlement house leader who later became the first woman member of the U.S. cabinet, said of Mary Richmond after her death that "a new state of mind, a social state of mind, is her indestructible monument" (1929, 339). A contemporary of Richmond's who reviewed her book *What is Social Case Work?* (1922) likewise underscored her contribution to a holistic view of social work purposes:

> It is this ability to gain an intimate understanding of environmental factors, to appreciate the molding effect of home surroundings, neighborhood conditions, community life, . . . to utilize environmental resources . . . that the distinctive claim to professional status lies. . . . The caseworker is a specialist in "environments." Not environment in the mass sense of the social reformer . . . but in a new and individualistic sense, looking at the environment through the eyes of the individual. (Buell 1922, 70)

Although both the charities and the settlements sought to transform social conditions, their efforts were directed at different points in the social system. The primary interest of the charities was the person and his or her immediate circumstances: their overriding concern was to ameliorate the effects of poverty at the individual and family level. The settlement movement, on the other hand, was concerned primarily with people as part of larger social systems and structures (though, like the COS, it too was essentially a white, middle-class movement with its own class-based and cultural expectations (Berman-Rossi & Miller 1994). For the settlers, the primary locus of change was the wider social and political environment. In the particular consciousness of the Progressive era, these two streams of experience—the reformist environmentalism of the social settlements and the pragmatic, person-focused, neighborhood-based practice of the friendly visitors and social caseworkers—were maintained in productive balance. For social work, as for the wider society, however, the experience of World War I brought significant change.

The 1920s: Freud and the Americans

Their idealism spent, Americans were in a different mood after World War I than they were before it. The reform spirit of the prewar years dissipated along with America's hopes for a glorious peace. In part the mood of the 1920s was one of profound disillusionment: neither the Progressive movement nor the outcomes of the war had lived up to expectations. One result was a retreat from public issues to the more controllable domain of private life: Americans, as historian Arthur Schlesinger has said, had "had their fill of crusades" (1986, 31). Public cynicism was matched by indifference in the state and national legislatures and the courts, and by malaise among the professionals and intellectuals who had been at the center of the Progressive movement (Hofstadter 1955).

In retrospect, World War I marks a defining shift in social work's relationship with environmental practice. The settlement movement, such a vibrant presence in the prewar years, lost momentum and coherence in the face of public intolerance for social activism and shifts in the composition of urban neighborhoods (Trattner 1989; Trolander 1987). In social casework, new priorities and preoccupations also emerged. Before the war, when almost all of the extremely varied activities of social caseworkers were directed to adjusting poor clients to the "disciplines and pressures" of the social environment (Lubove 1965, 81), Mary Richmond's environmentally oriented practice met most of the needs of workers in the field. Even then, however, many of the problems of poor families had emotional sequelae for which caseworkers had few answers. After the war, faced with human problems framed increasingly in psychological terms, social workers became more urgent in their desire for knowledge and skill in psychological treatment.

By 1919, at least in the Northeast and among those who attended the National Conference of Social Work, there was intense interest in the relationship between social work and psychiatry, specifically Freudian theory. In 1918, spurred by the demands of the war, Smith College initiated a six-month training course for psychiatric aides, a program that by 1919 had evolved into a training school for psychiatric social workers. At the National Conference in Atlantic City in the same year, enthusiastic social caseworkers crowded the halls to hear a slew of papers rooted in dynamic psychiatry (Day 1937). The susceptibility of social caseworkers to the "new psychiatry" was, as Ann Hartman (1972) has argued, overdetermined. A key factor was the mental hygiene movement, founded in 1909 but increasingly influential during and after World War I, which provided dramatic evidence of the need for effective psychological help, not only for war victims, but in the population as a whole. During the war, social workers with the Red Cross Home Service also had their first, extensive experience with servicemen and their families who were "above the poverty line" (Black 1991). After the war, middle-class individuals and families began to use social casework services on a voluntary basis, in the family agencies and the newly developed child guidance clinics, and in the tentative beginnings of private practice among psychiatric social workers (Courtney 1992).

The move away from environmentally oriented practice can be linked also to a concurrent shift in the location of social casework practice. In the postwar period, social casework expanded further into new institutional settings, such as medical and psychiatric hospitals and child guidance clinics. Although still considered to be experts in environments, these agency-based workers were less likely to derive their knowledge and skill from direct, everyday experience with clients in their homes and communities. This shift toward practice in centralized agencies at a distance from local neighborhoods further distanced social casework from its commitment to environmental knowledge and practice.

A narrower focus on the person and a psychodynamic approach to practice gave social caseworkers more likelihood of success with the psychological troubles of their clients. But efficacy was bought at a price. The assumptions and priorities embedded in Freudian theory—for example, the emphasis on individual change and on a therapeutic role for the caseworker—connected with and revived the individualism lying just beneath the environmentalist veneer that overlaid casework ideology in the Progressive years. At the same time, a more relational and individualized view of environment replaced the primary concern with the objective conditions of poverty that was typical of the prewar years.

Continuity amid Change:
The Depression Years

Although widely heralded as one of social work's glorious periods of social activism, in social casework the depression years were more a period of continuity and consolidation than of change. The psychodynamic paradigm dominated developments in casework just as it did in psychiatry (Abbott 1982), and neither the miseries of the depression nor the intellectual challenges of iconoclastic social caseworkers dislodged it.

At the outset of the depression, casework agencies struggled to provide material relief along with psychological help. As the depression deepened, however, the level of need became overwhelming. Social caseworkers in the private agencies, ambivalent about returning to their traditional role as providers of relief and concrete services to the poor, looked to government to provide for the unemployed, a strategy that enabled them to define their own contribution primarily in therapeutic terms. As a contemporary caseworker said in 1939, "From 1922 on, caseworkers were having increasing difficulty adjusting the environment to the client, and so it was natural that their interest should center, not on whether he [sic] had a job, but on how he felt about not having a job" (Millar 1939, 347). In part this emphasis on personal adjustment may be seen as a defensive attempt to carve out a zone of efficacy in the midst of a deluge of structural problems far beyond the reach of the casework mandate. Social casework was never designed, as Bertha

Reynolds (1935) once pointed out, for the amelioration of large-scale social problems. But the depression also magnified the inherent unmanageability of environmental factors, and caseworkers were understandably frustrated by their lack of impact.

Relieved, eventually, of the responsibility for providing material relief by the provisions of the Federal Emergency Relief Act (1933) and the New Deal, caseworkers in the voluntary agencies concentrated on developing their skills in psychological treatment. The separation of casework from relief had several important consequences for the profession's approach to the environmental domain. First, it institutionalized the tendency, emergent since World War I, for private agencies to serve more capable, middle-class clients (Cloward & Epstein 1965). This was partly because people from all walks of life suddenly found themselves in need of help, but it also reflected the increasingly selective practices of the family agencies, many of which had begun screening clients at intake. This selectivity enabled social caseworkers to focus on the refinement of insight-oriented psychotherapy and on the enhancement of professional status (Austin 1948). The redistribution of relief services to the public agencies likewise freed caseworkers in the voluntary agencies to concentrate on treatment. In a classic parallelism, the private agencies specializing in psychodynamic treatment came to be seen as more prestigious than the public agencies providing relief—a situation that served the professional aspirations of the casework mainstream but further deepened and underlined the relegation of environmentally oriented practice to the second tier of social work services.

In the depression years, factors thus converged that resulted, paradoxically, in a strengthening of social casework's commitment to individual treatment and to a view of practice framed essentially by psychotherapeutic thinking. The publication in 1930 of Virginia Robinson's book *A Changing Psychology in Social Case Work* was a significant marker in the shift toward the person, for it defined social casework not in terms of its environmental content (the material issues bringing people for help), but as "individual therapy through a treatment relationship" (p. 187). To this point, social casework practice had been centrally concerned with the conditions and effects of urban poverty. Robinson's approach, however, brought the client, rather than his or her material circumstances, to the center of attention. Casework thus moved from a concern with the *actual* environment, to a concern with the *metaphorical* environment: the environment as described by the client, and/or as represented in the dynamics of the helping relationship.

From the 1930s until the 1960s, social work was dominated by social casework, and in social casework the main preoccupation was the refinement of a clinical approach based on psychodynamic theory. Nonetheless, a small but influential group of casework theorists—key among them Ada Sheffield, Gordon Hamilton, and Bertha Reynolds—continued to see environmental and social issues as central to social casework theory and practice. In the following vignettes, we present brief outlines of the work of these important social work theorists.

Gordon Hamilton

Gordon Hamilton, perhaps casework's most influential theorist in the period from the depression until the early 1960s, was exposed early to Mary Richmond's person-environment framework. As a young Red Cross worker, Hamilton met Richmond and on Richmond's recommendation went to the New York COS as a caseworker in 1920. In 1923 Hamilton joined the faculty of the New York School of Social Work (later the Columbia University School of Social Work), which became her intellectual base for the next thirty-four years. Her book *Theory and Practice of Social Casework* (1940, 1951) was for many years the defining text in the field.

Like Mary Richmond, Hamilton believed that social work was true to itself only when attending to both personal and environmental factors:

> It is this essentially dualistic relationship which consistently has shaped social work and given it its distinguishable if not yet wholly distinctive pattern. . . . No one can understand a problem of poverty without some reference to human behavior, and no one can treat a problem of human behavior intelligently without reference to its economic and social framework. (1940, 4)

Hamilton framed the focus of social casework as being the "living event"—the dynamic, living interaction between people and their external circumstances:

> A social case is a "living event" within which there are always economic, physical, mental, emotional, and social factors in varying proportions. A social case is always composed of internal and external, or environmental, factors. . . . Fundamentally all social cases have "inner" and "outer" characteristics, and consist of person and situation, of objective reality and the meaning of this reality to the one who experiences it. (ibid., 34).

This organismic approach represents a major conceptual leap from Richmond's thinking and is a hallmark of Hamilton's work. Drawing on gestalt psychology, in particular Kurt Lewin's field theory, she overcame, at least in theoretical terms, separation of person from situation and the implication of linear causality inherent in such fragmentation. In Hamilton's work, the focus of social casework shifted from the more dualistic "person-and-environment" to the integrative "person-in-environment."

Although conceptually brilliant, Hamilton, like Mary Richmond, offered the practitioner few new techniques for intervention. In *Theory and Practice of Social Case Work,* her classification of interventions followed the traditional Richmond schema of direct (psychological) and indirect (environmental) treatment. Hamilton separated indirect treatment into "administration of a practical service" (often termed provision of concrete services) and "environmental manipulation," which she defined as "all attempts to correct or improve the situation in order to reduce strains and pressure, and all modifications of the living experience to offer opportunities for growth and change" (1951, 247). Although Hamilton made it clear that she considered both direct and indirect treatment powerful methods for intervention, in the field priority continued to be accorded to direct, or psychological, methods. Surveying the social work scene in 1953, Hamilton remarked thus: "Process has it. She is queen and her realms have been widening . . . the social causes of disturbed behavior . . . and the social engineering tasks for dealing with them have been lost sight of, and interest in them has evaporated" (cited in Klein 1968, 139–140).

Ada Sheffield

Ada Sheffield, a Boston-based caseworker and social work theorist, is a neglected figure in social casework history. Though a friend of Mary Richmond (indeed she helped Richmond with parts of Richmond's famous book *Social Diagnosis,* published in 1917), Sheffield disliked the tendency to dichotomize person and situation that she perceived in the writing of Richmond and other social work leaders. She considered this separation to be "too sharp and mutually excluding," particularly since it tended to result in a primary emphasis on the individual (Sheffield 1937, 76–77). To conceptualize the interconnectedness of person and environment, Sheffield, like Gordon Hamilton, looked to the field theory of Kurt Lewin, to the work of other gestalt psychologists such as Koffka, and to a range of other social psychologists, including John Dewey (Sheffield 1920, 1931, 1937). Sheffield (1937) was also one of the earliest social casework theorists to use the term "psycho-social" to represent a dual and simultaneous concern with inner and outer factors.

Ada Sheffield conceptualized social casework as "social treatment," a process encompassing both assistance to individuals and attention to social and environmental factors, particularly the "web of relationships" (1920, 201) that make up the social context of personal life. She stressed that the components of a case should be viewed as an interdependent system, or organismic whole, and was interested in "clients in complex relationships with their physical and social setting" (1931, 474).

For Sheffield, the test of effective intervention was sufficient change in the *situation* (not necessarily the client) to resolve or at least ameliorate the problem. Her formulation retained a casework identity, since the focus of intervention—the reason for involvement—was the individual client. She avoided, however, the expectation of attitudinal and personality change or adjustment that dominated casework theory in this period, and denied the supremacy of psychological intervention and (as she called it) the client-centered approach.

Though Ada Sheffield reached for transactional and mediating ideas, she lacked the conceptual tools to articulate them clearly for direct practice. As Florence Sytz once aptly noted of casework in general, "We can think in wholes but we act in relation to parts" (1946, 136). Sheffield's approach raised technical questions for the social caseworker with a job to do. It was not clear, for example, how one could proceed from holistic assessment to intervention, without being overwhelmed or ineffective, or both.

More fundamentally, Sheffield challenged the prevailing psycho-dynamic orthodoxy. She rejected the focus on client dysfunction inherent in the psychodynamic approach, endorsed a contextual and social-psychological approach to the "case," and advocated an interventive model framed primarily in terms of education rather than treatment. Sheffield's critique left social caseworkers with the choice, therefore, of dethroning psychodynamic theory and relegating it to the status of one useful theory among several, or of rejecting her point of view. That they took the latter route is not surprising given their investment in the psychodynamic approach and its embeddedness in their sense of professionalism. Sheffield's work was rejected or ignored by the majority of social caseworkers, and the possibility of a helpful integration between social psychology and psychoanalytic theory through the articulation of a situational approach was, for the moment, lost.

Bertha Capen Reynolds

From the 1920s and 1930s until her death in 1978, Bertha Reynolds—psychiatric social worker, educator, union social worker, activist, and thoroughgoing iconoclast—fought to keep social work attention on both the broad variety of needs that bring people for help and the social circumstances that give rise to such needs. She was interested in helping people to function better in relation to the practical circumstances of their daily lives, and saw very clearly that the environment has an enormous impact on ability to cope. The proper focus of social casework attention was, she believed, the dynamic relationship between the person and his or her social reality. She did not reject psychoanalytic theory. On the contrary, she was very clear as to its usefulness. But she considered it just a part of the knowledge base of social work, to be used as appropriate.

From the 1920s Reynolds sought to resolve, in her own way, the emerging separation in casework theory and practice between the psychodynamic approach and the demands of the environment. She was concerned particularly that the developing emphasis on individual treatment of voluntary clients removed social caseworkers from the places where they were most needed, and from their characteristic commitment to neighborhood-based practice and the poor (Reynolds [1934] 1982, 1938). As the country slipped into the depression and social caseworkers continued to be preoccupied with treatment, Bertha Reynolds's personal and professional discomfort increased.

From this sense of dissonance came seminal integrating ideas, many of which the profession would not assimilate until it was again faced with social upheaval in the 1960s. Three in particular are salient here: (a) the notion that social caseworkers have a mediating role between person and environment (Reynolds 1935); (b) recognition that the proper point for social work intervention is the intersection of person and environment (Reynolds 1933, [1934] 1982); and (c) the related idea that behavior is an adaptive response to a particular environment, rather than just an adjustment to it (Reynolds 1933, 1942).

Unlike many social casework theorists of her time, Reynolds was concerned not with pathology, but with helping people to deal with the "normal hazards of living" (Reynolds [1934] 1982). She believed, as she famously said, that social workers and the people they serve must meet "at the crossroads of life where ordinary traffic passes by" (ibid., 13), and began to think, in holistic terms that would now be considered ecological, of the need for attention to the "life situation" of the person:

> One essential in all our thinking about social case work is to keep constantly in mind the fact that it has two poles of interest—the individual and his [sic] environment. After all, what is life but the continuous adaptation made by a complex and ever-changing human being to an equally complex and changing environment? Probably we should say environments, for we have to think not only of the person's adaptations to his [sic] own body and means of subsistence in the biological sense, but to think of the world of social relationships and, beyond that, of the world of ideas and ideals which is as real an environment as any other. Not even are we limited to environment in the present, for the individual who is failing in his [sic] attempts to adapt is often living as if a long past environment were still about him [sic], or as if a hoped-for future one were a reality. (p. 337)

During the depression, Bertha Reynolds's social commitments became increasingly politicized, and specifically Marxist, as she searched for a "science of society" as powerful as the Freudian "science of personality" (Freedberg 1984; Reynolds 1935, 1938). Frustrated by the profession's fixation on the inner life, by the distance between social agencies and social circumstances, and by the conservatism of social workers in general, all in the face of the desperation of millions, she reached for answers in social and political theory. In 1935, she asked of social work's traditional emphasis on adjustment: "Adjustment to what?" (Reynolds 1935). As the depression deepened, so did her conviction that society was essentially inequitable and conflict-laden, and that social workers served dominant groups to ensure social control and compliance (ibid.). Her view of the environment was therefore inherently political, underpinned as it was by a social-structural analysis indicating that social and environmental conditions are toxic for many members of a capitalist society.

Reynolds's perspectives were not those of the mainstream of social work, let alone social casework. By the summer of 1938, the distance between her views and those prevailing at the decidedly psychoanalytic Smith College School for Social Work led to her resignation from the faculty, a departure that "presaged her dismissal from the traditional cadres of the social work profession" (Freedberg 1984, 149).

No longer welcome in academia, Reynolds took a casework position with the National Maritime Union, an experience that was fundamental to the development of her thinking about social work practice (Reynolds 1963). The provision of casework services within a membership organization defined by a sense of ownership and participation was an experience qualitatively different from that in the traditional casework settings in which she had previously worked. The atmosphere of belonging, mutuality, and reciprocity at the Maritime Union taught Reynolds that it was not necessary to make people into clients in order to help them. Increasingly, her interest centered on "the stream of normal living" and on helping people to deal with the challenges in their external reality for themselves. With this understanding came a more proactive and environmentally grounded perspective on the function of social casework:

> Social casework helps people to test and understand their reality, physical, social, and emotional, and to mobilize resources within themselves and in their physical and social environment to meet their reality or to change it. (1951, 131)

Reynolds' emphasis on people within their everyday circumstances and her understanding that mediation, education, and competency-building are key to mastery of the environment were as central to her work as her activist commitments. As with Sheffield's work, however, such ideas denied the supremacy of psychological approaches and did not fit comfortably within the dominant psychodynamic paradigm. Although Bertha

Reynolds continued to develop and refine her thinking, the validity of her work was fully recognized only after her death, and in her lifetime she was never readmitted to the ranks of the "great and the good" in the social work profession. Powerful ideas about the environmental domain of practice were thus bypassed once again by the mainstream of social casework.

Casework in Prosperity: 1945–1959

Few histories of social work dwell on the years after the Second World War. In retrospect they seem a barren time, at best a backdrop for the dramatic social upheavals of the 1960s, at worst a period of grinding conservatism in which social work was defined increasingly in terms of the treatment of individual problems. Featureless as they may appear from a contemporary perspective, however, the late 1940s and 1950s were formative to the redefinition of social work in the 1960s and beyond.

After the Second World War, Americans lived in peace but in fear of war. The prosperity and business-as-usual ethos of the postwar era did little to reduce anxieties about the cold war, the possibility of nuclear holocaust, the reach of the McCarthy witch-hunts, or the power of the corporate-military complex (Graebner 1991). The experiences of the Second World War also further underscored the need for psychological services, not only for servicemen and refugees, but also in the general population. In the postwar period, in a climate of doubt, uncertainty, and fear, psychological interests and services flourished. Social casework established a niche for itself in the market for psychotherapy, and in the shadow of McCarthyism became even further dissociated from environmental issues and practice (Ehrenreich 1985; Reynolds 1963).

To support their professional interests, social caseworkers continued to be heavily invested in the development of technique, particularly the systematization of social work treatment grounded in Freudian theory. Once again, as in the period after World War I, the trauma of war and its effects gave the psychodynamic perspective external validity. This time, however, social caseworkers were already deeply committed to articulating Freudian theory for practice (Hamilton 1958; Hollis 1949, 1951). That the mood and needs of the times supported this commitment only strengthened the grip of psychoanalytic theory on social casework's sense of self.

In the 1940s and 1950s, social caseworkers added the work of the neo-Freudians to the Freudian theoretical foundation they had adopted before the war. Ego psychology, with its emphasis on the active response of the person to environmental conditions, provided an important theoretical bridge between person and environment (Goldstein 1984). The view of the environment embodied in ego psychology was, however, limited in two particular respects: First, it focused in the main on the immediate experience and relationships of the client. Second, although Heinz Hartmann's (1958) notion of adaptation included the potential for change in the environment, his core concept of the "average expectable environment" implied acceptance of environmental conditions as they stood (Saari 1991). In practice, therefore, ego psychology supported an approach to the environment focused on individual adjustment rather than on change in environmental conditions.

A balanced approach to person and environment thus continued to be elusive. Indeed in 1948, Irene Josselyn, a practicing psychiatrist and psychoanalyst, pointed out that insight therapy had become social casework's pièce de résistance and that environmental therapy, once so central to social casework practice, had become its stepchild. Josselyn chided social caseworkers for relegating environmental treatment to a secondary status since it was, she argued, the unique therapeutic contribution of social casework; the one area in which social caseworkers could be credited with a distinctive role. Gordon Hamilton said of social casework in these years that it had dug deep into a relationship terrain (cited in Klein 1968). Although by the end of the 1950s there was increasing awareness of the importance of conditioning factors such as cultural and class variables, the environment continued to be defined primarily in relational terms, environmental intervention was identified largely with the provision of concrete services, and within the profession there was increasing tolerance of psychotherapeutic practice. Notably absent, in social work as in the broader society, was any critique of prevailing social conditions, perhaps because the McCarthy era taught everyone just how risky the role of social critic could be.

Toward a New Paradigm:
The 1960s and Beyond

The social tumult of the 1960s was all the more dramatic for its juxtaposition to the quiescence of the 1950s. The rhetoric of John F. Kennedy's inauguration set the tone for the decade: in these years, American society was defined by the need and desire for social change. Social unrest peaked in 1968, the year of the Tet offensive, the assassinations of Martin Luther King and Robert Kennedy, the tumultuous Democratic National Convention in Chicago, and the election of Richard Nixon as president.

As in the 1930s, the social work mainstream responded sluggishly to escalating social unrest (Bartlett 1970; Ehrenreich 1985; Hall 1963). Though there were calls for more attention to social issues, in the short term the topography of casework theory and practice changed little. The trend toward a psychotherapeutic model continued and there was increasing interest in private practice, which offered social workers greater autonomy, status, and economic advantage (Merle 1962). Articles in the leading social work journals remained heavily focused on individual treatment at least through the Kennedy years.

Scholarly interest began to shift only after President Lyndon Johnson's poverty program got under way in 1964: from this point, articles on poverty and civil rights proliferated. Even so, as Meyer (1970) and Ehrenreich (1985) have pointed out, professional social workers had become so distanced from public welfare (and so associated with the establishment) that they played a minimal role in the development and implementation of poverty programs. Indeed, as Cloward and Epstein (1965) have documented, the private family agencies continued to move away from the provision of services to low-income clients.

At the same time, social workers began to look more carefully at their practice. External events supported the need for professional self-scrutiny; those calling for change could point to a society in turmoil for validation of their argument that traditional person-centered paradigms were no longer a sufficient basis for social work practice. Much of this professional self-castigation was directed to social casework.

To a growing critique of casework's effectiveness (Briar 1968; Briar & Miller 1971; Fischer 1973a, 1973b, 1975; Mullen, Dumpson, & Associates 1971; Woodward 1960) was added the argument that it was not relevant to contemporary social problems or to the needs of many clients (Cloward & Epstein 1965). The individualistic discourse of social casework and the lack of a race or class analysis in casework theory seemed to offer little to the struggle for civil rights, or to efforts to alleviate poverty. Further, a series of research studies on the outcomes of social casework intervention appeared to demonstrate that it was inherently ineffective (Mullen et al. 1971). Calling these "serious criticisms of the most fundamental sort," Scott Briar, editor of *Social Work* and dean of the School of Social Work at the University of Washington, argued that social caseworkers had committed a double error: they had elevated method over purpose, and they had put their faith in methods that were not effective. Helen Harris Perlman later asserted that social casework became the "whipping boy" of social work (1968, 435). Certainly it was a lightning rod for the profession's struggles to redefine itself in concert with changes in its external environment.

Many social workers, caught up in the social movements of the decade, accepted the criticism of social casework and looked toward other models of practice, particularly community organization and development, to redress social ills. The "new social work" of the 1960s, exemplified by New York's Mobilization for Youth program (Zimbalist 1970), repudiated social casework and took instead a social issues approach, oriented more to the rights than to the needs of clients. Activist practice, marked by consumer participation and a focus on community organizing, advocacy, and brokering, was inherently environmentalist. It was, however, also fundamentally polarized from the casework mainstream.

In social casework, therefore, the demands of the 1960s did not result in a linear shift to a more socially oriented perspective. Though some social caseworkers became very interested in socially active practice and in the impact of the environment on clients, at a deeper level social casework clung tenaciously to its identification with psychological theory and preoccupation with treatment.

If anything, this period was marked by splitting and polarization, particularly in its resurrection of the hardy dualism of social reform and social casework. Social activism, being noisier and more in keeping with external events, dominated the profession. But social casework did not wither on the vine. Perhaps the radical critique was too strident or too threatening to be heard, or the lack of conceptual openness in social casework simply too ingrained. There was also growing recognition that, one by one, people were still in need of skilled services. A hardy core of social caseworkers thus went forward much as before, affected by the radical critique but not transformed by it, and perhaps even more wedded to their point of view as a result of having to defend it so forcefully.

BRIDGING PERSON AND ENVIRONMENT: ECOLOGICAL AND SYSTEMS THEORY

In social work, as in the wider culture, the activism of the 1960s lost momentum in the 1970s. Yet the concerns and challenges of sixties carried over into the next decade. In social casework, this period is marked by a series of efforts to develop conceptual frameworks that would encompass both the diversity of methods in the profession and the two poles of person and environment. At this point the question of the environment in casework theory shifted dramatically, as the problem of the environment became part of a larger discussion about the need to develop consensus about social work purposes along with new and more encompassing theoretical frameworks (Bartlett 1970; Gordon 1969; Meyer 1970, 1973A, 1973B, 1981; Minahan & Briar 1977; Whittaker 1974).

Systems Theory

The search for new ways to conceptualize the relationship between the personal and environmental dimensions of social work practice led several authors to explore emergent ideas in general systems theory (GST), which focuses on the transactional processes within and among systems (Greif & Lynch 1983). In a classic paper, "Social Study: Past and Future," Carel Germain (1968) suggested that new knowledge about systems would enable the conceptual integration of social and psychological phenomena, and thus support a shift in social casework from a static to a dynamic view of the environment.

From the perspective of the environmental domain of practice, the systems approach raised many exciting possibilities. Not only did the transactional nature of systems theory refocus attention on the environment, but it revitalized the potential of the environment as a site for intervention and change, along with approaches to the individual. "In a systemic view," Carol Meyer said, "there is no inner and outer, but rather an operational field in which all elements intersect and affect each other" (1983, 127).

The attempt to articulate systems thinking for direct practice was not entirely welcomed by the field. Reactions, as Hartman noted, "ranged from enthusiasm, to caution, to resistance, to downright hostility" (1970, 467). Those aspects of GST most troubling to practitioners were, she suggested, its level of abstraction, the range of competing perspectives within systems theory, and the mechanistic, nonhuman nature of much of its language. Germain (1979) further noted that although GST brings the complexity of the client's life space into focus, it does not provide the worker with guidance for intervention.

Ecological Theory

In an attempt to bridge the gap between the abstraction of systems theory and the demands and realities of practice, Carel Germain, a leader in efforts to reconceptualize the environment for social work practice, introduced ecological concepts into social work theory.

Central to the ecological perspective, which Germain and others consider a subset of systems theory (see, e.g. Germain 1978; Germain and Gitterman 1987; Meyer 1983), is the idea of the continuous, transactional relationships between organisms, or living systems, and their environments:

> People and their environments are viewed as interdependent, complementary parts of a whole in which person and environment are constantly changing and shaping the other. (Germain 1978, 539)

Germain argued that ecological thinking presented an organic worldview, relevant to living systems and closer to human experience, and thus more compatible with the value base of social work than general systems theory. From an ecological perspective, social work attention is directed to enhancing the growth, development, and adaptive capacities of people, to removing environmental obstacles, and to increasing the responsiveness and nutritive properties of the social and physical environment (Germain 1979, 1980). Intervention may be addressed to the person, to the environment, or to the transactions between the two, and is concerned with restoring adaptive balance (the fit between person and environment), reducing stress, enhancing coping, or promoting stability (Germain 1981b).

The ecological perspective provided Carel Germain with the theoretical means to develop a more complex and dynamic view of the environment in social work practice. To further articulate this for practitioners, she and Alex Gitterman developed the life model of social work practice (Germain & Gitterman 1980, 1996; Gitterman & Germain 1976), which applies the ecological metaphor to direct practice. In the life model, stresses that flow from a maladaptive fit between people and environments (reframed by Germain and Gitterman as "problems in living") are conceptualized as occurring in response to three major life areas: stressful life transitions, maladaptive interpersonal processes, and unresponsive environments. Professional intervention is formulated in terms of two central efforts: (1) liberating, supporting, and enhancing people's adaptive capacities (coping), and (2) increasing the responsiveness of social and physical environments to people's needs.

A significant contribution of the life model is the degree to which it focuses attention on the environment and environmental intervention as a core social work function. Indeed, the authors advocated

> maintaining a continuing vigilance with regard to the impact of environmental variables on clients; keeping sensitively attuned and open to clients' overt and masked requests for help with environmental issues;

maintaining clarity about the legitimacy and primacy of this area for joint worker-client attention and action. (Germain & Gitterman 1980, 156)

While the ecological perspective opens up rich possibilities for more holistic and integrative practice, like systems theory it also has limitations. Chief among these is a strong emphasis on evolutionary adaptation, a concept that unfortunately connotes adjustment to rather than change in environmental conditions (Gould 1987). The underlying ecological assumption that successful adaptation equates to health and well-being, and that the individual who does not adapt is coping less well than the one who does, is also open to question. Given the remarkable plasticity and adaptability of the human organism, there are many instances in which people adapt to environmental circumstances they should never be asked to tolerate. Similarly, there is a possibility that failure to adapt may wrongly be attributed to individual pathology or failure rather than to toxic or hostile environmental conditions.

The Ecosystems Perspective

Social work theorist Carol Meyer (1979, 1983) approached the "search for coherence" in the profession by combining systems and ecological theory in an overarching conceptual framework that, in keeping with similar work in other disciplines (see, for example, Auerswald 1968; Bronfenbrenner 1979), she called the "eco-systems perspective":

[E]co-systems theory is a metatheory that offers social work practitioners/clinicians a way of thinking about and assessing the relatedness of people and their impinging environments; it does not specify the what (problem-definition) or the how (methodology) of practice. For that it relies upon the increasingly large repertoire of available practice models, each one to make those specifications consistent with its particular theoretical orientations. (Meyer 1983, 29–30)

The ecosystems perspective is not a model of practice. Rather, as Meyer (1983) has repeatedly pointed out, it is a metatheoretical framework—a way of thinking about social work practice that enables the complexity of variables in the case to be viewed without the bias (often person-centered) inherent in a perspective grounded in a particular method or theory. Such an approach provides for a complex assessment of a case, and allows for the use of any practice model in keeping with social work purposes, values, and ethics. In particular, the ecosystems perspective offers social workers a way of conceptualizing the relationship between people and environments, and encourages a balanced approach to both domains of practice.

By applying ecological and systems concepts in tandem, the ecosystems perspective also overcomes, at least conceptually, some of the constraints inherent in reliance on one or the other. The ecological perspective balances the abstraction and mechanism of the systems theory, while systemic concepts encourage a focus on relatedness and the processes of change as well as on adaptation. The broader systems perspective also enables the construction of a metatheoretical framework that subsumes various methodological approaches in practice.

The ecosystems perspective has been very influential, particularly in social work education and as an encompassing intellectual structure for social work practice (Wakefield 1996a, 1996b). Conceptually, it has many advantages, including the "rich expression" it gives to social work's traditional concern with both person and environment; its comprehensive, holistic approach to assessment; its status as a nonprescriptive, open system of ideas; and its encouragement of a creative, eclectic approach to intervention (Siporin 1975).

As with any ambitious theoretical framework, however, there are weaknesses in the ecological-systems approach (for a recent critique, see Wakefield 1996a, 1996b). Key among these is the lack of a critical perspective. Almost without exception, the leading exponents of ecological-systems theory have given priority to the interdependence of person and environment, and have failed to explore the tension or dialectic between them. Further, as an open system of ideas, and one that is explicitly nondirective as to the interventive choices of the practitioner, the ecosystems perspective fails to provide sufficient protection against the continued erosion of the social purposes of the profession. It is assumed that social workers will act in terms of the tasks generated by the ecosystemic assessment, and in accordance with professional purposes, ethics, and values (Meyer 1983). The strong potential thus exists that workers will use those methods they are most familiar and comfortable with, and that often these will be person- rather than environment-centered.

The nondirectiveness of the ecosystems perspective also raises the possibility that approaches will be employed that are fundamentally inimical, either to each other, or to the purposes and values of the profession. In the politically laden and fiscally contingent environment that is the context of social work practice, a host of variables direct the attention and choices of the worker. Many of these, as we note in Chapter 7, direct attention away from the environmental domain of practice and from related social and structural issues. The profession's intellectual commitment to inclusiveness notwithstanding, the "problem" of the environment thus persists in contemporary theory and practice.

CONCLUSIONS

At the broadest level, shifts in social work's concern with the environment seem to follow shifts in society as a whole. In periods of social action and reform, such as the Progressive era or the 1930s depression, social work has likewise been more activist and environmentally oriented. In relatively introspective times, such as the 1920s or the years after World War II, social work has tended to be more person-centered (Franklin 1990).

Complexity emerges, however, when we look closely at the response to the environment in direct practice. Despite its environmentalist foundations, the central thrust in direct practice since the 1920s has been toward the conceptualization and refinement of interpersonal helping, constructed largely in psychological terms. Relegated to the sidelines, environmental intervention became the Cinderella of social casework—homely, commonplace, somehow lacking the importance, dignity, and status of person-centered practice. This hierarchy of value can be seen even in periods of considerable social upheaval, such as the depression years or the 1960s.

Our historical overview suggests three primary and interlocking contributory factors to the persistent marginalization of the environment in direct social work practice: (a) the impact of professionalization, (b) the lack of a comprehensive theory of environment and associated practice methods, and (c) the association of the environment with poverty and thus with marginality. We conclude the chapter with a brief discussion of these major influences.

Professionalization

The "problem" of the environment is in large part a function of the choices made by a developing profession in search of external recognition and status. As a minor profession, linked inextricably in the public mind with poverty, dysfunction, and social marginality, social work has always been particularly sensitive to the charge that it lacks a defined practice supported by a distinctive and transmissible body of knowledge and skill. This has been the case at least since 1915, when Abraham Flexner, who had been instrumental in bringing a Germanic model of the professions into American medicine, told social workers that they lacked the attributes of a profession (Flexner 1915). Stung by his judgments, social workers have made considerable efforts, over a long period of time, to frame the developing profession in his terms.

Flexner's model, which stressed abstract, scientific knowledge, graduate education, and professional accountability structures, created enormous tensions for a profession heavily reliant on case-based knowledge and an apprenticeship approach to training. Though the early social workers were experts in environments, their knowledge and skill, derived largely from everyday practice experience, lacked the professional credibility and authority of knowledge developed in the academy for application in the field. Furthermore, as Mary Richmond (1922) once observed, environmental practice suffered from "the handicap of the familiar"—to many of the early social workers (and their critics) it looked too much like "everybody's business," always in danger of being considered as being no more skillful than everyday neighborliness. On both counts, environmental knowledge and practice have been marginalized and devalued, contributing to the development of a hierarchy of knowledge and skill in direct practice, with psychological knowledge and treatment accorded priority.

Knowledge for Practice

Of the numerous explanations put forward for the relative neglect of the environment, the profession has taken most seriously the suggestion that the environment gets overlooked because social workers lack knowledge and skills for environmental intervention as powerful, conceptually appealing, and systematic as those available for person-centered practice (Germain 1979, 1981a, 1981b, 1983; Grinnell 1973; Grinnell & Kyte 1974; Siporin 1972). There has been both a lack of theoretical clarity about what constitutes the environment and, flowing from this, a failure to develop an extensive repertoire for environmental intervention.

In large part the profession's struggles to articulate a theory of environment have been reflective of the state of knowledge development more generally. Until quite recently, much of the knowledge available on the environment has, paradoxically, been seen as either too commonplace or too abstract to fit the profession's need for high-status knowledge that is also useful for everyday practice. Knowledge derived from daily practice was regarded as too simplistic and commonsensical. Environmental theory from the social sciences, on the other hand, was associated with "ivory tower" academics, was relatively abstract, difficult to link to practice, and often concerned with generalizing about large, messy, and overwhelming environmental factors that seemed largely unavailable to social casework intervention (the urban studies of the Chicago School provide one example of such knowledge).

The appeal of Freudian theory lay precisely in its ability to span this apparent contradiction: it had demonstrated utility for practice but at the same time met the criteria for "professional" knowledge established by the major professions. It offered hope of effective intervention, a "scientific" base for practice, and an organizing framework for professional development. By recentering the individual, it was in keeping with social casework's professional need to create a compact and definable focus. Further, it provided an effective and communicable method and a coherent body of knowledge. And, by association with psychiatry, it conferred a desirable measure of professional status. As a problem solution, Freudian theory was thus irresistible.

Association of Environment with Poverty

We suspect that the story of social work's ambivalent relationship with environmental intervention also has a subtext, which is that social workers struggle with the environment in part because of what it represents, or signifies, both in the profession and in American society more generally. In the early history of the profession, the environment was associated primarily with the needs and conditions of the urban poor. At a deeper level, the environment thus became associated also with deviance, dysfunction, and danger, since fear of the poor has always been a defining part of the larger social response to poverty and its consequences. In the Progressive era, for example, the early social workers and reformers were concerned not only to alleviate the effects of urban poverty but also to curb the excesses of the "dangerous classes" (Boyer 1978) and, hopefully, to restore social stability. Linked thus with poverty and danger, the environment has, it seems, been marginalized along with all that it represents.

Undoubtedly, these associations are reflected also in the profession's move away from the environment in the process of professionalization. Professions accrue status from their clientele as well as from the nature of their services. In social work, as in the public mind, there is very likely a link between the profession's historic commitment to the poor and oppressed and its own marginality in the system of professions. The search for professional status and public recognition has thus involved a shift away from the provision of services to the poor. Implicit in this shift was a concurrent move away from environmentalism and environmental intervention. When, for example, during and after World War I, the opportunity came for social workers to provide services "above the poverty line" to voluntary, fee-paying clients, and to break their primary identification as providers of services to the poor, they were eager to do so.

In the years after World War I, schools of social work proliferated, a series of professional associations were developed, and Freudian theory became increasingly influential as a base for practice. Though muted in the depression years, the desire for professional status remained firmly in place in the years between the wars, and indeed was sharpened by a broader social interest in defining human problems and their solution in scientific terms.

The conservative sensibility of the years following World War II both accommodated and supported the professional preoccupations of social caseworkers. In the main, social work attention was taken by old concerns: the continuing desire for professional status (Greenwood 1957; Kadushin 1958), the ongoing interest in the refinement of technique (Bisno 1956; Schorr 1959), and a preoccupation with fitting psychoanalytic theory to casework practice (Hamilton 1958). A new and related temptation, the increasing movement of social workers into private practice, also emerged. In the years after the war, the cleavage between public and private social services deepened as the casework mainstream pushed further toward a middle-class, fee-for-service clientele, and attempted to break the profession's identification with the disadvantaged (Pray 1947). Though rationalized in terms of the need for social work to develop a professional practice similar in form to that of other professions, the effort to develop universalistic services moved social casework further away from its traditional commitments to urban neighborhoods and to the poor.

Such issues are rarely explored on the surface of social work discourse. But they are of critical importance as social workers attempt to struggle more effectively with issues of race, class and marginality. Without critical awareness both that the environment stands as a code word for poverty, and that the profession's deep ambivalence about environmental practice is to some extent an expression of this identification with marginality, it is unlikely that environmental intervention will be fully recognized in social work practice.

NOTES

1. The historical "neglect" of the environment by social workers in direct practice, despite ongoing efforts by theorists to develop knowledge and skills on both sides of the person-environment equation, has long been recognized (see,

for example, Germain 1981b, 1983; Grinnell 1973; Grinnell & Kyte 1974; Meyer 1989).

2. For reasons having to do with our own recent research interests, the materials in this chapter focus largely on the history of environmental helping within the social casework tradition, or direct practice with individuals and families. We fully recognize that there is likewise a rich history of environmental practice in the groupwork tradition, beginning with the neighborhood-based settlement houses and continuing with the classic work of Grace Coyle, Robert Vinter, William Schwartz, and many others. The task of revisiting this tradition and reclaiming it for current environmental practice will be an important contribution to future work in person-environment practice.

3. This chapter is based in large part on Kemp (1994).

3

Knowledge Foundations:
Rethinking Environment for Social Work Practice

Our thinking about person-environment practice is informed by a diverse body of scholarship, both well established and emergent. A hallmark of this literature is its interdisciplinary and cross-paradigm nature, reflecting both a growing interest in context across a range of disciplines and awareness of the need to reach across professional and disciplinary boundaries to fully capture the complexity, variety, and multidimensionality of environmental experience in everyday life. Taken as a whole, it enables us to think in new ways about the contexts of social work practice and the environmental influences on our clients and their communities.

In this chapter, we set out the theoretical and empirical sources that frame the more detailed discussion of environmental assessment and intervention in person-environment practice that follows in Chapters 4 and 5. From the voluminous literature pertaining in some way to interactions between people and their environments, we have chosen that most relevant to direct social work practice and to social workers in their everyday work with individuals, families, groups, and neighborhoods. We present material that we hope will stimulate new thinking about the environmental contexts of social work practice, even though some of this material represents emergent thinking even in its own disciplinary settings. We recognize that our choice of material is selective, and that we do not encompass all that is typically included in social work discussions of environmental practice (see, for example, Neugeboren 1996), nor all that is available in the wider literature. We reiterate that this is not a book on all of social work practice, but one that is written with direct practice explicitly in mind. Our efforts here are just the beginning of what we anticipate will be renewed interest in more fully drawing into social work the rich array of interdisciplinary research now focused on the environmental domain.

The materials in this chapter are organized into three major groups: First, we discuss the relevance to person-environment practice of two interrelated practice perspectives: empowerment practice and the strengths perspective. Second, we overview an emergent interdisciplinary literature that addresses the multidimensional and socially structured nature of environmental experience. Third, we review past and current scholarship, primarily from an ecological-systems perspective, which enriches our understanding of the environmental contexts of human development and behavior. In conclusion, we provide definitions of environment, environmental assessment, and environmental intervention.

SOCIAL WORK PERSPECTIVES

Empowerment Theory and Practice

Our approach to person-environment practice is consistent with and draws on the rapidly expanding body of social work scholarship on empowerment theory and practice. Empowerment practice has deep roots in the earliest traditions of social work as well as in the social protests of the 1960s, the civil rights and women's movements, and a host of grass roots activities (Simon 1994). It is increasingly accepted both as a philosophical framework highly congruent with the mission and purposes of the profession and as a key approach to practice with people who are disadvantaged, marginalized, or oppressed. Women, people of color, the chronic mentally ill, the elderly, poor families, and the developmentally disabled are among the many groups who can benefit from efforts to enhance their personal, interpersonal, and collective power. Rappaport defines empowerment in the following terms:

> [Empowerment] suggests both individual determination over one's life and democratic participation in the life of one's community, often through mediating structures such as schools, neighborhoods, churches, and other voluntary organizations. Empowerment conveys both a psychological sense of personal control or influence and a concern with actual social influence, political power, and legal rights. It is a multilevel construct applicable to individual citizens as well as to organizations and neighborhoods; it suggests the study of people in context. . . . There is built into the term a quality of the relationship between a person and his or her community, environment, or something outside one's self. (1987, 121–130)

Empowerment practice is thus inherently, indeed inevitably, environmental and ecological, for it assumes that external circumstances lie at the center, not the margins, of client issues. The goal (whether short or longer term) is for people and communities to develop the capacity to resist and change external conditions adversely affecting their quality of life and opportunities for equitable access to resources and services. Central aspects of the empowerment process include critical analysis of the relationships between people and their environmental contexts, transformation of perspectives and beliefs about one's place in the world, the development and expansion of personal and group competencies, and action in relation to oppressive social and environmental conditions (Gutiérrez & Lewis, in press; Freire 1970; Parsons 1991).

Empowerment has personal, interpersonal, and social dimensions (Breton 1994; Gutiérrez & Ortega 1991), and encompasses both processes and outcomes (Breton 1994; Riger 1993). Personal empowerment includes the development of personal power, efficacy, and competence as a foundation for enhanced well-being and for action in the wider environment. Interpersonal empowerment involves interactions with others that develop critical awareness and enhance problem-solving, assertiveness, and the ability to be influential in critical life contexts. Social empowerment or political empowerment is centrally related to collective participation in social action and change activities.

While the overall process of empowerment is often represented as a developmental continuum from personal to social empowerment (see, for example, Kieffer 1984), we conceptualize it as ongoing and transactional, such that involvement in environmental action inevitably feeds into and supports personal and interpersonal empowerment, and vice versa. Empowerment practice thus provides, as Gutiérrez (1990) notes, an important bridge between personal transformation (or micropractice) and social/environmental change (macropractice).

From this it should be clear that empowerment is more than an individual-level construct (for example, increased self-esteem, self-efficacy, or the perception that one is more powerful or can influence external conditions). Necessary also is the practical application of these transformative processes to effect change in the everyday environment (Breton 1994; Freire 1973; Riger 1993): "The goal of effective practice is not coping or adaptation but an increase in the actual power of the client or community so that action can be taken to change and prevent the problems clients are facing" (Gutiérrez, DeLois, & GlenMaye 1995, 249). A combination of critical reflection and emancipatory action, or praxis, thus lies at the heart of empowerment practice.

The action-oriented, critical stance of empowerment practice vis-à-vis the environment goes beyond the emphasis on adaptation inherent in social work models informed primarily by an ecological perspective. In Chapter 2 we noted our concern that an overemphasis on adaptation can result in accommodation to inappropriate or even toxic environmental circumstances, particularly given the remarkable plasticity and adaptability of the human organism. Empowerment practice, which is predicated on a critical approach to person-environment transactions, encourages workers and clients to assess carefully the range of environmental impacts and to focus on environmental change, along with person-centered interventions.

Core dimensions of person-environment practice, derived from an empowerment perspective, include (O'Melia, Dubois, & Miley 1994; Simon 1990, 1994):

1. Participation

Active participation in the process of change by clients and consumers is an essential building block of effective practice. Key elements of participation include the formation of partnerships between clients and workers, and the development of mutual and reciprocal alliances between and among clients and consumers.

Client-Worker Partnerships. Simon points out that empowerment is not something that can be provided to or performed for others. Rather, it is "a reflexive activity, a process capable of being initiated and sustained only by the agent or subject who seeks power or self-determination" (1990, 32). A social worker can facilitate this process through collaborative, nonhierarchical roles such as consultant, advocate, systems guide, organizer, and resource broker. Though power differentials inevitably exist, and should not be denied, clients as well as workers deserve recognition for their expertise and skills. The goal, Simon (1994) suggests, is the achievement of "equal moral agency" between client and worker, including mutual respect, valuing what each brings to the process of change, and open acknowledgement of the power imbalances inherent in professional worker-client relationships.

A commitment to participation is realized also through client participation in program planning and service delivery. Studies of community participation, for example, demonstrate that active involvement results both in personal empowerment for community members (Rich, Edelstein, Hallman, & Wandersman 1995; Zimmerman & Rappaport 1988) and in more positive and durable outcomes for community projects (York & Itzhaky 1991). Participation can take many forms: the involvement of clients in program planning and management, involvement in community committees and coalitions, and increasing roles for consumer-providers in service delivery.

Client-Client Partnerships. The development of participatory and col-laborative relationships between and among clients/consumers is also fundamental to empowerment practice. Such relationships enhance in-terdependency, mutuality, and reciprocity among those experiencing similar issues, provide a forum for the development of collective per-spectives, and at the same time reduce unhelpful dependencies on social workers and other formal systems. This emphasis on interdependency and relationality stands in marked contrast to more traditional practice approaches, which typically reflect the wider social value placed on independence and self-sufficiency.

Groups, as we have already noted, are thus a central modality in empowerment practice. Small groups are an important context for mutu-al aid and support, for discussions that explore social realities and shift the focus from "individual discomfort" to the environmental causes of that discomfort (Brown & Ziefert 1988), and for the development of the sense of common purpose that is an important catalyst for collective action:

> Just as others help us validate our reality, the identification with others makes it possible to construct new perceptions of social realities, new social contexts for our behaviors. . . . *Out of these new perceptions comes the identification of change points in the environment. . . . Empowerment is that stage of development when one begins to confront the environmental sources of stress with the goal of social change.* (Brown & Ziefert 1988, 101–102 emphasis added)

Similarly, as we make clear in Chapters 4 and 5, social networks are an important focus of empowering and environmentally oriented prac-tice: "When they function well, social networks provide members with material assistance and services (caretaking), emotional nurturance and counseling, problem-solving advice and referral, and a forum for collec-tive action and advocacy" (Kemp 1995, 193). We explore the research literature on social networks in more detail in the last section of this chapter.

2. *Education*

The deep, intricate connections between knowledge and power (Foucault 1980; Freire 1973) point to education as a central modality in empowerment practice. First, as teachers, mentors, coaches, and guides, social workers provide and interpret essential information for individu-als, groups, and communities. Second, social workers have many op-portunities to collaborate with client systems to generate knowledge that will facilitate empowerment. Third, social workers teach valuable and much needed skills and competencies (Breton 1994).

Although educating clients about issues and resources has always been a integral part of direct practice, the educational role has typically not been highly valued in the social work repertoire. There is growing evidence, however, that education is a critical component of empowering and collaborative practice. In the mental health field, for example, families of the mentally ill have lobbied to be included as full partners in the caregiving process and have argued forcefully that shared knowledge and skill are essential elements of such a collaboration (Hatfield 1994). Family education models, a widely used intervention with families of the mentally ill, focus on the provision of comprehensive information, practical help, and the development of generic problem-solving skills for the longer term. These interventions are nonstigmatizing, responsive to individual and family needs, normalized, and often relatively brief, since their focus is not family treatment but the building of effective alliances with families.

A second important educational role involves collaborations with clients to develop knowledge about client system issues, resources, and challenges. Robust models for collaborative knowledge-building can be found in Participatory Action Research (PAR) (Finn 1994; Herr 1995; Sohng, in press), feminist research (Maguire 1987), and community psychology (Conti, Counter, & Paul 1991). Sohng notes that PAR "arose as an attempt to decentralize knowledge and the power it confers through participation of ordinary people in gaining knowledge" (in press, 8). She claims the involvement of ordinary citizens in the creation of "people's knowledge" as a central element in the process of giving people a voice in decision-making. Further, as "experts on their own lives," clients and consumers are a primary source of sturdy, ecologically valid data on the everyday realities facing individuals, families, and communities. Powerful examples of the links between empowerment and participatory knowledge-building can be found in self-help movements such as the disabilities movement, mobilizations by homeless groups, and AIDS activism and advocacy.

The benefits of participation in knowledge development extend beyond the generation of information. When we are actively involved in something, we frequently feel more sense of ownership, come to see the issues involved in new ways, learn new skills, and are more committed to the outcomes of the activity (Conti et al. 1991). The capacities gained through such participation become a resource for action and thus are a critical component of the process of emancipatory change. Since they are self-generated, they are also more likely to be maintained and thus to sustain learning and change into the future.

A third educational role for social workers involves teaching important skills and competencies (Germain & Gitterman 1980, 1996; Richey 1994). Although empowerment practice assumes that all clients and communities have strengths that can be mobilized, it is also true that disadvantaged and oppressed groups have significant gaps in the knowledge and skills they need to gain full access to resources and opportunities. The process of capacity-building at the individual, group, and community levels thus constitutes an important role for social workers committed to empowerment and self-sufficiency.

A focus on education, particularly in the context of collaborative and group-based practice, also provides important opportunities for clients to be both learners and teachers as they share knowledge and skills with others (Freire 1973; Riessman 1990). Since disempowered groups often believe that expertise lies only outside themselves and their local experience (Simon 1994) it is very important for social workers to provide opportunities that counter this perception. Lightburn and Kemp (1994) describe, for example, the potential for family support programs to become "learning collectives" that provide opportunities for parents to experience new roles as teachers, mentors, and experts on their cultural and community experience. Indeed, as Lynd (1992) points out, participatory learning has three key transformative aspects: outsiders educate insiders, insiders educate each other, and insiders educate outsiders.

3. *Critical Reflection*

Critical reflection is a multidimensional process that includes critical examination and discussion of everyday "lived, concrete experience" (Freire 1973); reflection on internalized beliefs and behaviors that reinforce oppression (i.e., the interaction between external conditions and internal processes; Lichtenberg 1990); and reevaluation and reinterpretation of individual and group experience in relation to wider social and environmental factors and forces, including analysis of the power relationships that determine access to resources and services (Dodd & Gutiérrez 1990). This ability to critically evaluate one's life circumstances and life experience and to "think against" the status quo opens up perspectives and provides the opportunity to conceptualize alternative ways of "being in the world." Freire and others have described this as a process of "conscientization" or consciousness-raising (Freire 1973; Longres & McLeod 1980).

Although reflectiveness is often thought of as primarily an introspective, private, or cognitive process (see, for example, the literature on critical thinking; Gibbs & Gambrill 1996), in empowerment practice, "critical reflection" is essentially outer-directed, action-oriented, and dialogical: "Conscientization . . . becomes part of an empowering strategy only if the cognitive structuring it entails leads to seizing or creating

opportunities in the environment" (Breton 1994, 32). Empowerment theorists also suggest that the process of critical reflection occurs most
powerfully and readily through dialogue with others.

Through dialogue, people have the opportunity to examine their assumptions from the perspective of others, to explore common ground
and areas of difference, and to externalize and contextualize their personal experiences (Rose 1990). Since dialogue is typically constructed as
a process that moves outward from personal experiences and preoccupations to a wider collective and social analysis (Hart 1990), group
work is emphasized as an ideal modality for dialogical and empowerment practice (Dodd & Gutiérrez 1990; Gutiérrez 1990). Our own perspectives on dialogue are informed by multiple influences, including
Freire's (1973) emphasis on dialogical process as the foundation for critical consciousness and social action, the work of physicist David Bohm
(1980) on dialogue as a form of "participatory consciousness" that provides the basis for the construction of common meanings, and the robust feminist tradition of "speaking out," "naming," and "talking back"
(hooks 1990), all of which encompass collective strategies for the development of new understandings and perspectives on self/group-in-
environment.

4. Transformation of Perspectives

Through critical reflection, dialogue, and action, people develop new
perspectives on themselves and their relationship to the external world.
These perspectives provide the conceptual or cognitive foundation for
effective participation in social and environmental action. To act differently in the environment requires the belief that this is possible. Key
elements of this transformation of perspectives include a sense of self-
efficacy (the belief that one has power and control over the outcomes of
one's life), assertiveness, and, at the cognitive level, a realistic appraisal of
environmental barriers and obstacles and of the impact of wider social
conditions on life opportunities. While the development of such critical
perspectives is sometimes conceptualized as a shift in perceived locus of
control from externally to internally directed, this construction should be
used cautiously given cultural and class variations in the valuing of inner-
directedness and individually oriented forms of coping (Bechtel 1986).

5. Competence-Building in Clients and Communities

From an empowerment perspective, competence is conceptualized as
a function of the transactions between people and environments rather
than as some innate ability or personal characteristic (Breton 1984, 1994).
In his ground-breaking book, Maluccio described "ecological compe-

tence" as the "repertoire of skills, knowledge and qualities that enable people to interact effectively with their environments" (1981, ix). Included under the rubric of ecological competence are the multiple skills required for effective action in one's environment or life space, including "problem-solving; skills for community or organizational change; 'life skills' such as parenting, job-seeking or self-defense; and interpersonal skills such as assertiveness, social competency, or self advocacy" (Dodd & Gutiérrez 1990, 72–73). Kieffer (1984) defined "participatory competence," which he considered essential to empowerment, as having three interconnecting dimensions: sense of personal competence, critical understanding of the sociopolitical environment, and the development of personal and collective resources for action. Competence-oriented practice thus encompasses both individual and environmental change: emphasis is placed on identifying and clarifying client system competencies, mobilizing actual or potential client system strengths, using natural helping networks and other environmental resources, and developing a mutual and authentic relationship between client and worker (Maluccio 1981).

6. Social/Environmental Action

While the dimensions described above, including critical reflection, education, and personal transformation, are all necessary components of empowerment, they are not decisive to it. For empowerment to be fully realized, individuals, groups, and communities must also have real access to social and material resources such as employment, housing, decent schools and affordable health care. The work of sociologist William Julius Wilson (1987, 1996), for example, makes clear the essential relationships between welfare dependency and the lack of employment structures in poor neighborhoods. Robert Halpern (1995b, 1995c) similarly points out the limitations on neighborhood-based initiatives in impoverished communities created by resource and opportunity constraints in the larger society: "The idea that poor neighborhoods contain the resources and capacities for their own regeneration can be, and often has been, used to promote self-help without the requisite external supports and linkages" (p. 222). Efforts at the local level must thus be linked with larger efforts to increase social equity and access.

A Note on Culturally Competent Practice

Of the many aspects of an empowerment perspective that are consistent also with a commitment to culturally competent practice, two seem particularly salient:

1. a commitment to social justice,
2. a commitment to recognizing, valuing, and building on diversity.

In both respects, a concern with the environment is of central importance. Indeed, our research for this book has made us increasingly aware of both the deep structural relationships between environment and oppression, and the complex and intimate connections between environmental experience and diversity. Since we explore these connections in more detail in Chapter 6, our purpose here is only to remind readers of the salience of an environmental perspective to culturally competent social work practice.

In the next section of this chapter, for example, we describe an emerging body of scholarship that explores the ways in which everyday environments produce and reinforce wider social patterns of privilege and oppression (consider, for example, formal and informal mechanisms of residential segregation). A critical understanding of the relationships between environmental experience, class, and culture is thus an important dimension of effective cross-cultural practice. This perspective is demonstrated in the work of Nagda and Gutiérrez (1996), who distinguish between *ethnocentric practice,* which focuses on adaptation and conformity to dominant cultural values, beliefs, and behaviors; *ethnic-sensitive practice,* which is primarily concerned with cultural awareness and the development of group pride and identity; and *ethnoconscious practice,* which blends ethnic-sensitive practice and an empowerment perspective and is centrally concerned with social justice and equality of participation and access.

The links between cultural competence and person-environment practice come with the understanding that there are vast differences in the ways everyday environments are perceived and experienced, and that many of these differences have deep tap roots in culture, ethnicity, gender, sexual orientation, and other forms of diversity. Increasingly, feminist, postmodern, postcolonial, and multicultural scholars reject a narrow reliance on universalistic, monolithic, and "objective" views of reality in favor of a partial, positional, "situated" awareness of the rich and complex diversity of social and environmental experience (Bondi & Domosh 1992; Collins 1986; Haraway 1988; Harding 1986; Hartman 1992; Rose 1993; Smith 1987). Though not without its own problems and contradictions (Hekman 1997; Leonard 1994, 1995), this literature is a valuable pathway to deeper and more complex understandings of the particular ways in which social and geographic locations interact with individual and collective experience. This enhanced understanding of multiple and overlapping spatial and environmental realities is a core but neglected dimension of culturally competent practice. Our efforts in

Chapter 6 represent only a small beginning in the work still to be done in this area.

The Strengths Perspective

Empowerment theory, which by its nature is concerned with redressing the negative impacts of environmental forces on individuals and communities, provides an important foundation for a more critical understanding of the environment. We consider such an analysis to be much needed, and indeed long overdue, as a component of direct social work practice. At the same time, this critical understanding of environments as a locus of oppression and inequality must be balanced by the equally valid understanding that they are also a vital source of support and opportunity. For this we turn to the strengths perspective, which has a long provenance in social work (Longres 1996) but only recently has received sustained theoretical and methodological attention (Saleebey 1992, 1996, 1997; Sullivan & Rapp 1994; Weick, Rapp, Sullivan, & Kisthardt 1989). The strengths perspective reminds us of the positive attributes, resources, capacities, potentialities, and competencies of clients and communities. Attention is focused on resilience in the face of adversity and on the many ways in which clients cope, survive, and thrive, rather than on pathology, risk, and dysfunction. "In a strengths approach," Weick and Saleebey point out, "we are obliged to make an accounting of what people know and what they can do. We are beholden to render a roster of resources that exist in and around individual, family, and community" (1995, 4). This focus on local resources is quite different, as Delgado notes, from the profession's historical reliance on a "paradigm of scarcity," or the belief that "outside resources are the only answer to a community's needs" (1996, 169).

In large part a philosophy of practice, the strengths perspective is grounded firmly in the social purposes and humanistic values of the profession, including a concern with empowerment and social justice. Key assumptions of the strengths perspective (DeJong & Miller 1995; Saleebey 1992, 1997), include:

1.   The belief that all persons and environments have strengths that can be harnessed to improve quality of life.
2.   The belief that client motivation is enhanced by a consistent emphasis on strengths, particularly as defined by the client.
3.   The understanding that discovering and building on strengths is best achieved through collaboration and partnership between client and worker.

4.   The belief that all environments contain resources, actual and potential, which can be mobilized for change.

Conceptually, if not always in practice (Longres 1996), the strengths perspective gives equal weight to both personal and environmental factors. A particular challenge for social work, with its commitment to poor and oppressed populations, is to identify strengths and resources in environments that often seem devoid of opportunities and hope. America's poor urban neighborhoods come immediately to mind—environments that have been at the center of social work concern since the turn of the century (Boyer 1978). Faced with potent images, in the media but also in more scholarly writing, of inner cities as "tangles of pathology" (Wilson 1987) and "urban war zones" (Garbarino, Kostelny, & Dubrow 1991), it is frequently difficult to see the complex and varied tapestry of everyday life present in these communities as in all others. This is particularly so if our primary contact with clients takes place outside their natural settings, in welfare offices, mental health clinics, substance abuse programs, or hospital emergency rooms.

Because public perceptions of poverty, violence, drugs, and urban decay form such a powerful filter, and our agencies are often both physically and culturally distanced from our clients, we may fail to notice the networks of kin and friends, churches, natural helpers, and store-front agencies, the times when neighborhoods come together to play or to grieve, and the opportunities this complex web of interactions present for further enrichment and development (Kretzmann & McKnight 1993). Nor do we always recognize and validate the resourcefulness and tenacity of the individuals and families who negotiate life in such neighborhoods on a daily basis (Cook & Fine 1995; Swadener & Lubeck 1995). A strengths perspective, as Sullivan points out, is one pathway to a more complex and contextualized view of client systems:

> A strengths perspective of social work practice offers an alternative conception of the environment. This perspective promotes matching the inherent strengths of individuals with naturally occurring resources in the social environment. . . . Recognizing, recruiting and using these strengths can help maximize the potential of our clients and our community. In addition, when the environment is viewed as a source of opportunities for clients, rather than as an ecology of obstacles, the sheer number of helping resources we perceive expands dramatically. (1992b, 148–149)

This perspective comes to life in Feldman and Stall's (1994) ethnographic study of African-American women in a public housing project in Chicago. The women's efforts to improve their daily living environment became a vehicle for individual and collective empowerment: as they worked together to reclaim recreational facilities and to create and staff a community laundry, the women built a relational community that provided support and a base for future action. Through such interactive processes, the authors note, "individuals purposefully transform the physical environment into a meaningful place while in turn transforming themselves" (p. 172). Carol Stack's (1974) seminal study of African-American kin networks likewise offers powerful evidence of the networks of care and mutuality that enable survival in the midst of urban poverty.

We are not suggesting a romanticized view of poverty-stricken or oppressive environments or of the people who live in them. Stack's work, for example, demonstrates very clearly that kin networks are a barrier to upward mobility as well as a source of strength and survival. David Harvey (1989) likewise points out the potentially limiting effects of place-attachment in poor communities and of social movements that are overly defined by local issues and resources.

All environments present obstacles as well as opportunities, and the people who live in them struggle with real problems. It is not our intention to deny these realities; indeed we encourage a more critical and dialectical view of environmental impacts on people in all walks of life and of every experience. Our stance is one of acknowledging complexity—both increased awareness of the negative impacts of environmental structures and conditions on human life and increased efforts to acknowledge, build on, replenish, and enhance naturally occurring strengths, potentialities, and resources, wherever these are found in the lives and everyday environments of our clients. In the following section, we present material from a range of perspectives that helps us to think about the environment in this more complex way.

CRITICAL AND CONSTRUCTIVIST VIEWS OF ENVIRONMENT

Wider intellectual currents increasingly reflect a critical awareness of the diverse and complex relationships between person and place (see, for example, Agnew & Duncan 1989; Blunt & Rose 1994; Friedland & Boden 1994; Gregory 1994; Keith & Pile 1993; Kirby 1996; Massey 1994). This renewed interest in the environmental contexts of human life, evident in scholarship from a range of disciplinary and theoretical perspectives, challenges the taken-for-grantedness of space and place in traditional social theory—a tendency, critics suggest, that both naturalizes and normalizes existing spatial arrangements and conditions. In contrast, recent scholarship raises important questions about the inevitability, reasonableness, and neutrality of physical and social environments. As geographer Edward Soja argues:

> We must be insistently aware of how space can be made to hide consequences from us, how relations of power and discipline are inscribed in the apparently innocent spatiality of social life, how human geographies become filled with politics and ideology. (1989, 6)

This more recent scholarship is helpful on many levels. In general, it moves our thinking away from static and monolithic views of the environment toward the understanding that "the environment" is perceived and experienced in many different ways, depending on one's view of the world and position within it. As we point out, however, it is important that we understand not only the subjective experience of particular individuals and communities, but also the relationships between environmental experience and larger social categories, such as race, ethnicity, gender, sexual orientation, and personal capacity. Framing both these levels, but also woven through them, are the "hidden realities" of environment: the intersection of race, class and power with environmental experience, and the understanding that environments are fundamentally expressions of larger social arrangements.

Meaning and Environment: Constructions of Environmental Experience

The understanding that "reality" is mediated by individual and collective systems of meaning and belief is increasingly influential across a range of disciplines (Berger & Luckmann 1967; Bruner 1990; Geertz 1983; Mishler 1979). As Carolyn Saari observes, "current theories outside of social work are now suggesting both that meaning is created in interpersonal interaction and that the content of the meaning system of the individual is basically reflective of that person's experiences in an environment that is both social and physical" (1991, 14). In the helping professions, this influence can be seen in a growing interest in constructionism, and meaning-making, including the use of narrative and story as elements of practice (Berlin 1996; Franklin & Nurius 1996; Laird 1994; Saari 1991; Saleebey 1994; Scott 1989; White & Epston 1990). Community psychologist James Garbarino (1993), for example, describes narrative reconstruction, including journal writing and storytelling, as an important tool for helping children who live with daily experiences of community violence and trauma to make meaning of growing up in an unsafe world. Writing from a clinical perspective, Saari (1992) like-wise suggests that meaning provides the bridge between person and environment.

In geography, scholars such as Yi-Fu Tuan (1977), David Seamon (1979), and Peter Jackson (1989) have drawn on humanism and phenom-enology to conceptualize the ways in which individuals and groups experience and actively interpret their everyday environments. A con-siderable body of work in cultural geography, for example, has explored the idea of "sense of place," which has been defined as "the meaning, intention, felt value, and significance that individuals and groups give to places" (Gesler 1992, 738). We become attached, in different ways, to the places we inhabit. Through everyday living and doing, "space" is trans-formed into "place": over time, places become part of individual and community identity as they accrue memories, images, and symbolic meaning (Kirby 1996).

Consideration of the "meaning" of environments is useful also as a way of thinking about the fluidity of environmental experience. Not only is there wide variation in the ways that different people experience the same place, but individual experiences of place vary significantly by mood, experience, and developmental stage. The special places of child-hood often seem very different when we revisit them as adults; home may no longer feel like a refuge after it is the site of a rape or a burglary; the busy urban environment that energizes a younger person may terri-fy that same person in old age. Korbin and Coulton (in press) provide vivid evidence of the differences between "objective" and "perceived" realities when they observe that mothers in dangerous urban neighbor-hoods prefer their children to play in dead-end alleys rather than in public playgrounds. To the mothers, the playgrounds were dangerous and unprotected, while the alleys, though seemingly bleak and inhospi-table, were seen as a "protected, restricted environment, one in which children could experience the freedom of being outdoors without being exposed to danger from traffic or from the deleterious conditions of the neighborhood" (Korbin & Coulton, in press, 20).

Contemporary interest in "meaning-making" extends and revitalizes a rich tradition of scholarship on the experiential environment. Both Kurt Lewin's (1935, 1936) concept of "life space" and Husserl's (1970) concept of the "lifeworld" evoke the particular, individualized ways in which each person constructs his or her physical and social world. Building on these ideas, Urie Bronfenbrenner (1977) emphasized the importance of the perceived environment, reminding his readers of the famous dictum by W. I. Thomas: "If men define situations as real, they are real in their consequences." Michael Rutter likewise points out that a person's responses, for example to environmental stress, are influenced by "his appraisal of the situation, by his capacity to process the experience, attach meaning to it, and to incorporate it into his belief system" (1985, 608). These ideas are reflected in the work of medical sociologist Aaron Antonovsky (1979, 1987), who suggested that well-being is centrally related to a construct that he termed a "sense of coherence," or the extent to which the world is perceived as meaningful, manageable, and comprehensible.

Constructivist and humanist perspectives on the environment shift our understanding of the environment from unitary conceptions of reality (the "reality," for example, to which we assume that "sane" people are oriented) toward the awareness that the world contains many realities, and that any environment thus has multiple dimensions. These perspectives also help us to understand the complex relationships between place, collective identity, and self-definition. In addition, and of particular importance, they remind us that people are active agents in the environments that they inhabit. For all these reasons, they fit well with social work practice perspectives that emphasize individual and collective agency and empowerment.

Though conceptually fruitful, these perspectives are not, however, unproblematic. Of particular concern is the tendency (evident, for example, in the social work literature on the strengths perspective) for authors who are strongly influenced by humanist and phenomenological thinking to overemphasize subjective experience and individual agency, and to underestimate potent social and historical realities, such as power inequities, racism, and poverty. To encompass more fully these critical dimensions of environmental experience, it is helpful to turn to scholarship that explores the relationships between environments and larger social, structural, and political arrangements.

Power and Environment:
The "Politics of Place"

An emerging body of critical scholarship examines the ideological, structural nature of environments. Key themes in this literature include the ways in which the power relations of capitalist society are expressed in space and place, and the means by which space produces and reinforces prevailing patterns of privilege and social inequity. Critical theorists focus on the impact of structures of domination and oppression on environmental experience, and on the spatial inequalities that result from class, gender, ethnic, and other socially constructed divisions (Harvey 1989; Soja 1989). Social structure is seen as embedded in spatial structure, and in the myriad of spatial devices (boundaries, territories, in-groups and out-groups, margins and centers, "closets" and free spaces) that maintain hierarchies of power and privilege. A "subtle geography of enclosure, confinement, surveillance, partitioning, social discipline, and spatial differentiation" (Jezierski 1991, 179) separates the more powerful from the less powerful, the socially accepted from the socially marginal. As geographer Joni Seager has observed, "Street harassment keeps women in their place. Residential segregation maintains racial hierarchies. Men's clubs and old-boy institutions keep power and knowledge literally behind closed doors" (1993, 3).

A class analysis, for example, suggests that the built environment and access to it are shaped by class power and privilege. Individuals and groups with more power and resources determine not only how the environment will be used, but by whom and on what terms (consider, for example, the siting of waste transfer stations, freeways, and airports; the bylaws and curfews that determine who can be on the streets and at what times; or the constellation of banking and real estate practices that create and maintain residential segregation). Such classifications of space underline and perpetuate oppressive social arrangements and strengthen social categories based on various forms of "difference." As geographer David Harvey argues:

> Those who have the power to command and produce space possess a vital instrumentality for the reproduction and enhancement of their own power. They can create material space, the representation of space, and spaces of representation. (1989)

Affluent groups have much greater control of space, have more spatial freedom, and are considerably less susceptible to external controls and surveillance than the poor. The recent proliferation of gated communities provides a salient example of the intersection between class and use of geographic space. Like racially segregated suburbs, these affluent enclaves intensify social polarities and, ironically, probably heighten perceptions of danger by minimizing opportunities for interaction between diverse groups. One resident of a gated community, interviewed for a recent article in the *New York Times*, described a neighborhood "totally devoid of random encounters. So you develop this instinct that everyone is just like me" (Egan 1995, 1). Such spatial segregation intensifies the "Otherness" and marginality of disadvantaged populations, for the affluent are insulated not only from people different from themselves, but also from the realities of life in poor neighborhoods.

Critical perspectives counter the more common tendency to regard the environment as a neutral backdrop for human activity. So accustomed are we to the spaces we inhabit that it is difficult to see them as expressions of larger social/structural arrangements and preferences. By pointing up the ways in which ideology is imbedded in environmental structure and experience, this body of scholarship provides an important foundation for critical analysis of the relationships between people and their environmental contexts. For social workers, however, a limiting factor is the extent to which this literature tends to deny human agency in favor of social and environmental determinism.

Person-Environment Transactions

Mindful of the unhelpful polarities generated by setting individual and collective agency against social and structural conditions, much current scholarship usefully blends both humanist and materialist perspectives. In this literature, which is perhaps best described as social constructionist in orientation, the focus is on the recursive or dialectical interaction between structure (material conditions) and individual agency and experience. Place is seen as a "negotiated" reality, the outcome of reciprocal negotiations between people and the places they inhabit. Environments, in other words, are "enacted": people both act upon and are shaped by the contexts of everyday life.

Geographer David Harvey (1989) observes, for example, that oppressed populations have little power over "space," but that they can and do construct "place," and that it is through the construction of and attachment to places—home, neighborhood, community—that poor and oppressed groups create identity and meaning. Cultural critic bell hooks gives life and meaning to this idea in her work on the historical importance of "homeplace" in black culture: "that space where we return for renewal and self-recovery, where we can heal our wounds and become whole" (1990, 49). hooks eloquently describes, for example, the historical efforts of black women to create, in their domestic lives, "spaces of care and nurturance in the face of the brutal, harsh reality of racist oppression, of sexist domination" (ibid., 43). For hooks, such places are crucial not only as sites of connection and nurturance, but also as "sites of resistance"—free and private spaces that afford oppressed and minority groups the opportunity to connect and organize beyond the gaze of mainstream society. Further, by claiming marginality as a place of power and emancipation, hooks denies its traditional association with exclusion and otherness.

The idea that marginal space has the potential to be liberating as well as oppressive has also been explored by Evans and Boyte (1986) in their work on "free spaces" as locations for the development of a sense of citizenship and commonality. Describing the historical and contemporary importance of black churches, for example, they argue that for

> alternative cultures to emerge and survive, people need community places that they own themselves, voluntary associations where they can think and talk and socialize, removed from the scrutiny and control of those who hold power over their lives. (pp. 27–28)

James Scott (1990) builds on this idea when he marks the importance of "sequestered" social spaces that provide oppressed groups with the opportunity to develop "hidden transcripts of resistance." Like hooks, Scott affirms the important role of domestic spaces, but he also describes a range of public and semipublic venues that afford subjugated groups the opportunity to express their true feelings and to reach mutual agreements:

> None of the practices and discourses of resistance can exist without tacit or acknowledged coordination and communication within the subordinate group. For that to occur, the subordinate group must carve out for itself social spaces insulated from control and surveillance from above. (p. 118)

Black churches, lesbian and gay bars, self-help and mutual aid groups, the proliferation of new social movements, a host of voluntary associations: all of these, Evans and Boyte (1986) suggest, are "participatory environments" that nurture collective understandings and action.

For the disenfranchised, however, attachment to place also has its costs. Low-income and minority communities, for example, are subject not only to the opportunity structures and surveillance of the wider society, but also to the "leveling" effects that result from an ethic of communal, rather than individual responsibility (Stack 1974). In the gay community, spatial separation affords opportunities for connection and affirmation but also limits access to wider social opportunities.

Taken as a whole, the three interdisciplinary perspectives we have presented—constructions of environmental experience, the politics of space and place, and person-environment transactions—along with the strengths and empowerment perspectives, point to the importance of more complex understandings of the interactions between "objective" environmental conditions and human agency, with their inherent tensions and contradictions. In addition, however, direct practitioners need solid foundation knowledge regarding the transactions between people and their particular everyday life contexts. For this, we turn next to ecological systems theory and the rich body of research that has flowed from this perspective.

ECOLOGICAL SYSTEMS THEORY

Our perspectives on person-environment practice have been stimulated and continue to be shaped by the numerous social work and social science scholars who have added to our understanding of the practical implications of an ecological systems perspective. From social work these include, but are not limited to the substantial contributions of Carol Meyer, Carel Germain, Alex Gitterman, Max Siporin, and Anthony Maluccio. From social science, they include such giants as Kurt Lewin, Urie Bronfenbrenner, and Nicholas Hobbs, as well as more recent contributors such as James Garbarino, Arnold Sameroff, Edward Seidman, Julian Rappaport, and Carl Dunst. From them and many other scholars, we have learned much of the power of proximate and distal environments to shape optimum as well as adverse outcomes for individuals, families and communities. We have learned as well from many interventionists operating from an ecological perspective of the elasticity of environments and their amenability to change.

Ecology refers, simply, to the relationship of an organism to its (multiple) environments. Ecological processes refers to the ways in which the organism and its environments affect and respond to each other. Bronfenbrenner's definition of human development captures these notions:[1]

> [Human development is] the progressive, mutual accommodation between an active, growing human being and the changing properties of the immediate settings in which the developing person lives, as this process is affected by relations between these settings, and by the larger context in which the settings are imbedded. (1979, 2)

As Garbarino points out, Bronfenbrenner's basic concept of development contains an important social component: "An individual's social field increases concomitantly with his or her overall development" (1983, 10). Bronfenbrenner suggests three features of his definition of development worthy of note: First, the developing person is viewed not merely as a tabula rasa on which the environment makes its impact, but as a growing, dynamic entity who actively moves into and restructures the environment. Second, interaction between individual and environment is bidirectional, i.e., it requires a process of *mutual* accommodation characterized by reciprocity. Third, environment, as conceived here, is not limited to a single immediate setting such as the family or peer group, but extends to incorporate interconnections between such primary settings, as well as external influences emanating from the larger community and society. This ecological environment is conceived topologically as a nested arrangement of concentric structures, each contained within the next (Bronfenbrenner uses the example of a set of "nested Russian dolls" to capture this image; 1979, 21–22). What are these different levels of environment? Bronfenbrenner posits a four-part categorization:

The *microsystem* represents the smallest developmental context directly experienced by the developing person. Interaction consists of direct, face-to-face contact, including, for example, the family, a friendship group, a school classroom, a neighborhood play group, and so on. Key elements of the microsystem are activities, roles, and interpersonal relations as they are played out, say, in the context of the family. A central concept is experienced, suggesting the importance not only of the objective properties of the microsystem but the ways in which these properties are perceived by the people in that environment (ibid., 22). For most children, the microsystem is, at the beginning, quite small. It consists, perhaps, of relationships with one or two primary caretakers in the essential activities of daily living. Over time, these relationships expand and the nature of the activities becomes increasingly more complex. This expanding capacity for ever greater levels of complex interaction is, for Bronfenbrenner, the essence of human development.

The *mesosystem* (meaning, literally, "in between") describes the interrelations among two or more settings in which the developing child actively participates. Examples here include the links between the family and a primary school, a neighborhood and a family daycare home, or between a church-sponsored nursing home and its local congregation. A central notion here is that the stronger and more diverse the linkages between microsystems, the more powerful the resulting mesosystem will be as an influence on development. As Garbarino suggests, a rich range of mesosystems is both a product and a cause of development. For example, a "well-connected" child's resulting sense of competence increases her or his ability to form further connections (1981, 23).

While individuals clearly play a prominent role in shaping and elaborating their own mesosystems, external forces often play a role as well. Bronfenbrenner refers to these as *exosystems,* meaning one or more settings that do not involve the developing child as an active participant but nonetheless influence the primary developmental settings: the parent's workplace, or a school class attended by an older sibling. Cochran and Brassard (1979) suggest multiple ways in which the parents' network of friends can influence the developing child in indirect ways, as well as directly, face to face. As family constellations and patterns change, the impact of the exosystem becomes greater. Consider, for example, the critical nature of workplace hours to mothers of preschool children, whose participation in the workforce has increased dramatically in recent years.

Finally, all of these levels of environment are influenced by the *macro-system:* the general culture of a society underpinned by such intangibles as ideology, belief systems, custom, and law. Bronfenbrenner speaks of the macrosystem as providing the "blueprints" for society: how and in what form basic services such as health care, education, and social services are to be cast. For example, to what extent have American cultural norms on violence and family privacy influenced the incidence and re-medial approaches to child abuse and related problems of family vio-lence (Garbarino 1977)?

Other key concepts from the ecological paradigm include *ecological transition*—a change in a person's position that results from an alterna-tion in role, setting, or both—and *ecological validity,* which, in the context of person-environment practice, refers to the extent to which the environment that is experienced by clients has the properties that it is supposed or assumed to have by the practitioner (Bronfenbren-ner 1979). For example, to what extent do public and voluntary child and family service agencies understand the patterns of informal care-giving and child rearing among minority families they serve? In fact, the presence of just such criticism was one element that spurred the growth of culturally sensitive practice in services such as adoptions and foster care (Billingsley & Giovannoni 1972; McAdoo 1988; Stack 1974).

For each of the four levels of environment, Garbarino (1981) suggests the potential for sociocultural *risk* and *opportunity.* By opportunity, he means a person-environment relation in which the developing person is offered material, emotional, and social encouragement compatible with his or her needs and capacities at a given time. Conversely, risk suggests danger to development that comes from outside the individual in the way in which his or her world is organized.

The ecological paradigm offers us a set of lenses for examining person-environment fit at different levels of size and complexity (Ger-main & Gitterman 1996). It orients us to the multiple contextual influ-ences on human behavior, the notion of reciprocity between person and environment, and the implications for what has been called in social work "environmental" or "indirect" helping. As we saw in Chapter 2, the idea of understanding the person-in-environment has long been part of the tradition of social work practice. In short, our field builds on a rich and diverse tradition of understanding and of aiding the individual person in an environmental context. In fact, much of our present inter-est in areas such as social support networks and environmental helping flows from this tradition. Today the social work focus on ecological assessment and intervention is carried on in the work of many practitioner-researchers (Biegel 1987; Germain & Gitterman 1987, 1996;

Hartman & Laird 1983; Maluccio 1987; Meyer 1993; Polansky & Gaudin 1983). This work parallels that in sister disciplines such as community psychology (Gottlieb 1983, 1985; Seidman 1991; Seidman, Aber, Allen, & French 1996; Shinn 1996) and applied behavioral analysis (Dumas & Wahler 1983; Jeger & Slotnick 1982; Jones, Weinrott, & Howard 1981; Rogers-Warren & Rogers-Warren 1977), where issues of maintenance and generalization of behavioral change are forcing clinician researchers to pay closer attention to environmental-contextual factors. This is also the case in early childhood and parent-child intervention programs where the "unit of service" is increasingly a composite of person-centered and environment-centered interventions (Barnard et al. 1985; Dunst & Trivette 1986; Lightburn & Kemp 1994; Olds 1988). Taken together, this work affirms the simple eloquence of Kurt Lewin's equation: $B = F(P, E)$ (Lewin 1935, 73). *Behavior is, indeed, a function of person and environment in continuous, reciprocal interaction.*

While useful as an orienting framework for practice knowledge, the ecological paradigm offers no panacea. Indeed, its lack of domain-specific content feeds the skepticism of many practitioners and practice researchers toward elegant theories, or "systems" frameworks that offer few specifics for practice (Wakefield 1996a, 1996b). For our present purpose, however, the following quotation from Holahan, Wilcox, Spearly, and Campbell captures the critical significance of the ecological orientation for practice:

> The environmental emphasis of the ecological view supports environmentally oriented interventions directed toward strengthening or establishing methods of social support. . . . [T]he transactional emphasis of the ecological perspective fosters individually oriented interventions directed toward promoting personal competencies for dealing with environmental blocks to achieving personal objectives. (Holahan et al. 1979, quoted in Whittaker & Tracy 1989, 26)

SOCIAL AND PHYSICAL ENVIRONMENTS

Social Networks and Social Support

The term *social network* refers to the structure and number of a person's social relationships. *Social support,* on the other hand, refers to exchanges within a network (emotional encouragement, concrete assistance or tangible aid, and advice and information) that are perceived as beneficial. Social support can occur spontaneously through natural helping networks of family, friends, neighbors, etc., or it can be professionally designed or mobilized, as in support groups or volunteer matching programs. A social support network is the subset of a network that provides support on a regular basis (Whittaker & Garbarino 1983).

More social network resources does not necessarily imply more social support. Social network size, for example, neither reveals what types and amounts of supportive behaviors are exchanged, nor how the person experiences those exchanges. People may be surrounded by large social networks, but may not feel supported or may not be receiving the supports they need. Some existing social networks may be negative, in the sense that they are critical or that they encourage harmful antisocial behaviors such as drug abuse. Some networks may be a source of excessive demands and caregiving responsibilities, particularly for women (Fischer 1982; Belle 1982). Therefore not all social ties are supportive; supportive ties may come as part of networks that also contain nonsupportive ties. Social support is a multidimensional construct, consisting of social network resources, types of support, perceptions of support, and skills in accessing and maintaining support (Heller & Swindle 1983). Research has documented the significance of such variables as the types of support provided (Unger & Powell 1980), the timing of support delivery (Jacobsen 1986), the source of support, and the characteristics of the support recipient (Vaux 1985). For these complex reasons, comprehensive and individualized assessment of social network resources is very important.

A wide range of studies documents that people with more social and environmental resources are in better physical and mental health and are better able to adapt to and cope with life changes (Barrera 1988; Cohen & Wills 1985; Thompson 1995). These results hold across people of various age groups and those facing different life situations and challenges (Whittaker & Garbarino 1983). In our own earlier work regarding the evidence base for social support interventions with children, youth, and families, we found compelling studies on the role of social support in mediating parenting attitudes, parent-child interaction, and child behavior (Tracy & Whittaker 1987). Informal helping networks provide emotional and material support, serve as role models for parenting, and often link parents with outside sources of help and advice (Powell 1979).

There is evidence that, without social support, people are less likely to maintain the changes achieved from social work interventions (Wahler 1980). Some clients do not have a social network that supports their efforts for change; they may be receiving conflicting advice from network members or outright discouragement in their pursuit of change. Consider, for example, the role of social networks in substance abuse treatment and recovery. Those working with chemically dependent women often find that understanding the woman's connections with others is central to treatment (Corrigan 1991; Finkelstein, Duncan, Derman, & Smeltz 1990). For women, initial use of alcohol and drugs, as well as entry into treatment, is typically tied to social relationships (Boyd & Mast 1983). Supportive relationships have also been associated with completion of treatment and length of time abstinent (Havassy, Hall, & Tschann 1987; MacDonald 1987). Social relationships thus play a key role in the development, maintenance, and resolution of alcohol and other drug problems in women; treatment programs have begun to emphasize the development of healthy relationships in women as a result of these findings (Finkelstein et al. 1990).

In sum, we continue to follow with interest the ever-increasing spiral of research and theoretical work on social networks and social support. While the precise mechanisms of social support continue to elude the test of final empirical validation, researchers from many social science traditions have enhanced our understanding of what might be thought of as components of the support process. For example, a recent review by Pierce, Sarason, and Sarason posits three overlapping and mutually influencing components of social support: (1) "support schemata"— roughly equivalent to the more common construct of perceived support and encompassing an individual's expectations about the forthcoming-ness of the social environment in providing aid should one need it; (2) "supportive relationships"—which the authors view as relationship-specific support schemata; and (3) "supportive transactions," including supportive behavior, support-seeking behavior, and support receipt (1996, 5–18). As one corpus of research proceeds to probe the nature and relationship of these and related components, another continues the applied tradition of design and evaluation of social support interventions. Thompson's recent review (1995) of social support in the area of prevention of child maltreatment identifies many useful pathways for future intervention design, while acknowledging that social support alone is unlikely to be an effective preventive intervention:

> The operative concept to be underscored is *integrated* (cf. Miller & Whittaker 1988; Tracy & Whittaker 1987). Social support interventions that exist at the periphery of other ongoing social services are likely to lose their effectiveness because they are not tied to other resources that are of value to target families (Thompson 1995).

We agree with this caution and seek throughout this volume as in our teaching and research to place social support interventions squarely in the center of comprehensive case planning for clients.

Neighborhood and Community

The increasingly rich body of knowledge now available on characteristics of neighborhoods and communities is of considerable value in direct social work practice. While social workers in direct practice have typically been concerned mostly with clients as individuals, groups, or families, many "new-old" practice models, such as family preservation and family support approaches, are intrinsically concerned with the transactions between clients and their communities. The Homebuilders model (Kinney, Haapala, & Booth 1991), for example, is constructed largely around home-based services. Family support programs, one of the "growing points" of child and family services, are primarily neighborhood-based and deeply concerned with community-building as both a focus and framework for program activities (Dunst 1994; Kagan 1996).

Such practice models, which have much in common with the Progressive era settlement houses, exemplify an ecological approach to practice in their focus on the transactions between participants and their environmental contexts. In neighborhoods and communities riven by poverty and violence, for example, community-based family support programs can serve as vital sanctuaries in a hostile environment. Within Head Start, Family Service Centers provide an alternative community of parents and providers (Lightburn & Kemp 1994). In such "fields of care," to borrow a phrase from geographer Yi-Fu Tuan (1977), participants whose intimate and community environments have been dominated by failure, alienation, abandonment, and isolation have the opportunity to develop new meanings and perspectives. The program community becomes a sustaining environment, providing consistent and multidimensional support, opportunities, and connections with others in similar circumstances. In this environment, parents and families can recover, learn new skills, and access support, all of which help them both to manage their lives in a different way and to function more effectively in their wider communities (Dunst 1994).

Accurate, multidimensional, and textured information on neighborhood environments is an essential foundation for practice that incorporates a community perspective. The work of Coulton and her colleagues in Cleveland, Ohio (Coulton, Korbin, & Su 1996; Coulton, Korbin, Su, & Chow 1995; Coulton, Pandey, & Chow 1990; Korbin & Coulton, in press) provides an excellent example of ecologically oriented research at the neighborhood level.

A multidimensional study by Korbin and Coulton (in press), combining both quantitative and ethnographic measures, highlights, for example, the importance of neighborhood quality for child outcomes in urban communities. The authors report that neighborhoods with many children per adult, few elderly residents, and a low proportion of adult males are at highest risk of adverse child outcomes, a finding that reflects the smaller numbers of adults available to care for children and to become involved in neighborhood social institutions and networks. In the high-risk neighborhoods in Korbin and Coulton's study, residents saw themselves as less able to intervene with neighborhood children. Reasons for this perception included erosion of the sense that all adults in a community are responsible for children; the belief that parents would align with children against an intervening adult; shifts in perceptions of acceptable and unacceptable behavior (erosion of expectations and standards); fear of anger/violence by parents (and the related belief that should such tensions occur, these would create problems among adults in community); the belief that intervention could exacerbate the situation (child's behavior escalates); and concern about retaliation by parents of children and adolescents. These findings closely mirror Halpern's conclusions about inner-city communities, which he describes as having crossed some kind of "invisible threshold":

> It was a threshold of isolation and problem density, of risk over protective factors, and of the proportion of negative versus positive social interactions. Historic norms developed to pass on positive values and to cope with hardship and depredation—norms such as communal responsibility for children, social control by elders, and the sharing of resources, religious faith, oral stories, music, and humor—did not disappear completely. But they were simply swamped by the new ones that grew out of the ghetto context. (1995b, 142)

Outcomes for children in such settings reflect also the relative geographic and economic isolation of low-income urban communities. Korbin and Coulton report an inverse relationship between the resources available in neighborhoods, such as supermarkets, banks, and other retail and cultural amenities, and rates of adverse conditions for children (in press, 18–19). The lack of resources other than small local stores or bodegas undermines neighborhood-based networks and increases feelings of marginality among community residents, many of whom strongly resent the lack of amenities in their neighborhood. In ways both obvious and subtle, a lack of resources and amenities reinforces social and environmental isolation. This finding resonates with our own work with an urban family support program (Lightburn & Kemp 1994), located in a city so stripped of social amenities that there was no bookstore in the downtown shopping area. For a surprising number of the children and families participating in this program, program outings were the first time many of them had been outside their immediate community (Lightburn 1991).

In all communities, the extent to which residents feel a "sense of community" (Chavis & Wandersman 1990; Glynn 1986) seems to be a key mediating factor between individual and community well-being. Sense of community is related to the degree to which members believe that they can have an influence on their immediate environment (Chavis & Wandersman 1990), the extent to which there is interaction between residents in a neighborhood (Chavis, Hogge, McMillan, & Wandersman 1986), and membership in neighborhood organizations (Chavis & Wandersman 1990; Wandersman & Florin 1990). Neighborhood quality and social cohesion have been linked with effective parenting (Brooks-Gunn, Duncan, Klebanov, & Sealand 1993; Coulton et al. 1995; Garbarino & Kostelny 1993), school success (Baker, Barthelemy, & Kurdek 1993), improved health outcomes (Taylor & Covington 1993), and general quality of life (O'Brien & Ayidiya 1991).

Recently, Brodsky (1996) has pointed out that while sense of community has been conceptualized primarily in positive terms, and this positive relationship to the community has been viewed as a protective factor, negative psychological sense of community may also be associated with positive outcomes. In an ethnographic study of resilient single mothers resident in an inner-city housing project in Washington D.C., Brodsky found that a negative view of their community was an important coping strategy in an environment perceived as hostile and dangerous. By keeping a distance from the community, the women protect themselves and their children. As Brodsky notes:

> [F]or the resilient single mothers in this study, relative isolation from their community is a prized and very important attribute. In their view, it is crucial that they remain independent as well as non-conforming. (p. 360)

Such adaptive mechanisms are not without their costs. Brodsky notes the self-fulfilling nature of negative psychological sense of community, for these mothers isolate themselves not only from the negative but also from the potentially positive aspects of their communities. Nonetheless, their fierce independence and sense of autonomy is central to their resilience. While on balance efforts to enhance community connections and involvement still seem very worthwhile, Brodsky's work highlights the need for community interventionists to think carefully about the potential costs as well as benefits of such interventions: to recognize, in other words, the value of both distance and affiliation in some environments.

The growing evidence that child and family well-being is fundamentally tied to the well-being of neighborhoods and communities (see, e.g., Elliot et al. 1996) points to the importance of a focus on the development of community resources and supports as a component of direct practice. In Chapters 4 and 5, we present comprehensive information designed to promote effective practice with natural social networks. The work of Kretzmann and McKnight (1993) on community-building is also a valuable resource for interventions designed to develop community assets and strengths. An increasingly diverse array of community-based services, including the family support movement (Kagan, Powell, Weissbourd, & Zigler 1987; Weissbourd 1990) and community-centered mental health services (Crosby & Barry 1995; Carling 1995), likewise offers social workers robust models of community-based direct practice.

RESILIENCE, PROTECTIVE FACTORS
AND ENVIRONMENTAL RISK

The 1990s mark a significant transition in the prevention literature from a primary focus on risk factors such as family dysfunction, child abuse, or parental mental illness to an equal concern with the promotion of resiliency and well-being. Though both strands have always been present in prevention research, there has typically been a greater emphasis on deficits, disease, and dysfunction (i.e., on risk) than on the correlates of individual and social well-being (Cowen 1994). More recently, however, attention has shifted to the emerging evidence that risk is mediated by a range of protective factors, both personal and environmental, and thus to the potential for interventions that buffer as well as reduce risk (Brewer et al. 1995; Hawkins, Catalano, & Miller 1992; Haggerty, Sherrod, Garmezy, & Rutter 1994).

What the risk-based research of the 1980s does provide is strong evidence that the negative impacts of environmental risk factors become increasingly profound as risk accumulates (Garbarino 1993; Garmezy 1993). In the Rochester Longitudinal Study (RLS) of children born to schizophrenic mothers, for example, Sameroff and Seifer (1995) found (contrary to their expectations) that environmental context, in particular the number of risk factors being experienced, was significantly more powerful as a predictor of childhood dysfunction than the specific psychiatric status of the mother. Children experiencing four or more risk factors fared particularly poorly. On intelligence scores, for example, on average each additional risk factor reduced the child's IQ by four points, resulting in a difference of more than thirty IQ points between those children with no environmental risks and those with eight or nine risk factors. In the RLS study, no single variable was predictive of child outcomes: "[O]nly in families with multiple risk factors was the child's competence placed in jeopardy" (ibid., 244). Garmezy and Masten (1994) likewise found that while two stressors in family life resulted in a 5 percent increment in the rate of child psychiatric disorders, four or more stressors accounted for a 21 percent increment. In a landmark longitudinal study, *The Children of Kauai,* Emmy Werner and her colleagues also found that combinations of risk factors (for example, early trauma combined with poor environmental circumstances associated with chronic poverty) were highly correlated with later difficulties (Werner, Bierman, & French 1971; Werner & Smith 1977, 1982; Werner 1989). These findings underscore the extreme vulnerability of children and families whose every-day, long-term experience involves multiple and chronic risk factors.

Embedded in these and other studies, however, are the seeds of optimism. All these groups of children included some who not only survived but thrived, despite their exposure to environmental conditions of great adversity. To explain these "resilient" children, as Garmezy points out, "It is necessary to search for the presence of 'protective' factors that presumably compensate for those 'risk' elements that inhere in the lives and in the environments of many underprivileged children" (1993, 129).

Although "a younger and less mature sibling to the older and more adequately studied effects stemming from actualized risk factors" (ibid., 127), the growing literature on protective factors represents, we believe, an area that is particularly relevant to social work practice. Where a preoccupation with risk tends to result in a preoccupation with the remediation of deficit and dysfunction, a focus on resilience, which can be thought of as the ability to bounce back or recover from adverse experiences, is more likely to result in the promotion of capacities and strengths in individuals and communities (Benard, 1993).

The shift in emphasis—from ameliorating risk to enhancing resiliency —is highly consistent with the philosophical shift in social work toward strengths and empowerment practice discussed earlier in this chapter (Saleebey 1996). It is congruent also with the emerging interest in wellness and the promotion of well-being that is increasingly evident in the prevention literature. Community psychologist Emory Cowen argues, for example, that there is a need to focus on what goes right in development and adjustment, rather than on what goes wrong: "The orienting concept of psychological wellness directs attention to new conceptual formulations and derivative phenomena . . . that differ sharply from those that now guide the mental health fields" (1994, 150). As Werner and Smith point out:

> Our findings and those by other American and European investigators with a life-span perspective suggest that these buffers make a more profound impact on the life course of children who grow up under adverse conditions than do specific risk factors or adverse life events. They appear to transcend ethnic, social class, geographical and historical boundaries. Most of all, they offer us a more optimistic outlook than the perspective that can be gleaned from the literature on the negative consequences of perinatal trauma, caregiving deficits, and chronic poverty. They provide us with a corrective lens—an awareness of the self-righting tendencies that move children toward normal adult development under all but the most persistent adverse circumstances. (1992, 202)

Put simply, "risk accumulates, and opportunity ameliorates" (Garbarino 1993). The resiliency literature brings to the center of attention Bronfenbrenner's (1979) emphasis on the progressive, mutual accommodation between the developing person and the immediate and broader contexts in which the person lives. This body of scholarship underscores the remarkable adaptability of the human organism to environmental conditions, even those that are manifestly undesirable or toxic, and points the way to interventions and services that build on these inherent strengths and capacities.

The foundations of resilience are environmental, interpersonal, and constitutional. Critical elements of resilience include (the following lists are adapted from Kaplan, Turner, Norman, & Stillson 1996; Werner 1989, 1995):

Individual Attributes

- An engaging, easygoing personality or temperament (Garmezy 1985; Werner 1989, 1995).
- Cognitive competence, good communication and problem-solving skills, an "action" orientation, and active coping abilities (Masten, Best, & Garmezy 1990; Werner 1995; Werner & Smith 1982).
- Experiences of self-efficacy (confidence that one's world is predictable, controllable, and hopeful), achievement, and responsibility; faith that one can make a difference in one's life and environment (Beardslee 1989; Cowen, Wyman, Work, & Parker 1990; Werner 1995).
- Realistic expectations and appraisal of the environment (Cowen et al. 1990; Werner 1989).
- The capacity to understand and respond to others' feelings (empathy; Wyman et al. 1992).

- Adaptive distancing, for example, the ability to think and act separately from troubled caretakers (Beardslee 1989; Berlin & Davis 1989).

Family/Interpersonal Factors

- A stable, committed, positive relationship with a caring adult (Werner 1989, 1995).
- Positive parental modeling of resilience and coping skills (Rutter 1985; Werner 1995).
- Extended support networks, including family and friends (Garmezy 1993; Werner 1989, 1995).

School/Community/Neighborhood Factors

- Opportunities for involvement in decision-making and community life (Rutter 1979).
- High but realistic expectations (Rutter 1979).
- Consistent social support (Werner 1989, 1995; Werner & Smith 1982).
- Positive community norms and role models (Garmezy 1993; Werner 1995).
- Community resources for children and families (Garmezy 1993).

To support resilience, it is necessary to look at protective factors, which Rutter defines as "influences that modify, ameliorate, or alter a person's response to some environmental hazard that predisposes to a maladaptive outcome" (1985, 600). In a review of the literature, Garmezy (1985) identified a triad of protective factors: (a) temperamental factors that mediate interactions with the environment, including activity level, reflectiveness, cognitive skills, and a positive responsiveness to others; (b) family factors, including warmth, cohesion, and the presence of a consistent, stable, and caring adult; and (c) external social and environmental supports, either personal social networks or institutional supports such as church, school, or a caring agency. Empirical support for Garmezy's protective triad has come from Werner (1989, 1995), who describes a similar trio of protective qualities (individual dispositional attributes, affectional ties in the family, and external support systems), and from a range of other studies (Rutter 1993; Sameroff & Seifer 1995; Seifer, Sameroff, Baldwin, & Baldwin 1992).

It is noteworthy that many protective factors at the individual level are characteristics that promote positive experiences and interactions with others in the environment. It is also clear that resilient children possess active coping skills and are able to make good use of environmental resources and supports. From an environmental perspective, factors of critical importance to the development and maintenance of resilience seem to be consistency, nurturance, and support in at least some aspect of the environment, whether this be family, extended family and friends, school, or a helping agency.

The literature on resilience and protective factors strongly underlines the critical importance of environmental contexts, for good and ill, in human development and well-being. In this regard, it is important to note that resilience is not a fixed attribute, but rather varies over time and according to family and community circumstances (Rutter 1985). The Rochester Longitudinal Study (Sameroff & Seifer 1995), for example, provides some evidence that resiliency at one point in time can be eroded by prolonged exposure to adverse circumstances. At the same time, resilient coping can be promoted and enhanced by exposure to positive and protective environmental factors (Werner 1989). As Sameroff and Seifer (1995) point out, however, the environmental risks experienced by children in their study cohort remained remarkably stable over time (few children experienced diminished risk as they grew up). For all that environmental risk can be buffered and mediated, the fact remains that for most children, families, and communities, levels of environmental risk, whether high or low, remain relatively constant over considerable periods of time. As an inner-city youth interviewed for a *New York Times* series, "Children of the Shadows," put it, "[E]verything that goes wrong just keeps going on and everything that's right doesn't stay right" (cited in Halpern 1995a, 132).

Such findings have several important implications for direct social work practice. First, it is evident that the tendency to overemphasize vulnerability, risk, and disorder should be balanced by awareness of the protective impact of environmental factors, such as support, nurturance, and enrichment, on adaptation over time. This understanding speaks directly to the central importance of enhanced attention to strengthening the array of supports available to children and families in their immediate neighborhoods and communities. At the same time, evidence of the relative stability of environmental risks highlights the need for multilevel environmental interventions, including those that strike at the root causes of family poverty and instability and that are directly concerned with the empowerment of marginalized groups and communities.

DEFINITIONS

Environment

Our perspectives on the environment owe a huge intellectual debt to
the work of Carel Germain (1976, 1978, 1979, 1981b, 1983), whose wide-
ranging scholarship added breadth, depth, and complexity to the profession's understanding of the environmental domain. Germain defined
the environment as having physical, cultural, and social aspects:

> The physical environment comprises the natural world and the built
> world. The social environment comprises the network of human relations
> at various levels of organization. Both the physical and social environ-
> ments are affected by cultural values, norms, knowledge, and beliefs that
> pattern social interaction and determine how we use and respond to the
> physical environment. (1979, 13)

Additionally, as Germain pointed out in two landmark papers (1976,
1978), both the physical and social environment are framed by the "textures" of time (biological, psychological, cultural, and social) and space.

In this chapter we have focused on the transactions between people
and their physical and social environments, with particular emphasis on
the multifaceted ways in which space and place are integral to human
experience, agency, and opportunity. In reasserting the dialectics of the
person-environment nexus, however, we do not mean to understate the
importance of the objective physical world to everyday life and well-
being. The natural world—climate, seasons, weather patterns, flora,
and fauna, as well as that less definable but enormously significant
whole we think of as "nature"—is a constant and complex source of
enrichment and constraint in human life. Evidence of the intricate and
delicate relationships between people and the natural environment
comes from many sources. The growing body of knowledge on seasonal
variations in mood, for example, highlights the subtle and multilayered
connections between the human animal and the external world. The
deep appreciation that many people have for the natural environment as
a source of pleasure and renewal likewise speaks to the value and centrality in social work practice of a deeper and more nuanced awareness
of the relationships between clients and the physical world. This
is particularly so if we consider the environment in cross-cultural
perspective.

The built environment, as Germain terms it, is likewise central to a
full understanding of person-environment relationships. The built
world encompasses those aspects of the physical environment that are

man-made—buildings, transportation systems, communication systems, recreational facilities, indeed the whole structure of material culture. A huge and informative body of literature in environmental psychology (Altman & Christensen 1990; Stokols 1995, 1996; Moos 1996) explores the multidimensional transactions between people and their natural and constructed environments. Brought to attention are issues such as the relative effects of overstimulation and understimulation in the environment; the interconnections between architecture and design and human well-being; and people's responses to the symbolism as well as the material reality of their physical settings (Germain 1983; Gutheil 1992). This literature is extremely valuable to social workers in two respects. First, it adds to our understanding of the "external" environment as a domain that is at once objective, transactional, and phenomenological. Second, it reinforces our awareness of the potency of physical environments, and thus reduces the tendency to treat them merely as a "backdrop" (Germain 1981b) to more important social and psychological factors.

To Germain's definition of the environment we would add the linked ideas, explored earlier, that the environment is both personally and socially constructed and, further, that it expresses the power relationships inherent in the wider social structure. From this perspective, the environment is defined as a multidimensional entity, the levels of which include (see Figure 3.1):

- • *the perceived environment, i.e., the environment as constructed in individual and collective systems of meaning and belief,*
- • *the physical environment, both natural and built,*
- • *the social/interactional environment, comprised largely of human relationships at various levels of intimacy, and including family, group, and neighborhood networks and collectivities,*
- • *the institutional and organizational environment,*
- • *the cultural and sociopolitical environment*

Environmental Assessment

By environmental assessment, we mean:

An ongoing process in which client and worker, in partnership, gather and critically analyze information on the client or client system in transaction with multiple levels of the environment, including strengths, resources, potentialities, and opportunities, as well as risks, challenges, and issues of concern, and with attention to the meaning of these environmental experiences for the client.

DIMENSIONS OF ENVIRONMENT

- PHYSICAL ENVIRONMENT, BOTH NATURAL AND BUILT

- SOCIAL / INTERACTIONAL ENVIRONMENT
  - PERSONAL SOCIAL NETWORKS
  - FAMILY
  - GROUP
  - NEIGHBORHOOD AND COMMUNITY

- INSTITUTIONAL / ORGANIZATIONAL ENVIRONMENT

- SOCIOPOLITICAL AND CULTURAL ENVIRONMENT

- ENVIRONMENT AS CONSTRUCTED IN INDIVIDUAL AND COLLECTIVE SYSTEMS OF MEANING AND BELIEF

Figure 3.1. Dimensions of Environment

Environmental Intervention

We define environmental intervention as:

Action in the environment and transformation of individual and collective perspectives through critical analysis of the impact of environmental conditions (see Figure 3.2).

Core themes that underpin our approach to environmental intervention include:

1. Recognition that an environmental or contextual focus is central to efforts to facilitate the empowerment of individuals, families, groups, and communities.

2. A focus on the actual and potential resources available in the environment to bolster client strengths and resiliency.

3. The understanding that environmental practice is inherently developmental, i.e., that the progressive development of individual, family, group, and community competence and empowerment is supported by a spectrum of environmental interventions that themselves represent different levels of complexity and goals.

**ENVIRONMENTAL
INTERVENTION**

ACTION IN THE ENVIRONMENT

AND

**TRANSFORMATION OF INDIVIDUAL
AND COLLECTIVE PERSPECTIVES
THROUGH CRITICAL ANALYSIS OF
THE IMPACT OF ENVIRONMENTAL
CONDITIONS**

Figure 3.2.   Environmental Intervention.

4.   Recognition that the environment must be addressed both as objective reality and in terms of its meaning for individuals, groups, and communities, and that the meaning of the environment is strongly influenced by variables such as race, gender, sexual orientation, culture, and class.

5.   The related understanding that environmental intervention encompasses both intervention in the environment and the process of transforming individual and collective perspectives through critical analysis of the impact of environmental conditions.

6.   A commitment to incorporate into social work practice the understanding that the environment represents both opportunity and constraint, and that environmental intervention necessarily includes both critical reflection and action with regard to the impact of environmental conditions on individual and collective well-being.

NOTE

1.   Portions of this section are drawn from Whittaker and Tracy (1989, 22–26).

4

Environmental Assessment

Environmental assessment is a central but frequently underdeveloped component of comprehensive, multidimensional assessment with individual clients, families, and neighborhoods or communities. Social workers have always paid attention to environmental variables that may influence individual or group functioning, and nearly all definitions of social work assessment include generating information about the client's situation or environment (for example, see Hepworth & Larsen 1993; Whittaker & Tracy 1989; Kirst-Ashman & Hull 1996). In direct practice, however, environmental assessment has focused primarily on the immediate psychosocial environment. The assumption appears to be that environmental data beyond the client's immediate environment is not centrally relevant to assessment in interpersonal helping. At the same time, the many useful organizing frameworks available for understanding the wider environmental contexts of community or neighborhood are designed primarily for generalist or community organization practice (for example, see Kirst-Ashman & Hull 1996; Netting, Kettner, & McMurtry 1993; Sheafor, Horejsi, & Horejsi 1997; Johnson 1995).

Our intention here is to bridge this gap between micro and macro approaches to assessment. We consider a comprehensive and nuanced understanding of our clients' environmental contexts—at every systems level—to be at the heart of effective, appropriate social work practice. In the last chapter, we explored several current practice perspectives as well as theoretical and empirical perspectives that support more active attention to the range of environmental factors that impinge upon clients and to which clients relate and react. In this chapter, we build on this material to develop strategies for environmental assessment, which we see as a core component of person-environment practice.

89

If social workers are to embrace environmental interventions on a footing equal to that of person-oriented interventions, they need to think and assess contextually. Studies of attribution bias in social work assessment suggest that social workers tend to view client issues as person-centered or psychological, rather than as situational or environmental (Proctor & Rosen 1983; Rosen & Levine 1992). Subsequent interventions then tend to be focused on individual change and adaptation rather than on environmental change. As Kemp points out "faced with numerous depressed clients . . . a social worker in direct practice may feel more of a need to develop skills in treating depression than to think whether a community issue is contributing to his or her clients' problems" (1995, 187).

In this chapter, we present a rationale and a range of strategies for conducting environmental assessments in social work practice settings. We agree with Jordan and Franklin that "the practitioner who separates the client from the environment risks losing the breadth and depth of the client's life experiences" (1995, 5). In so doing, we stress that the primary goal of environmental assessment in person-environment practice is to empower the client to act in the environment, rather than to support worker treatment of environmental problems. We explore a number of assessment tools and techniques that allow both worker and client to gain a better understanding of environmental variables and their impact. We make a particular case for initiating environmental assessments at the level of personal social networks, for we believe that this level offers important opportunities for active consultation, collective exchanges, and empowerment. Furthermore, larger systems such as other human service organizations, neighborhood or community factors, or public policy become more accessible as targets of change when worker and client are armed with knowledge of the client's environment.

We begin by examining social work assessment generally and in person-environment practice. The major portion of this chapter is then devoted to detailed information on social network assessment, followed by practice guidelines for developing social environmental change goals with clients.

ASSESSMENT IN SOCIAL WORK

Accurate and timely assessment is critical to effective case planning and intervention. Social work assessments seek a systemic understanding of the case situation to guide practice decisions: a core practice task is to encompass relevant contextual features and to identify the interplay between the person and the impinging environment (Mattaini 1990; Meyer 1993). During assessment, the client and worker gather, analyze, and synthesize information in the following general areas: (a) issues of concern, (b) coping capacities of clients and significant others, (c) relevant systems involved in issues of concern and the nature of reciprocal transactions between clients and these systems, (d) resources that are available or are needed to remedy the issues of concern, and (e) the client's motivation to work on issues of concern (Hepworth & Larsen 1993).

Assessment in social work is best thought of as both a process and a product (Meyer 1993). For both worker and client the process is essentially cognitive: information is gathered, meanings are ascribed, a framework for organizing information is applied, and implications are drawn for goals and interventions. As a product, assessment generally leads to an oral or written statement of the issues of concern, description of the client system, how the client functions in relation to other systems, and formulation of a plan for change. Depending on the practice setting, the assessment statement assumes many forms of varying length and complexity.

The assessment framework applied in any given situation naturally flows from the agency setting and the responsibilities of the worker in this context. In general, however, social work assessments are focused on a consideration of the person and environment, encompass a multidimensional and multisystems perspective, and are strengths-based, client-driven, and client-centered. Franklin and Jordan (1992), for example, present an integrative skills assessment protocol, designed primarily for social work with individuals and families, which includes:

- information about the client,
- the nature of the presenting problem,
- intrapersonal issues (e.g., cognitive functioning, emotional functioning, behavioral functioning, medical information, mental status, ethnic/cultural considerations, motivation, roles and role performance, and developmental considerations),
- interpersonal issues (e.g., family composition and process, work/school relations, peer relations),
- agency context and social supports,
- strengths and resources at various systems levels.

ASSESSMENT IN PERSON-ENVIRONMENT PRACTICE (P.E.P.)

As a product or outcome, assessment in P.E.P. contributes to understanding the issues confronting the client and is the foundation for the development of a collaborative plan of action. As a process, assessment involves the client or client system and worker as partners in the process of knowledge development and opens up new ways of looking at the world, contributing to the development of "critical consciousness" (Freire 1970, 1973; Gutiérrez 1996), or transformed perspectives on person-environment interactions.

In Chapter 3, we described the process of empowerment and the critical role of the environment and defined environmental assessment as:

> *an ongoing process in which client and worker, in partnership, gather and critically analyze information on the client or client system in transaction with multiple levels of the environment, including strengths, resources, and opportunities, as well as risks, challenges, and issues of concern, and with attention to the meaning of these environmental experiences for the client.*

The environmental assessment methods presented in this chapter are central to empowerment practice for they allow for critical reflection and analysis of the environment through interaction and dialogue between client and worker and between client and others in similar circumstances. This process of meaning-making and consciousness-raising lays the foundation for effective planning and action. Figure 4.1 graphically displays environmental assessment as an ongoing process supported by the client-worker partnership.

Active client involvement in the generation and analysis of environmental information is the backbone of environmental assessment and intervention. In the assessment phase, the worker and client gather data about multiple levels of the environment, engage in a dialogue about the information gathered, and critically reflect on environmental impacts on the client's current situation. The very act of gathering information, asking questions about particular topics, and using strategies such as the visual display of information typically results in a shift in clients' perspectives on their situation. The process of gathering environmental information may change the client's definition of the presenting issue, toward more complex views of the interaction between personal and environmental factors. Careful environmental assessment is thus essential to the intervention or change process.

The notion here is that we are not merely completing an inventory of types and categories of environmental resources, but rather conducting a critical analysis with clients of their transactions with their environments. This process is supported by assessment methods that enable workers and clients to look at the clients' active responses to their environments and to realistically consider the opportunities and constraints in those environments, at various system levels, and in all their complexity.

How one defines the environment naturally sets boundaries on what

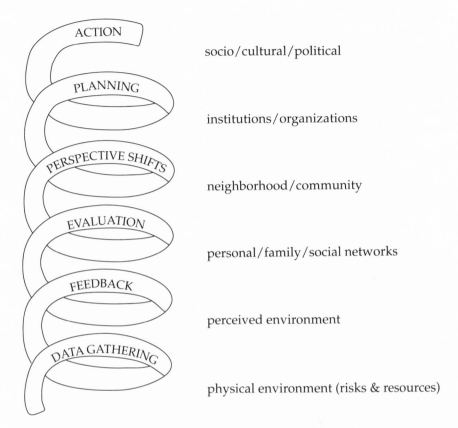

Figure 4.1. Environmental assessment: partnership and process.

factors are included in an environmental assessment. Our definition of environment (Chapter 3) includes both the objective environment and the many ways in which that environment is personally and socially constructed. Core dimensions of the environment include the physical environment, both natural and built; the social environment, largely comprising networks of human relationships at various levels of intimacy; the cultural, political, and institutional environment; and the perceived environment, as constructed in individual and collective systems of meaning and belief.

"Environment" does not mean the same thing to everyone nor is it experienced in the same way. In Chapter 6 we discuss how factors such as race, gender, age, or ability affect one's experience and construction of meaning at various levels of the environment. Environmental assessments must tap into individual and group experiences with the environment and the meanings these hold for our clients and incorporate the realization that the environment we see as workers may not be the environment our clients experience. Consider, for example, the differential impact of physical settings:

> [W]hen a flight of stairs leads to the entryway of a building, each person entering that building must alter his or her gait to accommodate the change in surroundings. However, while the weekend jogger may barely notice this shift and experiences no feeling of impediment, someone walking with the assistance of a cane may experience the stairs as an obstacle to be negotiated cautiously. (Gutheil 1996, 187)

A person's social and class position influences access to opportunities and power in the environment. This can be assessed through a power or stratification analysis (Gilgun 1994). A power analysis involves assessment of the ways in which conditions of powerlessness (based on race, age, social class, gender, sexual orientation, etc.) contribute to the current situation faced by the client. The analysis includes identifying sources of both power and emancipation, including sources that may have been neglected or underutilized, such as social network resources (Dodd & Gutiérrez 1990; Gutiérrez 1990; Hopps, Pinderhughes, & Shankar 1995).

Environmental assessments should not be overwhelmingly focused on environmental threats and deficits, but should attend equally to the strengths and resources, in individuals and communities, that form the basis for new connections and relationships (Kretzmann & McKnight 1993; Saleebey 1997). In Chapter 3, we noted that the strengths perspective represents a shift in social work focus consistent with empowerment and environmentally based intervention. In some areas of social work practice, however, such as the mental health field, the historical tradition has been to overemphasize the negative influences of the environment on people (Sullivan 1992a). A focus on environmental deficits may unnecessarily narrow our vision of helping resources and restrict client participation in the community. Within the community mental health system, for example, failure to recognize, recruit, and utilize naturally occurring environmental strengths results in further exclusion and social isolation of persons with chronic mental illness (Sullivan 1992a).

SOURCES OF DATA FOR ENVIRONMENTAL ASSESSMENT

As with all aspects of the assessment process, environmental assessment is strengthened if data are generated using a variety of assessment methods and drawing on multiple perspectives. As we employ various assessment methods, such as client self-report and participant observation, and explore more than one level of the environment, our environmental assessments become more complete and valid. Other social work assessment methods may include standardized interviews with clients, significant others, and "collaterals" (others who interact with the client); ethnographic interviews with clients, significant others, and collaterals; background information sheets and questionnaires; psychological, projective, or standardized assessment tests; client logs or diaries; and behavioral observations (Jordan & Franklin 1995). Typically, graphic and mapping techniques, such as an ecomap or genogram, are used to organize and display some of this information (Meyer 1993; Mattaini 1993). Computer-assisted assessment packages have also emerged as promising tools in the assessment process (Nurius & Hudson 1993). In P.E.P., priority is given to methods that most fully allow for the active involvement of the client in the generation of data and for discussion and reflection with the worker or others, as these methods support the goal of empowering environmental intervention.

In work with a community group, for example, environmental assessment techniques might include review of printed materials about the community, such as newspapers, maps, and newsletters; formal and informal interviews with key informants, residents, and other community stakeholders; interaction and participation with small groups and organizations within the community; and careful participant observation of community events and interactions (Johnson 1995). Much can be learned about a community from printed sources and other regularly collected demographic information, but physically driving or walking through a community gives the worker a firsthand sense of key factors such as physical surroundings, both natural and built, obvious geographical boundaries, and general impressions of safety (Kirst-Ashman & Hull 1996). Talking with major community figures likewise provides greater insight into residents' perceptions of themselves and their community. Warren and Warren (1977) stressed the importance of interviewing the elementary school principal, for example—someone who is in regular contact with families and is knowledgeable about the economic situation, racial tensions, and other issues in the community. Interviews with community residents also provide important information on residents' definitions of neighborhood or community boundaries, which may bear little or no resemblance to official census tracts or planning units (Kemp 1995).

Direct contact with informal, local sources of information is particularly important in work with communities of color. Dialogue with community members provides an understanding of cultural, political, and social factors and information about both differences and alliances among various groups within the community (e.g., religious, ethnic, racial, educational, social class groupings) as well as shared goals (Bradshaw, Soifer, & Gutiérrez 1994; Rivera & Erlich 1992).

The type and amount of information to be collected in the environmental assessment will depend on many factors, including the client's situation and commitment to involvement, the type of assessment tool or method selected, the purpose of social work involvement, and the agency's mission and goal. In child protective work, for example, risk assessment tools routinely screen for social and physical environmental factors that may place the young child or youth at greater risk. On the other hand, hospital discharge planners working with elderly stroke victims for their return home may assess a very different set of environmental factors. In each instance, the age and condition of the client, the immediacy of the need for service, relevant cultural features, and the agency's overall service mission will influence the choice and depth of assessment information collected.

FRAMEWORKS FOR ENVIRONMENTAL ASSESSMENT

Common sense tells us that environmental assessments should attend to those aspects of the environment most relevant to the client's situation (Hepworth & Larsen 1993). However, we have also seen that, depending on factors such as age, cultural background, and class, individuals experience the environment differently. Ultimately the fit between the person and the environment is the central focus of assessment. The environments of two clients may provide vastly different resources, for example, but for each the environment may be sufficient for present needs and interests. Conversely, two clients may share the same environment but experience it in very different ways (see the examples given in Chapter 6). These dramatic differences in how people perceive, experience, and utilize resources underline the central importance of individualization in the assessment and intervention process.

Aspects of the Environment

Aspects of the environment that should routinely be screened in any assessment include (a) the extent to which basic human needs are being met by the environment, (b) strengths and resources present in the environment, and (c) environmental toxins and hazards.

Does the Environment Meet Basic Needs?

Although the social work profession has always been concerned about the physical environment, many social workers proceed with intervention as though it does not really matter. Much credit for changing this perspective is due to the home-based and family support movement. Practitioners working in home and community settings, who are deeply involved in the physical environment and essentially become part of the client's milieu, simply cannot ignore it (Tracy & McDonell 1991; Whittaker, Kinney, Tracy, & Booth 1990). Teaching behavior management skills to clients in an office setting is one thing; it is quite another to help them implement behavioral changes when rats are dashing in and out, sounds and smells assault, and there is no clear wall (or refrigerator) upon which to hang a behavior chart (Kinney et al. 1991). Likewise the assessment of concrete needs is often the first priority in working with clients in home and community settings (Kaplan & Girard 1994; Kinney et al. 1991).

Hepworth and Larsen (1993) identify a number of universally needed social and physical environmental resources (Table 4.1). These range from the immediate home environment (e.g., ample space, sanitation, food) to the surrounding community (e.g., adequate police and fire protection). Zastrow (1995) suggests a similar list of basic environmental needs, with the addition of safety from environmental hazards and safety from air, noise, and water pollution. Zastrow also identifies some specific social support needs, such as emotional support from significant others and support from significant others to be drug-free, as basic universal needs. Vosler (1990), Dunst (1994), and Dunst et al. (1988) also provide assessment tools to determine the extent to which basic resources are available, accessible, and adequate to meet perceived needs, as well as the extent to which needs that are not adequately met contribute to stress and strain.

What Are the Environment's Strengths and Resources?

Despite considerable recent attention to the strengths perspective by the social work profession, the components of a personal strengths assessment have been articulated more fully than those of an environmental strengths assessment (Saleebey 1997). As with social work assessments in general, a strengths assessment should be multidimensional in nature, focusing both on internal and external strengths (Cowger 1994, 1996). In general, environmental strengths have been conceptualized as consisting of availability of and access to resources in the social environment, such as support from family, friends, or relatives,

Table 4.1.   Universally Needed Environmental Resources

Adequate social support systems
Access to health care
Access to day care services
Access to recreational facilities
Mobility to socialize, utilize resources, and exercise rights as citizen
Adequate housing that provides ample space, sanitation, privacy, and safety
Adequate police and fire protection
Safe and healthful work conditions
Adequate financial resources to purchase essential resources
Adequate nutritional intake
Predictable living arrangements with caring others
Opportunities for education and self-fulfillment
Access to legal resources
Access to religious organizations
Employment opportunities

Source: Hepworth and Larsen (1993, 268).

and basic concrete support services such as transportation or health care (Kretzmann & McKnight 1993; Sullivan 1992b).

One useful model for depicting environmental versus personal strengths is Cowger's (1996) assessment framework, which consists of four quadrants revolving around two axes (see Figure 4.2). The horizontal axis represents environmental factors versus personal factors as contributors to the need for service, and the vertical axis represents a strengths versus deficits continuum. Using this model, a complete assessment will ideally lead to sufficient understanding of both environmental and personal strengths and issues of concern.

Franklin and Jordan (1992) identify potential environmental strengths and resources as comprising availability of employment, adequate housing, supportive family, network of friends, community ties, religious network support, and financial security. Pecora and English (1993) provide guidelines for assessing environmental strengths within multicultural communities. In their review of risk and protective factors influencing child maltreatment, a number of community strengths are identified and operationalized, including community cohesiveness, community racial identity, community resources for children, community resources for adults, community groups and organizations, and community interaction with mainstream agencies.

It is important to remember that an assessment of environmental strengths and resources need not and should not be limited to tangible, physical aspects of the community. Attitudinal and experiential factors,

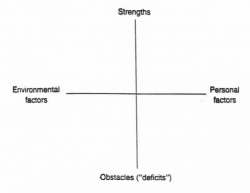

Assessment Axes

Figure 4.2. Assessment of client strengths. Source: Cowger (1996). Reprinted by permission of Longman Publishers, a division of Addison Wesley Longman Inc.

such as community identity, degree of attachment to the community, and shared community values, as well as relational factors, such as the community's ability to relate to other groups and institutions, are important domains of a strengths-based assessment. Finally, cultural narratives and folklore are extremely important sources of strength. These may include cultural accounts of origins, migrations, and survival, which can bring deep meaning and inspiration for change both to individuals and groups (Saleebey 1996).

Are Environmental Hazards Present?

Environmental hazards include substances and conditions in the environment that are known or suspected to cause or increase the risk of physical, mental, or social impairment (Soine 1987). In recent years, newspaper accounts and television news stories have been filled with reports of the effects of contaminated air, water, and food, hazards in the workplace and home (e.g., carbon monoxide), radiation exposure, noise, crowding, and dangerous consumer products. Though social workers frequently work with victims of environmental hazards (e.g., people with health problems related to exposure to asbestos or exposure to other occupation-related substances; veterans exposed to chemicals used during the Vietnam and perhaps Persian Gulf wars), our assessment tools and procedures rarely do justice to their impact. Consequently, many social workers are unaware or ill-informed about these and other environmental hazards. While the direct and indirect effects of many substances are still unknown or difficult to predict, there is growing empirical evidence to warrant further consideration of environmental hazards as part of a complete assessment. Consider for example some of the following examples of threats to physical and mental health from environmental pollution:

- The link between carbon monoxide levels and depression, among other aspects of cognitive and emotional functioning,
- the relationship between lead poisoning and mental retardation and other behavioral and developmental problems of children,
- the rise in the incidence of asthma and other respiratory diseases in response to air pollution,
- fetal deaths, miscarriages, and birth defects associated with exposure to toxic wastes in water and landfills (Hoff & Rogge 1996; Rogge 1993).

Environmental equity is a growing concern within the social work profession. Risk from environmental exposure to hazards is not shared equally but is borne disproportionately by low-income and minority communities: the racial makeup of the community, for example, is a strong predictor of toxic waste site location; poor neighborhoods and communities are at greater risk of industrial accidents (Hoff & Rogge 1996); and many indigenous groups are at increased risk due to use of their natural lands and resources as sites for mining or power production. Taken as a whole, the evidence strongly points to the need to ask about and consider environmental hazards when working with vulnerable populations. (We will discuss environmental injustice and racism more fully in Chapter 6.)

Levels of Environment

Jordan and Franklin (1995) provide a summary of significant environmental assessment factors at various levels of the environment that are consistent with the model of P.E.P. presented here. First is the family/significant other environment, which includes family of origin and present family constellation. The next level of environment to be considered is the social network of friends, including the quantity and quality of social support provided. The quality of the work or school environment is an important level as well, particularly in relation to work/school history, work/school environment (e.g., stressful, crowded, or dangerous conditions), and work/school relationships. The neighborhood and community environment is yet another assessment consideration; the adequacy of living conditions and the nature of the client's relationship with the community are examples of factors at this level. Finally, broader governmental and social forces are the last level to assess in conducting a person in environment assessment. Considered here should be the "relative economic and social state of affairs" (p. 177) and broader social forces that may be impacting access to or availability of basic social services. As Jordan and Franklin point out, some clients (persons of color, ex-prisoners, persons with mental illness, persons with AIDS) may lack access to certain community resources due to discrimination.

Classification Tools

Several useful instruments provide access to the various levels of the environment (family, neighborhood, community) and enable more careful assessment of environmental impacts. We summarize many of these environmental assessment instruments, tools, and techniques at the end of this chapter (see Table 4.2).

Person-in-Environment (PIE) System

The person-in-environment (PIE) system (Karls & Wandrei 1992; Williams, Karls, & Wandrei 1989) is a four-factor classification system designed by social workers to complement the classification system used by the psychiatry profession (the *Diagnostic and Statistical Manual of Mental Disorders—IV*), but focusing instead on social and environmental factors. Four factors are used to describe a client's problem situation: Factor I identifies problems in social functioning; Factor II describes problems emanating from the environment; Factor III describes mental health problems; and Factor IV lists physical health problems. This system provides a means to describe and code social functioning of adults in terms of role performance in the various contexts of the environment. Six categories of environment are included in Factor II of this system: economic/basic needs (e.g., food, shelter, employment, economic resources, transportation), education/training, judicial/legal system, health safety and social service system, voluntary associations (e.g., religion, community groups), and affectional support system. The worker manual accompanying the PIE system (Karls & Wandrei 1994) lists several problems that may be experienced under each category of environment. The presence of discrimination in the environment is also a coded problem category, along with ratings of severity and duration. This system is currently awaiting large-scale tests of reliability and valid-

ity (Karls & Wandrei 1995). While PIE is increasingly widely dissemi-
nated, this assessment system has some significant limitations for social
work practice. These include a focus only on individual adult functioning, a focus on discrete problems, the requirement that PIE be used in
conjunction with a psychiatric diagnosis, and the system's reliance on
lists of factors rather than a more transactional approach (Karls, Lowery,
Mattaini, & Wandrei 1997).

Ecomap

Perhaps the best-known and most frequently used environmental
assessment technique, the ecomap generates information on three major
aspects of environmental resources: those used by the client; those available but not fully used by the client; and gaps in resources, that is, those
needed by the client but not present or accessible in the community
(Hartman 1994; for further descriptions see also Mattaini 1993; Sheafor et
al. 1997) (Figure 4.3). The ecomap is a useful method for visually documenting the client's relationship with the outside world, including the
flow of energy and the nature of relationships experienced. Developed
initially in the adoption practice arena, the ecomap has since been applied and adapted in a large variety of practice settings.

To complete an ecomap, clients write and encircle the names of
people, groups, and organizations in their social networks. The distance
between circles indicates closeness of relationships. Lines drawn between the circles represent the quality of the relationship: stressful,
tenuous, positive. Arrows indicate reciprocity, the give and take of the
relationship. Ecomaps are generally constructed jointly by worker and
client, providing an opportunity for each to understand better the social
context of the client's life. The basic format can readily be adapted to fit a
variety of clients and settings.

Major Outcomes by Level of Environment

At various points in the process of conducting an environmental assessment with a client or a client group, both the worker and the client
will have information to guide the selection of a target goal and the
implementation of an intervention plan. In general, answers to the following questions (adapted from the work of Imber-Black 1988, Hartman
& Laird 1983, and Germain 1981a, 1981b) should be available in usable
form after completion of the environmental assessment.

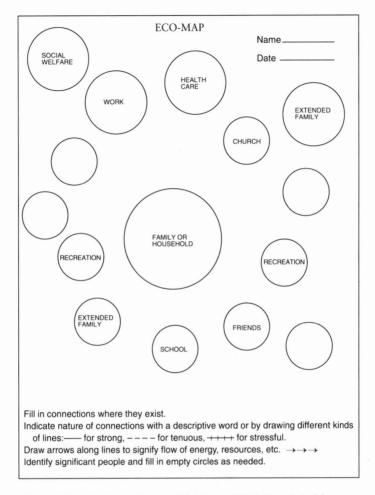

Figure 4.3. Ecomap. Source: Hartman (1978). Reprinted by permission of Families International Incorporated.

Overall Environment

What kinds of environmental strengths and resources are currently used by the client?

What is the nature of the relationship between the client system and the environment?

What strengths and resources in the environment are underutilized but could be mobilized?

What resources are needed or required that are lacking in the environment?

What obstacles (internal and external) prevent access to environmental resources?

To what extent does the client have an enhanced understanding of the environment?

Physical Environment

To what extent does the physical environment provide (or is perceived as providing)

- safety, security and shelter?
- social contact?
- pleasure and recreation?
- support for completion of developmental and life tasks?
- adequate stimulation for growth?

To what extent are the people connected with the physical environment

- dependent on that environment?
- lacking in power, skills, or resources to change the environment?
- involved in decision-making about environmental changes?
- involved in personal or collective action to achieve change in the environment?
- exposed to environmental disparities and risks as compared with other groups of people living in different environments?

Perceived Environment

How is the environment experienced subjectively by individuals, families, groups, and communities?

In what ways has the subjective experience of the environment been influenced by variables such as race, gender, and ethnicity?

In what ways has the experience of being involved in an environmental assessment changed or influenced the client's subjective experience and understanding of the environment?

Social/Interactional Environment

What is the size, structure, and composition of the social network?

What are the strengths and capabilities of the social network?

What are the types of social support available from the social network? Are there gaps in social support needs? Does reciprocity appear to be an issue?

Which network members are identified as responsive, effective, accessible, and dependable?

Which network members are critical of the client?

What obstacles (internal and external) prevent the client's utilizing social network resources?

How are social support needs prioritized in relation to other presenting issues or needs? Is crisis intervention an issue?

What would be a viable social support goal? What would constitute an appropriate social network intervention?

Within a family or group, how are individual members differentially connected to the social environment?

Institutional/Organizational Environment

What has been the nature of relationships and the place of larger systems in the client system's life to date?

What new relationships can be developed between the client system and the larger institutional system? How can viable relationships be maintained?

What constraints or barriers (internal and external) limit or prevent the development of viable relationships with larger systems?

An important set of environmental assessment questions relates to the agency context in which much of social work practice takes place. Here, it is important for the worker to consider how the agency is perceived by the client and the community, and how those perceptions may or may not influence the social work relationship and task (Maluccio 1979; Gutheil 1992; Seabury 1971). For example, in what ways does the physical structure of the agency influence the work with clients? In some settings, group or family sessions are discouraged due to lack of space. How is the agency perceived in the community: as a helpful resource or as an "alien" presence? Does the agency have a good or bad reputation, and on what basis was this reputation formed? How are staff and workers supported or not supported by the agency? Are workers frustrated by activities that do not appear to be directly related to meeting client needs, and how does this affect their practice? Home-based intervention programs, for example, have found it useful to attend to worker needs for support and recognition, inasmuch as their work is often stressful, demanding, and isolating. Assessment of the agency environment can take place formally, as in convening focus groups or conducting client surveys. Information about the client's perceptions of the agency may also emerge from social network data. In any event, the impact of the agency setting on the worker and client needs to be considered.

Social/Political/Cultural Environment

What is the nature of the sociopolitical and economic environment?

To what extent are oppression and discrimination dominant features of transactions with the environment?

To what extent does the immediate environment reinforce wider social patterns of power, privilege, or access to resources?

What opportunities exist for sharing/validating cultural, ethnic or religious meanings and values?

Environmental Assessment and Stage of Helping

Assessment is often viewed and experienced as an ongoing process, changing in response to the various phases of helping. As new data emerge in the life of a "case" and as the helping relationship evolves, the assessment statement is modified and enlarged. Frequently, the situation is most completely understood during the time period when worker and client are actively involved in implementing interventions. For this reason, when worker and client are stumped or slowed in their progress, it is often assessment to which they return. Although we cannot fully cover each stage here, it is helpful to be reminded of the role of environmental assessment in various stages of helping (Whittaker & Tracy 1989).

Environmental assessments can serve useful functions in the early stages of helping when worker and client are just beginning to know one another. For example, environmental assessment at intake helps identify the need for concrete services or referral to other resources. Environmental assessment techniques that fully involve clients and provide them with immediately useful information about their situation are particularly helpful in supporting engagement and the development of client-worker partnerships. We have found that use of a social network map early on in the working relationship fulfills the functions both of assessment and engagement. Clients learn more about their social network resources in a nonthreatening manner, and workers learn who else in the client environment should be included in ongoing assessments.

Environmental assessment also contributes to intervention planning, in that aspects of the environment that currently maintain the behavior of concern as well as potentially available resources to support behavior changes can be identified and mobilized as needed (Mattaini 1990). For example, in previous work we examined social network interventions across the continuum of child welfare services and outlined the types of social network assessments that should be an integral part of each stage in the continuum from preplacement to aftercare services (Tracy, Whittaker, Boylan, Neitman, & Overstreet 1995). Environmental assessment questions to be considered in working with families of children in placement include:

- Will the family's network reinforce the parents' behavior changes or will the network sabotage behavior change efforts in unanticipated ways?
- Will the family's network be able to play a role in supporting parental visitation, either through emotional support or through concrete assistance in providing transportation to and from visits?
- Are there culturally significant network members, such as grandparents, with whom the child can maintain contact and connection even if contact with biological parents is limited or impossible?

During the intervention stage, it is important to ensure that all the relevant people and environmental systems in the client's life situation are involved to the extent required to achieve the goal. Family group conferencing (Atkin 1991), a technique that is described more fully in the next chapter, is one strategy that both assesses the environment and makes full use of that environment in intervention. The extent to which the client has changed but the environment has remained unchanged is also a critical question. Rzepnicki (1991) emphasizes the absolute centrality of environmental supports and conditions to the maintenance of intervention gains. In a review of the literature on factors that increase the likelihood that progress will be maintained after formal intervention ends, she suggests that workers should (1) create as much similarity as possible between the intervention situation and the client's natural environment, (2) increase environmental support for improved client functioning, including both social support (from natural networks and helpers) and concrete resources (both currently and in the future), and (3) provide multiple opportunities for learning of new skills and competencies. At closure or termination, environmental assessment and intervention are thus crucial in guiding the transition from reliance on the helping relationship with a worker or agency to connections with other sources of formal and informal community support.

MAPPING SOCIAL NETWORK RESOURCES: THE SOCIAL NETWORK MAP

We have found that social network assessment is often the best and most time-effective method for beginning an environmental assessment.

Gathering information at the level of the social environment naturally opens a window of opportunity to learn about other levels of the environment. This is because the type and quality of the social network and social support resources available to a client are heavily influenced by other environmental variables, including physical features, institutional structures, and social/cultural/political systems. For example, Cochran and Niego, in a review of parenting and social networks, aptly point out that factors such as "poverty, unemployment, and lack of educational opportunity dramatically influence the networks of families, limiting their capacity to nurture and support parents and their children" (1995, 415).

A social network assessment can also be used to identify the different types of communities with which an individual maintains connections and the quality of those relationships as perceived by the individual. Community membership is based not only on residence, but on lifestyle, employment, interest, or experiences. Rubin and Rubin (1992) identify five major types of communities: neighborhoods (the most commonly used definition), solidarity communities, social classes, networks, and communities of interest. Kemp points out that "some clients who seem relatively isolated in their local neighborhoods may have connections with wider communities of interest" (1995, 185).

A further rationale for beginning the environmental assessment with a social network assessment can be found in the research evidence reviewed in Chapter 3 regarding the impacts of social networks and social support.

If social workers are to work with, and not against, the client's social network, completing an accurate assessment of social network resources is a necessary first task. This is especially true if, as is often the case, a large percentage of helping exchanges are occurring within the informal helping network. All too often, important social resources are not identified at all or are identified too late to be of any help in implementing a case plan.

Cultural differences between the client and the worker may exacerbate this difficulty; a social network perspective enables the worker to understand culturally specific patterns of help giving and receiving (Green 1995). The process of family group conferencing (Atkin 1991), for example, was informed by the traditional help-giving patterns of the indigenous peoples of New Zealand; this model was adopted from that group's definition of and preference for extended family involvement in decision-making. An understanding of coping and social support strategies used by various communities of color (e.g., Daly, Jennings, Beckett, & Leashore 1996) allows for more effective and early positive involvement of available resources.

There is also some evidence that naturally occurring sources of social support can be supportive of professionally based intervention with clients, thus allowing for more flexible and strategic use of time. In one study of network therapy, in which workers met the mental health client's entire social network, network therapy participants showed a 76 percent decrease in formal service contacts as compared with a 17 percent decrease in formal service usage for the comparison group (Gottlieb & Coppard 1987). Similar findings emerged from a social network case management project with homeless women (Jenny Kattlove, personal communication, October 30, 1996). When a support system is activated, the worker's role can become progressively decentralized. The decrease in service usage may be due to the fact that network members help detect and intervene with pending crises and help directly during periods of needed crisis intervention; in this manner, help provided from networks may be considered a factor in reducing phone calls to or face-to-face contacts with case managers.

As a research technique, social network mapping has been applied with many client populations (Biegel, Shore, & Gordon 1984; Fraser & Hawkins 1984; Hawkins & Fraser 1985; Kahn & Antonucci 1981; Lovell & Hawkins 1988). Network analysis has been used with personal networks as well as interorganizational networks for service delivery (Murty & Gillespie 1995). A number of tools are available for measuring such variables as social embeddedness, perceived social support, and enacted social support (for reviews of social support and social network scales, see Bruhn & Philips 1984; Rock, Green, Wise, & Rock 1984; Streeter & Franklin 1992). The social network mapping tool that we have developed was drawn primarily from the work of Fraser and Hawkins (1984) and Lovell and Hawkins (1988), with substance abusers and maltreating mothers, respectively. Whereas these researchers used the technique of gathering network member data and then developing a matrix to gather data on network member qualities and relationships, the current social network map enables collection of information on the total size and composition of the network and the nature of relationships within the network as perceived by the person completing the map (Tracy & Whittaker 1990).

Steps in Administration

Administering the social network map involves listing network members from each of seven domains (household, family/relatives, friends, people from work or school, people from clubs, organizations or religious groups, neighbors, and agencies or other formal service providers). Names or initials are initially recorded on the circle map and listed separately on small slips of paper or index cards (see Figure 4.4 for the map, grid, and complete instructions for administration). The next step involves asking a series of questions regarding the nature of network relationships. These questions cover (a) the types of support perceived to be available and (b) the extent to which network relationships are reciprocal, the extent to which network members are critical of the client, the closeness of relationships, the frequency of contact, and the length of relationships. The client is asked to sort the slips of paper or index cards into the appropriate response category (e.g., hardly ever, sometimes, almost always) using a sheet of paper as a sorting card. This procedure was informed by the work of Lovell (1986), who used such an approach with maltreating parents. Number-coded responses to these questions are then recorded on the network grid.

When analyzed, the social network map provides visual information

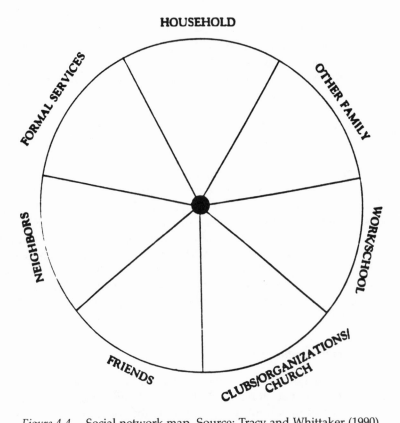

Figure 4.4. Social network map. Source: Tracy and Whittaker (1990).
Reprinted by permission of Families International Incorporated.
(continued)

(*Figure 4.4 continued*)

ID Respondent / Name	Area of life 1. Household 2. Other family 3. Work/school 4. Organizations 5. Other friends 6. Neighbors 7. Professionals 8. Other	Concrete support 1. Hardly ever 2. Sometimes 3. Almost always	Emotional support 1. Hardly ever 2. Sometimes 3. Almost always	Information/ advice 1. Hardly ever 2. Sometimes 3. Almost always	Critical 1. Hardly ever 2. Sometimes 3. Almost always	Direction of help 1. Goes both ways 2. You to them 3. They to you	Closeness 1. Not very close 2. Sort of close 3. Very close	How often seen 0. Does not see 1. Few times/yr. 2. Monthly 3. Weekly 4. Daily	How long known 1. Less than 1 yr. 2. 1-5 yrs. 3. More than 5 yrs.
#	7	8	9	10	11	12	13	14	15
01									
02									
03									
04									
05									
06									
07									
08									
09									
10									
11									
12									
13									
14									
15									
1-6									

Step One: Developing a Social Network Map

Let's take a look at who is in your social network by putting together a network map. (Show network map.) We can use first names or initials because I'm not that interested in knowing the particular people and I wouldn't necessarily be contacting any of the people we talk about.

Think back to this past month, say since [date]. What people have been important to you? They may have been people you saw, talked with, or wrote letters to. This includes people who made you feel good, people who made you feel bad, and others who just played a part in your life. They may be people who had an influence on the way you made decisions during this time.

There is no right or wrong number of people to identify on your map. Right now, just list as many people as you come up with. Do you want me to write, or do you want to do the writing?

First, think of people in your *household*—whom does that include?

How, going around the map, what *other family members* would you include in your network?

How about people from *work or school?*

People from *clubs, organizations,* or *religious groups*—whom should we include here?

What *other friends* haven't been listed in the other categories?

Neighbors—local shopkeepers may be included here.

Finally, list professional people or people from formal agencies whom you have contact with.

Look over your network. Are these the people you would consider part of your social network this past month? (Add or delete names as needed.)

Step Two: Completing the Social Network Grid

(If more than 15 people are in the network, ask the client to select the "top fifteen" and then ask the questions about only those network members. For each of the questions use the appropriate sorting guide card. Once the client has divided up the cards, put the appropriate code number for each person listed on the network grid.)

Now, I'd like to learn more about the people in your network. I'm going to write their names on this network grid, put a code number for the area of life, and then ask a few questions about the ways in which they help you. Let's also write their names on these slips of paper too; this will make answering the questions a lot easier. These are the questions I'll be asking (show list of social network questions), and we'll check off the names on this grid as we go through each question.

The first three questions have to do with the *types of support* people give you.

Who would be available to help you out in *concrete ways*—for example, would give you a ride if you needed one or would pitch in to help you with a big chore or would look after your belongings for a while if you were away? Divide your cards into three piles—those people you can hardly ever rely on for concrete help, those you can rely on sometimes, and those you'd almost always rely on for this type of help.

Now, who would be available to give you *emotional support*—for example, to comfort you if you were upset, to be right there with you in a stressful situation, to listen to you talk about your feelings? Again, divide your cards into three piles—those people you can hardly ever rely on for emotional support, those you can rely on sometimes, and those you almost always can rely on for this type of help.

Finally, whom do you rely on for *advice*—for example, who would give you information on how to do something, help you make a big decision, or teach you how to do something? Divide your cards into the three piles—hardly ever, sometimes, and almost always—for this type of support.

Look through your cards and this time select those people, if any, in your network who you feel are *critical* of you (either critical of you or your lifestyle or of you as a parent). When I say "critical," I mean critical of you in a way that makes you feel bad or inadequate. Divide the cards into three piles—those people who are hardly ever critical of you, sometimes critical of you, and almost always critical of you. Again we'll put the code numbers next to their names.

Now look over your cards and think about the *direction of help.* Divide your cards into three piles—those people with whom help goes both ways (you help them just as much as they help you), those whom you help more, and those who help you more. OK, let's get their code numbers on the grid.

Now think about how *close* you are to the people in your network. Divide the cards into three piles—those people you are not very close to, those you are sort of close to, and those you are very close to—and then we'll put a code number for them.

Finally, just a few questions about *how often* you see people and *how long* you've known the people in your network. Divide the cards into four piles—people you see just a few times a year, people you see monthly, people you see weekly, and people you see daily (if you see someone twice or more than twice a week, count that as "daily"). OK, we'll put their numbers on the grid.

This is the last question. Divide the cards into three piles—those people you have known less than a year, from 1 to 5 years, and more than 5 years.

Now we have a pretty complete picture of who is in your social network.

Figure 4.4.   (continued) Social network map. Source: Tracy and Whittaker (1990). Reprinted by permission of Families International Incorporated.

as well as absolute numbers and percentages along the following dimensions:

- *Network size:*   total number of people identified in the network.
- *Domain size:*   total number/proportions of people in each of the seven domains.
- *Perceived availability of emotional, concrete, and informational support:*   proportion of network members rated as "almost always" available to provide these types of support.
- *Criticalness:*   proportion of network perceived to be "almost always" critical.
- *Closeness:*   proportion of network perceived to be "very close."
- *Reciprocity:*   proportion of network relationships in which "help goes both ways."
- *Directionality:*   proportion of network relationships in which help goes primarily from client to network and proportion of network relationships in which help goes primarily from network to client.
- *Stability:*   length of relationships (how long known).
- *Frequency of contact:*   how often seen.

In addition to these specific variables, the social network map, when combined with other assessment information, may help the worker:

- understand culturally specific patterns of help-giving; culturally relevant definitions of family, and culturally specific help-giving roles;
- identify potential sources of support to aid in the maintenance of intervention gains;
- understand family system boundaries;
- pinpoint sources of conflict within the personal social network;
- appreciate the client's perception of support;
- encourage the client to actively restructure the immediate social environment;
- encourage client efforts at self-help;
- identify patterns of reciprocal helping;
- identify relevant others who may participate in future network interventions (Tracy, Whittaker, & Mooradian 1990).

Information on the reliability and validity of social network map data is often difficult to determine. Problems of recall, fatigue, and recent events all affect self-reports of social networks. In one test-retest study of the social network map's reliability, respondents identified 70 percent of network members when the map was administered a second time; ratings of network members were 76 percent reliable. Evidence suggests that some relational aspects of social networks, such as criticalness, were less stable than others (Tracy, Catalano, Whittaker, & Fine 1990). In another study, we attempted to address the issue of convergent construct validity, that is, correlations among dimensions of perceived social support as measured by the social network map and by other standardized social support instruments. Greater satisfaction with emotional support was associated with greater support satisfaction overall. On the other hand, the frequency of criticism from network members was significantly associated with less social support satisfaction (Tracy & Abell 1994). This study also confirmed our earlier findings that information about structural features alone, such as network size, provided little or no information about the quality, amount, or experience of social support (Tracy 1990). In general, further studies of reliability and validity of social network data are needed, particularly those which include shorter test-retest intervals, verification of reciprocated network membership, and measures of received support in addition to perceived support.

The Social Network Map in Practice

We have completed several pilot studies of the use of the social network map, in a home-based family service program (Tracy 1990; Tracy & Whittaker 1990, 1991; Whittaker & Tracy 1990; Whittaker, Tracy, & Marckworth 1989), in a large youth-serving organization (Tracy, Whittaker, Pugh, Kapp, & Overstreet 1994; Whittaker & Tracy 1990; Whittaker, Tracy, Overstreet, Mooradian, & Kapp 1994), and within Head Start early intervention (Tracy & Abell 1994). The clinical usefulness of the map in each of these settings was highly rated by participating staff: In all these contexts, the social network map also provides a significant baseline of environmental information. The map helped practitioners to systematically identify and assess stressors, strains, and resources within the client's social environment. Rather than describing social support in global terms (e.g., extended family lives nearby), the map provided specific information both to the workers and clients in areas such as the types of support available, the presence of close relationships, and the direction of help. Because of its general applicability, the social network map has been cited in numerous social work practice texts as a viable means of assessing client support systems (Garvin & Seabury 1997; Hepworth & Larsen 1993; Mattaini 1993; Meyer & Mattaini 1995; Sheafor et al. 1997; Webb 1996; see also Streeter & Franklin 1992, for a review of social support measures).

The social network map has also been adapted for use in a number of practice settings and within different cultures. The map and accompanying instructions have been translated into the spoken languages of targeted client groups, a process that requires careful attention to meaning and nuance. Even when English is the spoken language, words may hold different connotations within different cultural groups (Pat Dolan, September 1995, personal communication). It is important to use words and phrases that will be understandable to the people who will use the map. Some practitioners have made adaptations in the titles of the social network domains so as to be more meaningful to particular client groups. For example, one project in Canada, which translated the map into French and Inuktitut, used the title Elders rather than Clubs/Organizations/Church when using the map with native populations, and referred to the social network map as People and Groups in Your Life (Pennell & Burford 1995a, 1995b). Others have found creative ways to use the social network map with all the members of a family, engaging adoptive families, for example, in a problem-solving process to decide as a group who were the most important members of their social network (Groze 1996). The social network map has also been used to assess support systems for kinship foster care providers (Bonecutter & Gleeson, in press) and as a research tool in studies of child maltreatment (e.g., Moncher 1995).

The social network map is a versatile and flexible clinical assessment tool that helps to identify potentially useful resources and the client's perceptions of those resources. Often this process leads to the discovery of resources that are available but underutilized. For example, one client who spoke negatively of her neighbors realized after completing the social network map that those same neighbors did provide her with specific types of support. Another woman in desperate need of child care was able to identify two potential people to help with baby-sitting and, with the worker's coaching, was able to enlist these people and establish a child care schedule. One client realized in working on the map that she had become isolated due to a recent move; a specific intervention was developed to initiate contacts with her new neighbors. The case vignettes at the conclusion of this chapter illustrate the ways in which social network data are considered in relation to the presenting problems and needs of the client. Although there are variations depending on the type and orientation of social service agency, information gathered from the network map in all cases directly informs the goals and interventive techniques established with the client.

The social network map is also an empowerment tool, for it enables those completing the instrument to gain insight into and ultimately more control over their social environments. Completing the map gives people the opportunity to review current social ties, reconsider past social ties, and anticipate future social ties. This knowledge, in turn, often leads to an increased sense of competence and control. In fact, one proposed model of the mediating effects of social support in the face of life stressors suggests that perception of social support may prevent a stress appraisal response in the face of a stressor. In other words, the perception that there are others to help leads one to a redefinition of the event or situation as less stressful. Social network members may also provide a solution or coping behaviors in response to a stressful event (Thoits 1986). As an intervention example of this principle, a single father was provided a copy of his social network map to hang near his telephone, to remind him who might be available to help in an emergency. The simple act of learning about one's past and present resources is an empowering experience (Gutiérrez 1990), either because these resources become more immediately accessible, or the intervention required to make them accessible becomes more apparent. In one of our pilot projects, for example, the parents of a ten-year-old boy with a developmental disability were taught ways of establishing more productive relationships with the child's school staff; this in turn, unleashed sorely needed resources from which they had been previously alienated.

The experience of social network review is not always pleasant. In some instances, it becomes painfully clear that the current social network will not or cannot, even with help, support the changes desired or needed by the client. It may become clear in the network review, for example, that friends who are drug users will undermine progress during recovery. In such instances, a decision may need to be made to extricate oneself from a particular network or set of network ties and enlist new network members. On the other hand, a review of past network resources may lead to a plan to reconnect with these relationships as a means of generating renewed sources of support (Morin & Seidman 1986).

Before we leave this section on the social network map in practice, there are a few additional practical matters to address regarding its administration. Completion of the social network map involves filling in the circle map and the accompanying grid. The circle map can be enlarged, if necessary, to allow for more writing room. We have also used concentric circles within the map to depict closeness of relationships. In classroom and workshop exercises involving the map, we have routinely asked participants to draw arrows to indicate the flow of help and to use symbols directly on the map to illustrate the type of help provided by that source (see Tracy 1993, for classroom exercise description and instructions). Whereas the map can accommodate any number of network members, the grid has spaces for only fifteen names. We have typically asked people to list the top fifteen members of their network. However, it is not necessary to restrict the network in that manner. We suggest that another grid sheet be added to accommodate larger networks.

Finally, it is not uncommon for people to list unexpected supports, such as deceased network members, religious figures (e.g., Jesus), or pets, on social network maps. Our approach has been to list these supports on the circle map exactly as they are described to us. We have often created another circle for deceased network members in the recognition that the relationships these figures represent can influence the decisions people make and how they feel about themselves. Similarly, we recognize that various forms of spirituality serve important social support and coping functions. We believe that by not "editing out" or applying our own framework of thinking on the information provided, we reach a more informed and ecologically valid picture of the client's social environment.

GUIDELINES FOR SOCIAL NETWORK/SUPPORT ASSESSMENTS

The following questions are helpful in translating information generated from the social network map into appropriate social support change goals:

1. Who is in the network, how are they related to the client, and who could be potential members?

2. What are the strengths and capabilities of the social network? Among the strengths that need to be examined are number of supportive relationships, variety of supportive relationships, types of support available (emotional, concrete, and informational), and reciprocity among helping relationships. Again, there is no one perfect network: only a network that meets the client's need.

3. What are the gaps in social support needs? Is there a poor fit between the types of support that network members are willing or able to provide and the types of support the client needs or desires?

4. What relationships in the network are based on mutual exchange? Does reciprocity seem to be an issue for the client? Is the client always giving to others and thereby experiencing stress and drain? Or does the client appear to be a drain on the network, with the result that network members are stressed and overburdened?

5. What network members does the client identify as responsive to requests for help, as effective in their helping, and as accessible and dependable? Do sufficient numbers of network members meet these

conditions? These are the people and resources that would most likely be an asset to any intervention plan.

6.   What network members criticize the client in a negative or demanding way? Is the client surrounded by a network that is perceived as negative, nonsupportive, or stress-producing?

7.   What barriers exist to utilizing social network resources? Does the client lack supportive resources or lack skills to gain access to resources? For example, the client may lack some key social skills such as reaching out to others, offering feedback, requesting help, saying thank you when appropriate, and reciprocating to others. Are network members unable to provide more assistance due to lack of skills or knowledge, or have they provided support in the past and are now unwilling or unable to do so? Overwhelming family stressors, such as homelessness, may be present to interfere with the provision of support.

8.   How are social support needs prioritized in relation to other presenting problems and needs? What other levels of the environment need further examination?

The guidelines for assessing social support are useful for both worker and client to consider. At a minimum, the worker and client should be able to identify the structure of the network and the various patterns of support or conflict, assess the adequacy of the network for providing support, and pinpoint sources of conflict, identifying a strategy for dealing with at least one of them (Tracy, Whittaker, & Mooradian 1990). The social network map has other uses when administered repeatedly over set time periods; for example, the data can be used to track changes in network structure or functioning over time and thereby be used to monitor and evaluate progress toward goals. As a precursor to establishing network goals, clients may also be asked to visualize an ideal network, as they would like it to be in the future. This visualizing activity leads quite easily to the generation of goals; for example, if the client wanted to have more friends in his or her network, then the worker and client could begin to identify current obstacles and the first steps toward that goal.

The social network map should be considered in conjunction with other key pieces of information about the client and the client's environment. The information gathered from the social network map will often yield clues as to which other aspects of the environment are most important to assess. For example, a young mother living in a housing project may describe no relationships with neighbors due to the dangerous nature of the environment; in this instance further assessment of the physical environment and community/neighborhood setting would be indicated. A recent immigrant to the Unites States may describe a small network that is not able to link the client to vital resources; the worker may decide to use an ecomap or a culturalgram to explore culturally relevant connections with community resources. A parent, among the working poor, may describe overwhelming stressors, such as lack of health care insurance; the worker may opt for narrative assessment techniques to get at the client's experience and/or techniques of power analysis to assess larger social and political forces. As a final example, a parent involved with child protective services may identify a social network limited primarily to kin and formal service agencies; the worker may find it helpful to follow up to determine if insularity, that is, highly negative interactions with kin or formal service systems, is present. In previous work with high-risk families, insularity has been associated with poor maintenance of behavioral changes (Wahler 1980; see also Thompson 1995).

GUIDELINES FOR SOCIAL NETWORK/SUPPORT GOAL-SETTING

The most obvious use of environmental assessment information lies in the generation of appropriate change goals with the client. Typically goals in social work practice are prioritized in terms of such factors as how immediately the problem must be addressed, how important the issue is to the client, and how likely the intervention is to succeed in relation to other targeted areas for change. In prioritizing environmental assessment information with other sources of information about the client, it may become apparent that an environmental change must take place before other changes can occur; for example, the physical environment may be unsafe or below minimal standards of living, as with a client with no permanent living arrangements, no electricity, or substandard housing. In the same manner, the social environment may be noxious or stress-producing, as with a client living in a crack house, a child physically or sexually abused by another household member, or a "sandwich generation" adult caught between multiple and competing caregiving roles. In other instances, a change in the environment may support other targeted changes occurring in the client's life. Examples here would include participation in self-help groups, such as Alcoholics Anonymous or Parents Anonymous, as part of participation in other formal counseling services; participation in a residential program as part of substance abuse treatment for a mother; and involvement in a family support program as part of an early childhood intervention program.

In terms of social support, change goals may be directed toward either structural changes in the social network or functional changes in social network relationships. The choice of goal is dependent on an evaluation of the current social network and the changes that are desired by the client in this and other areas. As with goal selection in general, the client's expressed desires direct the choice of goals. Preferences and beliefs about help-seeking influence whether or not mobilization and utilization of social network resources would be considered an option. People hold different attitudes about asking for and receiving help from others, and their ideas are often culturally and socially determined (e.g., a good daughter "should," a grandmother "should"). In extreme cases of "negative network orientation" (Tolsdorf 1976), it is thought to be dangerous and inadvisable to utilize network resources. In such cases, the client may have a network but make little use of it or avoid its use for the purposes of social support.

Given client input and agreement, some examples of social support goals and accompanying interventions would include:

- increase or mobilize various types of needed support (e.g., concrete, emotional, or informational, as in enlisting volunteer transportation or respite care services for a family);
- change the composition of an individual or family social network (e.g., helping a person develop new friendships or linking a person with an informal community resource, thus reducing heavy reliance on formal services);
- increase skills in developing and maintaining supportive relationships (e.g., teaching social and interpersonal communication skills or teaching ways of dealing with network members who do not reinforce change efforts);
- improve or enhance the functioning of social network relationships (e.g., helping a family learn to reduce arguments among themselves or developing strategies for a person to use to handle criticism from others).

Most social work settings will require goals to be expressed or written in clear, behaviorally specific language. Dialogue with the client is often necessary to reach clear goal statements. Specific objectives are to be preferred over vague goals, because clearly specified targets for change can help maintain the vision and mobilize action toward the goal. For example, rather than establishing a goal "to increase social support," more behaviorally specific goal statements might be "to have at least one friend or contact in your neighborhood" or "to have one concrete service [such as transportation] provided by a network member, rather than by the social worker." Goal attainment scaling can be a useful way to document progress toward goal completion and to identify the sequence of steps that may need to take place in order to reach the final objective.

The choice of goal should also be based on an assessment of obstacles that prevent the client's benefiting from social support. For some clients, the major obstacle will be lack of or limited social network resources, or network resources that have been "burned out" or otherwise depleted by long periods of caregiving. For other clients, the social environment assessment may yield a stress-producing, nonsupportive, or antisocial network. Other clients may lack the social skills necessary to form and maintain interpersonal relationships; for these clients, interventions to address skills deficits may need to precede direct linking activities to strengthen social networks. Prejudice, stigma, and discrimination may be factors limiting social networks; for example, the stigma of mental illness has a negative effect on case managers' abilities to mobilize social network resources for persons with chronic mental illness (Cutler & Tatum 1983; Hatfield 1978).

Depending on the practice setting, systems barriers, such as paperwork, caseload size, and lack of time may prevent enhancement of social networks (Biegel, Tracy, & Song 1995). Finally, the success of many social network interventions is highly related to the level of resources in the community and the worker's ability to organize and develop formal and informal community resources (Biegel et al. 1984; Kisthardt 1997). Experience from at least one social support intervention project within the mental health system suggests that the implementation of social network interventions requires a blending of both direct clinical and community organization practice skills (Biegel & Tracy 1993; Biegel, Tracy, & Corvo 1994). Working toward changes in a client's or family's social support network may also require working toward a change in the service delivery system, the development of new community resources and services, or the forging of new linkages and relationships with informal resources. The next chapter will explore a range of environmental interventions that emerge from social network interventions.

SUMMARY

We end this chapter with a summary table: "Environmental Assessment Tools and Methods" (Table 4.2), which contains a wide range of environmental assessment techniques across different levels of client systems and environments. This information is not meant to be exhaus-

Table 4.2. Environmental Assessment: Tools and Methods

	Perceived Environment	Physical Environment	Social/Interactional	Institutional/ Organizational	Social/Political/ Cultural Environment
Individual	Perceived Support Network Inventory MSPSS Sociopolitical Control Scale	Assessment of universal environmental resources Environmental Assessment Index PIE System	Social Network Map Ecomap Community Interaction Checklist PIE System	Ecomap Nurturing/Sustaining Environment PIE System	Culturalgram Power Analysis
Family	Family Support Scale Narrative techniques	Family Access to Basic Resources Family Resource Scale	Ecomap Inventory of Social Support	Ecomap Family Empowerment Scale	Cultural Genogram Power Analysis
Group	Ethnographic interviewing Participant observation	Participant observation	Sociogram Socio-environmental context of group	Context diagram of environmental transactions Force Field Analysis	Power analysis Nurturing/Sustaining Environment
Neighborhood	Organizational history of neighborhood Participant observation	Physical description of neighborhood	Nomothetic ecomapping	Capacity Inventory Inventory of Local Associations Community Inventory	Framework for conceptualizing community Power Analysis

tive, but rather to illustrate the range of strategies and techniques that are currently available or being developed to assess various aspects of the environment. The interventions described here also meet many of the characteristics set forth earlier for in the definition of environmental assessment. All of these tools offer a means for the client or groups of clients to learn more about their environment—its strengths as well as its limitations—and its impact on their lives.

ENVIRONMENTAL ASSESSMENT: TOOLS AND METHODS

Perceived Environment

Perceived Support Network Inventory (Oritt, Paul, & Behrman 1985): A self-report paper and pencil questionnaire of perceived social support; respondents first generate a social network list and then rate each network member in terms of the type of support provided, satisfaction with support provided, and extent to which network member is asked to help and is responsive to requests for help, reciprocity, and conflicts.

Multidimensional Scale of Perceived Social Support (MSPSS) (Zimet, Dahlem, Zimet, & Farkey 1988): A twelve-item self-report paper-and-pencil instrument designed to measure perceived social support from three sources—family, friends, and a significant other; higher scores reflect higher perceived social support.

Sociopolitical Control Scale (SPCS) (Zimmerman & Zahniser 1991): A seventeen-item self-report paper-and-pencil instrument to measure sociopolitical control as distinguished from other types of perceived control; the scale can be used to measure a sense of empowerment in clients; higher scores indicate higher perceived leadership competence and policy control.

Family Support Scale (Dunst et al. 1988): An eighteen-item self-report paper-and-pencil measure of the perceived helpfulness of various sources of support to families raising young children.

Narrative Techniques (Saleebey 1994; see also Jordan & Franklin 1995): Narrative methods, such as case studies, self-characterizations, and repertory grids, take into account life stories, narratives, and myths, and the meanings that humans assign to their individual and collective experiences

Ethnographic Interviewing (Green 1995; see also Jordan & Franklin 1995): Interview techniques that seek to help workers understand cultural differences and value clients as cultural guides, explaining in their own words the meanings they attach to problems, relationships, and the help-seeking process, among others.

Participant Observation (Gilgun, Daly, & Handel 1992; see also Jordan & Franklin 1995): Method of assessment whereby the worker observes the client in everyday life and participates in the client's daily routines as unobtrusively as possible; especially useful when the view of the "insider" is needed or difficult to obtain; can be used with individual clients (e.g., observing a student in class), families (e.g., having dinner with a family), groups (e.g., attending a tenant group's meeting), and at the neighborhood level (e.g., participating in daily life in a housing project).

Organizational History of Neighborhood (Warren & Warren 1977, 70–71): Guidelines for organizing information about a neighborhood, considering recent history, divisive factors, organizational ties, identifiable neighborhood leaders, and individuals roles in community activities.

Physical Environment

Environmental Assessment Index (EAI) (Poresky 1987): A forty-four-item instrument to assess the educational/developmental quality of children's home environments via information gathered through a home interview with the caretaker and direct observation by the worker.

PIE System (Karls & Wandrie 1994): See Chapter 4 for information.

Assessment of Universal Environmental Resources (Hepworth & Larsen 1993): See Chapter 4 for information.

Family Access to Basic Resources (Vosler 1990): An assessment tool completed by both the worker and family to determine the extent of stress and stress pileup due to inadequate or unstable basic family resources; includes monthly expenses, current resources, potential family resources, and resource stability for the following resources: wages, child support, income transfers, housing, food, clothing, personal care and recreation, health care, education, family and developmental services, and transportation.

Family Resource Scale (Dunst et al. 1988): A thirty-one-item self-report paper-and-pencil questionnaire to measure the adequacy of different resources in households with young children; each item is rated on a five-point scale ranging from Not at All Adequate to Almost Always Adequate.

Physical Description of Neighborhood (Warren & Warren 1977, 194–195): Guidelines for describing the physical features of a neighborhood, including mapping of each block, types of automobiles, physical evidence of political activity, general upkeep, physical boundaries, number and variety of behavior settings, and extent of similarities and differences in the neighborhood.

Social/Interactional Environment

Social Network Map (Tracy & Whittaker 1990): Visual means to depict size and composition of social network, types of social support perceived to be available, and quality of relationships within a social network.

Ecomap (Hartman 1994): Visual means of placing an individual or family within the social context, particularly the organizations and factors impinging on their lives.

Child's Ecomap (Fahlberg 1991): Ecomap designed for completion by child entering placement; covers areas such as homes the child has lived in, friends, siblings, school, dreams, worries, and feelings.

Community Interaction Checklist (Wahler, Leske, & Rogers 1979): A self-observational listing of types of interactions occurring in the past twenty-four hours (or other) time period with members of the social network outside immediate household members; the nature and positive or negative rating of each interaction is recorded by the client.

Inventory of Social Support (Dunst et al. 1988): A paper-and-pencil matrix of personal social network in terms both of source and type of support; respondents indicate whom they would go to or receive help from for each of twelve different types of child-rearing supports.

Sociograms (Moreno & Borgatta 1951; see also Mattaini 1993): Graphically depicts patterns of affiliations and relationships between group members by using symbols for people and interactions; useful in identifying and assessing subdivisions and their impact on a group.

Socioenvironmental Context of Group (Yourdin 1989; see also Mattaini 1993): A visual representation of a group's situation and the environmental forces that may be critical to the group's functioning; exchanges that represent positive support for or opposition to the group from a variety of sources are depicted, including the larger agency structure, the families of the members and worker/facilitator, and other systems specific to the group, such as funding sources

Nomothetic Ecomapping (Mattaini 1993): Visual display of common supports and obstacles from a variety of systems for a particular neighborhood-level concern (e.g., school failure); results in a generic ecomap that may be used to inform choice points for intervention

Institutional/Organizational

Ecomap: See above.

Nurturing/Sustaining Environment (Norton 1978): Graphic representation of both the supports and problems a person experiences in the social environment; the positive, negative, or neutral effects of both the nurturing (immediate) environment and the sustaining environment (wider community and broader society) are identified; information can be generated with the client and leads to understanding of areas that need to be changed and areas of strength that might be resources for achieving change.

Family Empowerment Scale (Koren, DeChillo, & Friesen 1992): A thirty-four-item self-report paper-and-pencil instrument to measure empowerment of a parent or caregiver of a child with an emotional disability; the level and expression (through attitude, knowledge, and behaviors) of empowerment are assessed.

Context Diagram of Environmental Transactions (Yourdin 1989; see also Mattaini 1993): A visual representation of the transactions and exchanges occurring between an agency and other systems in its environment (e.g., clients, community agencies, schools, other service systems, etc.).

Force Field Analysis (Brager & Holloway 1978; see also Shaefor et al. 1997): A technique to organize information about the forces that may affect the success of a change effort: the steps include (a) specifying the desired change (usually at the organizational or community level), (b) identifying the driving and restraining forces that will affect whether or not the objective is met, (c) assessing the strength of each driving and restraining force in terms of potency, consistency, and amenability, (d) identifying the actors for each driving and restraining force and rating the likelihood that the actor will become involved, and (e) selecting a strategy for change based on the analysis of the various forces working for or against the change effort and the various actors that may be able to help.

Mapping Community Capacity (McKnight & Kretzmann 1990): A format for assessing the assets and capacities existing within communities;

three levels of assets are examined, those assets and capacities located inside the neighborhood and largely under neighborhood control (e.g., individual assets of residents and local resident-controlled associations and organizations), assets located within the community but largely controlled by outsiders (e.g., private and nonprofit organizations, physical resources, public institutions and services), and resources originating outside the neighborhood and controlled by outsiders (e.g., welfare expenditures, public capital improvement expenditures, and public information).

Inventory of Groups and Organizations (Center for Urban Affairs and Policy Research 1988): A booklet-length guide to finding out about the organizations and groups people belong to a city neighborhood; three methods of gathering information are described: using newspapers, directories, and other printed sources; talking to people at local institutions, such as parks and churches; and conducting a phone survey of a sample of local residents.

Frameworks for Analyzing a Community or Neighborhood (Kirst-Ashman & Hull 1996; Sheafor et al. 1997; Johnson 1995): Community assessment leads to organized information about strengths and limitations of the community, the manner in which the community solves problems, and the capacity for change (Johnson 1995). Most organizing frameworks consider such factors as physical setting, history and demography, economic and political system, and educational, health, and welfare systems.

Social/Political/Cultural

Culturalgram (Congress 1994): An ecomaplike assessment tool designed to assess the impact of several different aspects of culture on the family or individual, including reasons for immigration, length of time in the community, legal or undocumented status, language spoken at home and in the community, contact with cultural institutions, health beliefs, holidays and special events, impact of crisis events, and values about family, education, and work; also enables the worker to individualize for ethnically similar clients beyond cultural generalizations.

Power Analysis (Gutiérrez 1990, 1996): A critical component of empowerment-based practice, a power analysis is conducted with a client in two phases: first analyzing how conditions of powerlessness are affecting the client's current situation and second identifying sources of potential power available to or within the client.

Culturalgenogram (Hardy & Laszloffy 1995): Technique described to add cultural information to a genogram, including dimensions such as groups represented in culture of origin and intercultural marriages.

Framework for Conceptualizing Community (Netting et al. 1993, 91–92): Format for organizing information collected about a community or neighborhood; the factors to be considered include understanding characteristics of target population members, identifying community boundaries, profiling social problems, understanding dominant values, identifying formal and covert mechanisms of oppression, identifying evidence of discrimination, recognizing locations of power, determining resource availability, and identifying patterns of resource delivery and service delivery.

CASE VIGNETTES

Case #1

Mrs. Adams had recently moved and reported feeling isolated from her usual sources of support. Her social network map and grid revealed a network of five members: her husband and two teenage children, a pastor, and the pastor's wife. The family was heavily involved in church activities, attending church meetings four days a week. Among the many presenting problems, severe arguments figured prominently between the parents and children over church activities and rules. The mother expressed the strongest need for help with social support. She reported not feeling close to many people in her network, few reciprocal relationships, and several relationships highly critical of her. Although she did report sources of support, she lacked friendships and knew no neighbors in her new apartment building. Accordingly, she agreed to work toward developing friendships and expanding her network. The worker felt that enhancing the mother's social network resources would support her parenting efforts and complement other goals established with this family, for example, to reduce family violence. At termination, the mother's network had expanded to include several new neighbors and friends and, more importantly, she had learned ways to develop and maintain more supportive relationships.

Overall, findings from this study indicate that respondents did perceive a number of supportive resources within their networks. Opportunities exist, then, for strengthening and working collaboratively with these informal helping resources. At the same time, network composition and the functioning of the network can create additional stress on families. Efforts may be needed to assist families in creating or developing a supportive social network and to enable families to make use of available resources. Such interventions may ultimately allow practitioners to incorporate social and environmental factors more effectively in their work with at-risk families.

Source: Tracy, E. M. (1990). Identifying social support resources of at-risk families. *Social Work 35,* 252–258. Reprinted with permission of NASW Press.

Case #2

M is a twenty-nine-year-old African-American single mother with five children, ages two months to eleven years. She is an alleged crack/cocaine user who leaves the children unsupervised and sells her food stamps to support her crack habit. At first contact, M admitted to smoking crack two days earlier but stated that she wanted to stop using. She has four sisters and a brother, all of whom are in prison. She is not trustful of her own mother, who is described as "almost always critical" of her and who made the initial report to protective services. Five friends are listed on the network map, but on closer examination these friends provide little if any support. M lives with two friends, both of whom are suspected crack users. Review of the social network map information clearly showed the limitations she faced in getting or accepting help from her existing network. The worker reported that the network map was used as a tool initially to engage M in the helping process and address the issue of substance abuse. For example, the worker was able to initiate in a non-threatening way a discussion about the members of M's network and how she spent time with them. Out of this discussion grew an awareness of the role substance abuse played in her relationships. For this mother, the primary treatment goals were to locate her own housing away from drug-using network members, to enroll in drug-treatment services, and to begin to develop new nonusing social network contacts.

Source: Tracy, E. M., Whittaker, J. K., Pugh, A., Kapp, S., & Overstreet, E. J. (1994). Social networks of primary caregivers receiving family preservation services. *Families in Society 75,* 481–489. Reprinted with permission of Families International Corporation.

Case #3

J is a white, single parent in his twenties who assumed full child-care responsibilities while his partner was in drug treatment. J was not aware of resources to help with child care, nor did he actively use social network resources. After completing the map, names of people who might be supportive to him were circled, and then the map was left with him, as a prompt, to keep by his phone. In this way, he had access to the names of people who could help out when he needed respite or support. The map and its use were reviewed weekly.

Source: Tracy, E. M., Whittaker, J. K., Pugh, A., Kapp, S., & Overstreet, E. J. (1994). Social networks of primary caregivers receiving family preservation services. *Families in Society 75*, 481–489. Reprinted with permission of Families International Corporation.

5

Environmental Intervention

This chapter begins with a discussion of social work intervention in general, followed by our conceptualization of environmental intervention. The core of the chapter is a description of environmental interventions that are intended to gain access to or enhance social networks. Several other major environmental interventions that supplement and extend social network interventions are also reviewed. We conclude with some general thoughts about environmentally oriented practice and a summary table, "Environmental Interventions: Selected Strategies" (Figure 5.6).

We have chosen to provide an extended discussion of social network interventions because of their immediacy and relevance to the direct-service practitioner. In our view, the role of network consultant in large part defines the repertoire of direct service environmental intervention (Whittaker & Tracy 1989). In the social environment the practitioner works through the client's personal network and community systems to find social support in all its forms, to raise consciousness, and to promote solidarity for collective social action. The particular network interventions we have chosen as illustrations are based on and extend the building blocks of person-environment practice identified in Chapter 1.

Four types of social environment change intervention will be presented: natural-helper interventions, network facilitation, mutual-aid approaches, and skills-training strategies. *Natural-helper interventions* exemplify the notion of reciprocity by affording clients the opportunity to give as well as receive help. Further, by engaging helpers with whom the client shares similarities of socioeconomic status, culture, and region, natural helper interventions increase the probability of enhanced mutuality. *Network facilitation* expands the boundaries of current networks by introducing new helpers and by identifying new helping resources among present network members. *Mutual-aid groups* build a common consciousness and often become the vehicle through which private troubles become public concerns. *Network skills training* offers valuable strategies for gaining accessing to and increasing resources. These four interventions constitute a powerful resource for social work practice.

This chapter focuses on environmental change strategies because—as we have pointed out in earlier chapters—in large part our technologies for change and the organizational structures within which social workers practice are overwhelmingly person-oriented, despite a strong tradition of attention to person and environment variables. However, as will become clear later in this chapter both person-oriented change strategies, such as skills training, and community-oriented strategies, such as advocacy and case management, play an important role in prompting and supporting change in the social environment.

INTERVENTION IN SOCIAL WORK PRACTICE

The bridge between assessment and intervention—as ongoing and reciprocal activities—is provided by the mutual generation of goals and a contract for work (Hepworth & Larsen 1993; Shulman 1992; Whittaker & Tracy 1989). Workers and clients together plan and carry out change strategies as they work toward their stated goals. Depending on the setting, these activities may be called intervention, treatment, help, counseling, casework, or case management.

Successful movement in the direction of change presupposes the successful completion of a number of previous phases. The timing of this transition is crucial. Sometimes change efforts are implemented prematurely because of the worker's desire to be helpful (being "hasty to help"), before a full understanding of the issue is achieved or the client is fully committed to change efforts. Sometimes, when agency policies and funding practices dictate the length of the assessment period, workers and clients are propelled into the change phase at some arbitrary point. Ideally, the worker and client will have achieved a strong relationship before change is attempted; the client will be ready for change and committed to it; the worker and client will have completed a full assessment of the issue or concern and will have developed shared, realistic goals (Cormier & Cormier 1991).

Some social work intervention strategies seek to change behavior, cognition, or affect; others seek to enhance the functioning of families or other small groups; still other change efforts are directed at neighborhoods, communities, and organizations. The choice of intervention must flow from the situation as it is assessed, including assessment of the environment. The best intervention is the most relevant—one that provides the most promising means of achieving the stated goals. Interventions need to match developmental levels (e.g., children versus adults) and be responsive to ethnic, cultural, and racial dimensions (Leung, Cheung, & Stevenson 1994; Lum 1996; Proctor & Davis 1994). Mismatches can easily occur. For example, time-limited parent group education is probably not the most relevant and promising intervention for a family faced with multiple stresses, lack of support, and inadequate resources. Similarly, person-oriented interventions are so pervasive that workers may apply them in situations that clearly call for environmental and systemic change (Tracy, Green, & Bremseth 1993), underestimating the extent to which social-environmental problems affect their clients (Proctor, Vosler, & Sirles 1993).

Research on critical thinking has demonstrated that a number of worker behaviors during intervention planning are associated with less effective intervention. These include ignoring indigenous and natural helpers, generating vague goal statements, overlooking client assets, focusing on negative rather than positive behavior, and overlooking the physical environment as a constraint and resource for change (Gambrill 1990). Interventions that mismatch the problem and the target for change and those which do not make full use of environmental resources are less likely to be effective in goal attainment. For example, workers who provide services to clients in institutional settings understand the critical importance of the postdischarge environment (e.g., home, school, neighborhood) in maintaining gains from the structured treatment setting (Jenson, Hawkins, & Catalano 1986; Wells & Whittington 1990; Wells, Wyatt, & Hobfall 1991; Whittaker & Pfeiffer 1994). For this reason, many residential treatment programs have begun to shift to family-focused practice, including services such as family treatment, family reunification, and intensive case management before and immediately after discharge (Braziel 1996; Jenson & Whittaker 1987).

In selecting an intervention strategy, practitioners can be guided by the following question: Which strategy, or (more likely) combination of strategies will be most effective for this client with these desired outcomes? Unfortunately, this question is more easily posed than answered. Nonetheless, we offer some general guidelines for choosing among a number of social network interventions. The intervention strategy must make sense to the client, and implementation must be feasible with the resources that can be made available. The consumerism movement within the helping professions dictates that clients be active rather than passive participants, that client rights be made explicit, that the intervention process be demystified, and that clients consent to treatment or intervention (Cormier & Cormier 1991). We believe the following additional criteria, drawn from the key features of person-environment practice outlined in Chapter 1, are essential. Effective interventions

- are easy to carry out,
- match the unique characteristics and preferences of the client,
- match the characteristics of the desired goal,
- are positive rather than punitive,
- encourage the development of competence,
- strengthen clients' expectations of personal self-efficacy,
- are supported by the literature,
- are feasible and practical to implement,
- do not create additional problems for the client or significant others,
- do not require more of the helper than the helper is able to give or is responsible for giving,
- do not repeat previous unsuccessful solutions,
- build on client and community strengths,
- are based on principles of empowerment based practice (adapted from Cormier & Cormier 1991.)

ENVIRONMENTAL INTERVENTION IN SOCIAL WORK PRACTICE

The development of an effective repertoire for environmental intervention has challenged social work practitioners and theorists since the turn of the century (see Chapters 2 and 3). Frequently referred to as "environmental change" or "environmental modification," the purposes of environmental intervention have been to enrich environmental resources available to clients; to help clients make full use of resources available, and to reduce or modify environmental pressures and stresses impinging on clients (Grinnell 1973, 1983). Familiar practice roles in relation to the environment include those of broker, mediator, advocate (Grinnell 1973, p.219), and skills trainer (Hashimi 1981). As such, environmental interventions are closely aligned with the overall resource management function of the social work profession, including the goal of linking people with systems of resources, services, and opportunities (Dubois & Miley 1996; Zastrow 1995), and with the ethical responsibility of social workers to serve as advocates for clients as articulated in the profession's code of ethics (National Association of Social Workers 1996).

In the life model of social work practice, Germain and Gitterman (1996) discuss a variety of professional roles and methods in relation to specific environmental stressors. For people unwilling or unable to use available social or physical resources, the social work skills of enabling, exploring, mobilizing, guiding, and facilitating are suggested. Where there is a poor fit between client needs and social or physical resources, the social work roles of coordinating, connecting, and mediating may be employed. Advocacy is appropriate when resources are available but those controlling the environment are unwilling to provide them to a client who is otherwise eligible. Finally, organizing and innovating are the preferred practice modality when formal or informal environmental resources are unavailable. The professional methods employed thus match the type and source of environmental problem.

Neugeboren (1996) relates environmental practice to the micro–social work goal of changing service users' situations and the macro–social work goal of changing policies. He identifies six practice skills for environmental intervention: decision-making, monitoring, leading, staffing, negotiating, and representing. Intervention strategies include community resource coordination, linking clients with informal sources of support, developing new supportive services, social advocacy, and serving as change agent in organizations and the community.

As both the life model and Neugeboren's model illustrate, the scope of environmental intervention encompasses a variety of practice modalities. Hepworth and Larsen (1993, 475) identify many forms of intervention that may be employed to improve the environment:

- Enhance family relationships (e.g., family therapy, family support and education, family preservation and reunification, and family self-help groups).
- Supplement resources in the home environment (e.g., home help, home-based services, Meals on Wheels, respite care).
- Develop and enhance support systems (e.g., natural support systems, formal support services, organizations and institutions, indigenous helpers).
- Move clients to different environments (e.g., placements).
- Use case management (e.g., linking clients with essential resources).
- Enhance interactions between organizations and institutions (e.g., mediation).
- Improve institutional environments (e.g., staff training, physical improvements, programming).
- Empower clients (e.g., increase control over resources in the environment).

- Develop new resources (e.g., enabling, organizing, planning and program development).
- Employ advocacy and social action (e.g., case and cause advocacy, legal action, public education, lobbying for legislation).
- Plan and organize (e.g., organizing client groups, social planning, community organization).

For all this, there have been in our view, major problems in social work's treatment of the environment. Key among these have been the tendencies (a) to marginalize environmental practice; (b) to view environmental interventions as less professional than person-oriented interventions; (c) to draw distinct boundaries between direct, indirect, and macropractice; and (d) to ignore the many ways in which the environment is experienced and perceived differently, depending on the characteristics of the individual, group, or larger social structure.

ENVIRONMENTAL INTERVENTION IN PERSON-ENVIRONMENT PRACTICE

In P.E.P., we define *environmental intervention* as *both action in the environment and the process of transforming individual and collective perspectives through critical analysis of the impact of environmental conditions.* Core practice activities directed toward the environment include gaining access to, developing, and enhancing resources and services, including social networks and services that support, educate, and empower individuals, families, groups, and communities; and working to change toxic and oppressive environmental conditions. Environmental intervention also includes facilitating individual and collective discussion and analysis of the impact of environmental conditions. The ultimate goal of environmental intervention is twofold: to create an environment that nurtures and supports growth and change for individuals and groups and to enhance individuals' and groups' abilities to act in the environment on their own behalf.

The following activities all meet our definition of environmental intervention, though each focuses on a different level of the environment and brings to bear a different set of worker skills:

- Organizing a support and education group for family members living with a relative with chronic mental illness.
- Establishing a family resource center with educational materials and resource information in a public school.

- Setting up private visiting areas within a nursing home.
- Working with a consumer group to establish a client advisory group within an agency setting.
- Providing services based in the home and accessible twenty-four hours per day.
- Developing a "waiting room" support group for parents whose children are being seen in a pediatric AIDS clinic.
- Establishing a "buddy program" between first- and fourth-year college students.
- Mapping community assets and developing leadership skills as part of community-building efforts in a poor neighborhood.
- Using indigenous outreach workers to promote prenatal care for low-income pregnant women.
- Involving a youth group in a neighborhood enhancement project.
- Organizing a reminiscence group for elderly immigrants residing in a nursing home.
- Establishing a support and education program for those newly diagnosed as HIV-positive.

THE PROCESS OF ENVIRONMENTAL CHANGE

Figure 5.1 highlights the interrelationships that may exist among the various levels of the environment and the process of environmental change. The first aspect of environmental change is the acquisition of knowledge about the environment and its impact on one's life. In P.E.P., worker and client share equally in the acquisition of knowledge. Clients' direct participation in assessment and data collection and dialogue with the worker and with others in situations similar to their own contribute to their ownership of the process of change, partnership with the worker, and empowerment (Kopp 1993). The worker's task during this phase is to be "an engaged worker who helps clients to construct their experience in political as well as personal terms" (Kemp 1995, 190). Through the generation of knowledge and dialogue about its implications a shift in perspective can occur that enables people to see the ways in which individual experiences are shaped by events and conditions in the social, political, and physical environments. This "critical consciousness" is the foundation for empowerment-based practice and the basis for initiating change efforts.

The process of environmental change is well illustrated by the social environment intervention of network facilitation or network consultation. In this intervention strategy, the worker and client jointly assess

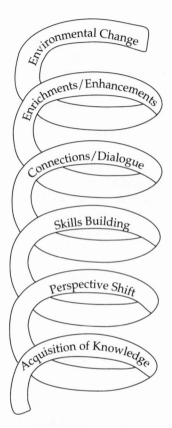

Figure 5.1.   The process of
environmental change.

the resources and capabilities of the surrounding social environment
using the social network map or some similar social support assessment
tool. The process of gathering and discussing this information leads in
most cases to new ways of thinking about the social environment. Resources that clients have ignored or neglected suddenly come into focus.
They may evaluate resources in a new way; a connection once referred
to as "friend" may be viewed differently after the client assesses the
types and amount of support exchanged between them. Barriers to more
supportive interactions with others become evident. From this analysis,
the need for skills training may become apparent—not only for the
client but also for network members or potential network members. The
need for community-building to develop more supportive resources or

to develop better coordination among resources may be identified. Through a variety of strategies, connections between people are initiated, maintained, and strengthened. Once connections are made, new supports and energy become available for producing change in other areas. Naturally, the cycle does not end at this point because, with new supports and resources, another perspective shift may occur. With a backdrop of new supports and new social resources, clients may view their situations as less stressful or more amenable to change. A client with a newly mobilized socially skilled network may say, for example, "I know how to get my needs met now; I am not alone." A new mother attending a drop-in program with other mothers of babies may report, "I think I am a more competent parent having others to turn to for advice and help."

Environmental interventions designed and implemented within an existing program need to be responsive to the context, goals, and values of the program within which the intervention is delivered. In our experience with social network interventions in a variety of practice settings, we have found that social network interventions should be congruent with other goals of the program or service. In our work with family preservation programs (Whittaker et al. 1994), for example, workers wanted social network interventions to be consistent with other home-based service goals, such as maintaining children safely in the home, defusing the precipitating crisis, preventing future crises from occurring, and maintaining change over time. They were interested in empirical evidence that enhancing support systems would in turn reinforce these and other important goals for families throughout the continuum of care (Tracy et al. 1995). These workers also believed that social support interventions should be congruent with the theoretical stance of the program and consistent with the family preservation values of meeting each family's unique social support needs; addressing concerns and needs of the parents, children, or entire family; building on family strengths; and showing sensitivity to culturally defined patterns of help-seeking. The plan for social network interventions that was established within the family preservation program thus specified that social network interventions should be congruent with agency values, philosophy, practice techniques, and goals.

SOCIAL NETWORK INTERVENTIONS

Although a comprehensive knowledge base forms the basis for social network interventions (Chapter 3), a few caveats are called for with regard to social environment interventions more generally. Overall, the practice technologies for environmental interventions are less clearly articulated than for person-oriented approaches, and in many areas of practice the requisite technology is still evolving. There is a critical need for practice evaluation and developmental research technologies that involve clients and workers in the evaluation process (Whittaker et al. 1994). We also recognize that many practice arenas currently do not or cannot support the full use of environmental interventions. In Chapter 7, we address some of the more common barriers to implementation experienced by workers, clients, and agencies.

Furthermore, the environmental interventions described here are typically not the only interventions made available to clients. For the purposes of this chapter, environmental interventions are somewhat artificially removed from their full context so that they may be clearly described. The reader should note that in most situations the environmental intervention employed was part of a larger service delivery plan. This is not to say that a great deal cannot be achieved through environmental interventions per se, but there are clearly instances when more traditional individual change techniques (e.g., behavior modification, family therapy, group work) are also indicated. Practitioners need to make a conceptual link between the environmental intervention selected, the overall assessment information collected, and any additional person-oriented change strategies or services to be utilized.

While each of the environmental interventions included in this chapter requires different practice roles and techniques for implementation, they also share a number of common elements, which constitute some of the key principles and values of environmental intervention.

1. *Linking* is the core practice skill underlying environmental interventions at all client system levels. Linking, and the related skills of resource referral and brokerage, involve at least three abilities. The first ability is to identify, engage, and assess resources (both recipient and helper resources). The second ability is to develop a plan and implement the steps required to make the linkage, whether the linkage is between two people, two families, or a person and a community resource. The third ability is to monitor the linkage, addressing barriers and problems that come up and ensuring that the linkage will remain over time.

2. All environmental interventions are based on strengths. In other words, linkages are made in order to capitalize on the resources to be shared among the parties involved. Thus a *strengths-based assessment model*, including interviewing for client strengths, is necessary at all levels of environmental practice. Deficits and problems are not ignored, but any new connection is based primarily on available strengths and resources.

3. Environmental interventions dictate a *collaborative worker-client relationship*, with power shared as equally as possible between the worker

and the client. The worker-client relationship provides a prototype of the linkages or relationships to be formed. Clients must be directly involved in environmental interventions because they are closest to and possess the most information about their environment, its boundaries, its strengths and limitations, and its meaning for them. To the extent the client is involved in the assessment and the change effort, the likelihood of lasting change is proportionately improved. Clients who view themselves as causal agents are more aware of the skills they have learned and how to apply them in future situations. Environmental interventions seek to increase the individual client's sense of self-efficacy and the group or community's sense of group consciousness.

Bernheim (1989) sums up the qualities of a collaborative helping relationship in the term "family consultant." Writing about the needs of families with a member who has a chronic mental illness, Bernheim states that "families generally want some combination of information, education, opportunities for emotional ventilation and support, professional availability in times of crisis, and contact with other families who have similar difficulties" (p. 562). As a consultant, the worker views the client (family) as competent, but lacking in information in which the consultant has expertise. The client retains the power of choice at all times; consultation is made at the request of the consultee and for the sake of the consultee. This clarity and openness regarding roles and responsibilities is at the heart of environmental helping and person-environment practice.

Social Network Interventions

Four major approaches to social network intervention are described here: natural helper, network facilitation, mutual aid/self-help, and social skills training. Social network interventions are typically directed toward either structural changes in the social network itself or functional changes in social network relationships (see Chapter 4).

Natural-Helper Interventions

Natural helpers are people to whom others naturally turn to for advice and support; often they are people who have "been there," having faced and overcome life challenges (Pancoast, Parker, & Froland 1983). Natural helpers are viewed by others as particularly resourceful and understanding people who possess the time and energy to help others. There are several categories of natural helpers. *Gatekeepers* are those people in a position to know how others are doing or to offer help. *Indigenous helpers* are people who perform culturally defined and sanctioned folk remedies. Germain and Gitterman (1996) point out that natural helpers may be children or teenagers and can be found in housing projects, workplaces, and churches.

Natural-helper interventions seek to develop consultative relationships with these key helpers in a community or defined geographical area (Collins & Pancoast 1976; Froland, Pancoast, Chapman, & Kimboko 1981; Lewis & Suarez 1995). Natural helpers provide various types of support, link people with professional and other needed services, and in some cases substitute for or supplement professional helping services. As such, natural-helper interventions can be used to achieve both structural and functional social network changes.

Natural-helper interventions are applicable to many client populations and service delivery systems. Such interventions extend the services of formal agencies, build connections with hard-to-reach clients, and enhance prevention and early intervention services. For example, Hooyman and Lustbader (1986) identify a number of ways in which natural helpers, such as hairdressers and barbers, apartment managers, and postal carriers, provide services and assistance to older persons living in the community. Some familiar program examples are:

- Teaching meter readers the early warning signals that an elderly customer might be in trouble (e.g., newspapers piled up, lawn unmowed) and the appropriate ways to make contact and referral.
- Recruiting and training community health aides to assist with transportation to medical appointments, basic health education, and early screenings.
- Recruiting and training mothers to reach out to other pregnant women in a defined geographical area and to assist in their obtaining prenatal care.
- Teaching school bus drivers basic empathic communication skills for use with parents at pick-up and drop-off points.

The "classic" form of natural-helper intervention, as defined by Collins and Pancoast (1976), is to develop a consultative relationship between central key helpers and social workers. The first step in this process is to gather information about the natural-helping network within a defined community (community of identity or place), e.g., how it operates, its rules and norms. Qualitative assessment techniques are helpful here, such as the use of narrative techniques and participant observation and use of key informants. The social network map described in Chapter 4 may also be used to identify natural helpers. Community capacity mapping is yet another method that may be used to identify which community members share or are willing to share skills and resources with others (McKnight & Kretzmann 1990). Delgado (1996) described an approach that used youth as field interviewers in a Puerto Rican community asset assessment to identify and enlist indigenous resources for participation in a substance abuse prevention program. In this project, youth who might otherwise be viewed as at risk were seen as a "resource." The benefits of hiring youth as community assessors included, among others, their ability to identify indigenous resources, the creation of community goodwill toward the youth, and youth leadership development.

Knowledge of the geographical locale is often essential to involving natural helpers, as the following vignette illustrates:

> A client wanted to attend GED classes. The worker arranged for classes two blocks from the client's apartment, but still the client did not show up for the first two classes. The worker was able to utilize working knowledge of the apartment building to locate another resident (not a client), who would be willing to walk the client to class. After three sessions, this concrete support was no longer needed and the client continued to attend classes on his own.

Interventions using natural helpers are best developed in partnership; co-optation can occur if the professional does not maintain a collaborative relationship, but rather assumes control over the natural helper. A directive and intrusive professional role may particularly be a problem when working with culturally diverse communities in which the worker cannot assume shared definitions of support and help (Collins 1983). On the other hand, natural-helper relationships can sometimes benefit from professional advice and involvement.

> One social network researcher tells the story of a client citing his barber as a significant source of support during a social network interview. When the researcher contacted the barber, another side of the story unfolded: the barber reported how frustrated and fed up he was with the client coming in every day to talk. The fact that he was so important and helpful to the client was new information for him. (as cited in Tracy, Biegel, & Corvo 1991)

Contracts with natural helpers have been used to outline clearly the roles and responsibilities expected vis-à-vis the identified client and to specify the limits of confidentiality between the parties (Gaudin, Wodarski, Arkinson, & Avery 1990/1991). Sometimes professionals question the quality and effectiveness of help provided by natural helpers (McFarlane, Norman, Streiner, & Roy 1984), and training programs have shown somewhat limited success in changing the way in which natural helpers deliver help (D'Augelli & Ehrlich 1982). We must remember, however, natural helpers are not volunteers or paraprofessionals; by definition, they are not trained to provide help. In addition, professional involvement with natural helpers may alter the help that is provided in unanticipated ways. For example, neighbors may drop off meals on a regular basis to a home-bound person, but is their help changed in any way if it is made part of a formal case management plan? Help that is provided as part of a formal plan may be perceived differently, both by the provider and the recipient.

Natural-helper interventions are viewed as especially useful in rural and in cross-cultural settings (Gaudin et al. 1990/1991; Patterson, Germain, Brennan, & Memmott 1988) (see box, The Social Network Intervention Project). Clients in rural areas may be miles away from formal treatment services; they and their social workers may need to rely on the help and support provided by natural helpers in the community.

Natural helpers are also important as cultural consultants and guides (Green & Leigh 1989). They may be able to help nonminority social workers understand traditional helping practices (e.g., where traditional healing ceremonies can be found among an urban native American population). Also, as the following example illustrates, they may serve to dispel some of the negative myths and stereotypes surrounding formal social services that may exist in cross-cultural service settings:

> Public health officials wanted to conduct hearing and vision screenings for all kindergarten-eligible children living on an Indian reservation. Most of the residents held a negative image of the public health hospital, as a place where people die, and for this reason parents were reluctant to bring their children to the hospital for screenings. Fortunately, there was a highly respected mother of five, a member of the tribe, with some nursing training, who was able to identify the children in need of screenings and persuade the parents of the benefits of participating. Without this natural-helper intervention, it was unlikely that significant numbers of children would have been screened.

Finally, natural-helper interventions can be an important component in community development and community organization efforts that seek to build upon the strengths of the community. Communitywide resource exchange networks, such as the Member Organized Resource Exchange of St. Louis, have been developed in some low-income communities. In these networks, goods and services are exchanged between the residents when help is needed (e.g., getting a car fixed). The contribution of labor, skills, and time that can occur in what have been traditionally defined as impoverished neighborhoods is impressive and demonstrates the power of natural-helper and self-help interventions (Rank 1994).

Network Facilitation

Network facilitation mobilizes the social network as a resource and support. This intervention may mobilize or supplement an existing network or may create a new personal network through the recruitment, training, and matching of volunteers. Network facilitation should be individually tailored, based on an identification of existing and potential network members and an assessment of the strengths and capabilities of the social network, including gaps in social support. These steps can be accomplished by completing the social network map and discussing it with the client (see Chapter 4). In order to generate appropriate network change goals, it is essential that an accurate analysis be made of the barriers that prevent supportive behaviors from occurring in the network. Answers to these questions among others will be useful in generating an appropriate goal and intervention plan:

- Are the network members currently providing little or no support?
- Is network member involvement noxious or stress-producing?
- Are network members unable to be more supportive because they lack knowledge or skills?
- Are network members burned out or overwhelmed with caregiving demands?
- Is the client unable to ask for help appropriately?
- Is the client philosophically opposed to accepting help from others?
- What skills are required in order for the client and network members to work together?

Linking network members and clients is most effective as part of a purposeful plan. To help ease the clients' concern about loss of control, it is important to set clear expectations and limits on services or tasks for which the network members will be responsible. This also allows network members to gain a more realistic appraisal of the time and energy they will need to expend. Careful matching of the task or service with the appropriate network member is also a key to success. For example, in the case of a child with a physical disability, one network member might be willing and able to construct special equipment for home use but be unwilling or unable to provide respite care. It may be helpful to develop a written network plan, listing which network member will carry out which activities under what time limits; performance contracts of this nature have been used to monitor the delivery of services and to determine if they were perceived as supportive by the client (Barsh, Moore, & Hamerlynck 1983).

Network meetings are frequently used to solidify new linkages and enhance the functioning of old linkages. During a network meeting, participants may discuss the client's situation, develop a plan of action and support, and learn new information to assist in helping. The Family Group Decision-Making Project (see box) illustrates the creative use of network meetings for decision-making consonant with the family's culture (Burford & Pennell 1995). Network meetings can be useful in reconnecting past network members; some network members may have dropped out of a client's network because they did not how to relate to the client or became alienated in some way (Morin & Seidman 1986). Network meetings may also be useful in maintaining and regenerating social networks. People who are unconnected to each other within a network are more likely to drop out over time (Hammer 1981). Connecting people who share similar roles and clusters of people who share similar functions are important elements of linkage (Morin & Seidman 1986). Connecting network members to each other, as in a network meeting, may help combat network burnout and enable the network to provide help more effectively. When network members know and communicate with one another, they are more able to support each other, deal with a crisis, and avoid duplication of effort.

The worker may facilitate a network meeting in consultation with the client, who is in the best position to nominate participants. There are some benefits, however, to the client's facilitating all or at least part of the session:

A support program for parents of children with handicapping conditions used network meetings as a means to convene a helping resource for the family. Extended family members, neighbors, baby-sitters, work colleagues, and congregation members were convened and became involved in the life of the child through such meetings. For one family, the negative views of the in-laws presented a significant barrier; the in-laws viewed the mother as the cause of the child's atypical development and saw her as an incompetent parent. At the network meeting, videotapes of the mother working with the child during therapy sessions were shown and the mother taught some of these techniques to the network members in attendance. The end result was significant. The in-laws, for the first time, saw their daughter in law working successfully and competently with their grandchild. Their comment "we never knew you could do that" and their subsequent change in behavior resulted in much more support for the child and mother. (Moore, Hamerlynck, Barsh, Spieker, & Jones 1982)

Skills Training and Network Facilitation

As the above example illustrates, it is sometimes necessary as part of linkage to train network members in the skills required to carry out their helping role. Even such simple tasks as providing car rides to medical or therapy appointments may require training. In the case of the child with a disability, for example, depending on the child's handicapping condition, the network member may need training in proper positioning and handling, safe use of car seats, and management of the child's behavior in the car.

The client may also need training in such social skills as asking for help, initiating conversations, appropriate self-disclosure, and saying Thank you (Tracy et al. 1991; Whittaker et al. 1989). Initiating, developing, and maintaining supportive relationships requires an ability to communicate and listen to others. Some people have difficulty getting help from their network because they do not know how to ask for help, or they ask for help in overly demanding ways. People may also have difficulty maintaining supportive relationships over time because they do not know how to express appreciation or carry on conversations. Initially, network members may need encouragement to continue to carry out their assigned tasks. If this encouragement does not come from the client, it may need to be provided by the professional involved.

Teaching communication skills is relevant to social network interventions because an ability to talk to people, expressing ideas and feelings and listening and responding to other people's ideas and feelings, is basic to social support. "I" messages are essential for communicating requests for help ("I'm really exhausted from being up all night with baby. I'd really appreciate some baby-sitting so I could sleep") as well as expressing thanks and appreciation ("I appreciate having a ride to the store. It made it so much easier to shop, not having to take the bus"). Active listening responses may be helpful in forming reciprocal relationships, as they foster understanding and closeness. Finally, the skills of engagement—to be friendly, show an interest in another person's activities, make small talk, start a conversation, show respect for another's life-style, and be comfortable in another person's environment—are prerequisite to developing supportive relationships. Many service programs routinely provide training in these and other related skills (Kinney et al. 1991). Role-playing new situations, either individually with a client or within a group, is often helpful in teaching and practicing new communication skills (e.g., attending a support group the first time, meeting new neighbors in the laundry room, meeting teachers and other professionals at a case planning session, asking someone over for coffee). The use of skill training as a means to enhance social support is discussed more fully later in this chapter, in the section Social Network Skills Training.

Reciprocity and Network Facilitation

Lasting informal helping relationships are generally characterized by mutuality and reciprocity (Lindblad-Goldberg & Dukes 1985). Until that kind of relationship develops, the client and members of the newly mobilized network may need some form of external support and recognition. This may be accomplished through a simple Thank you, certificates of appreciation, or other tangible gestures of thanks (for example, one mother reciprocated for the child care she received from a neighbor with the use of her washer and dryer).

For some clients, reciprocity may present a major issue, either because they cannot themselves reciprocate (Cutler & Tatum 1983) or because others do not. A first step to increase reciprocity would be to discuss the concept. Explore how being on the receiving end of help can lead to feelings of being beholden or obligated to the other person, thereby making the relationship unequal in power and perhaps leading to less confidence in oneself or one's abilities. On the other hand, being on the giving end of help can lead to stress, irritation, and resentment (Sokolove & Trimble 1986). Table 5.1 illustrates a number of strategies that can be employed for those disproportionately on the giving or receiving end of help.

Volunteer Linking and Network Facilitation

Although it is beyond the scope of this work to provide full discussion of the development and management of volunteer programs (see Dunn 1995; Ellis 1994; Scheier 1993), we will touch on some issues in the process of recruiting, selecting, training, and matching of volunteers, which are basic to network facilitation. Volunteer linking provides a means to increase social network size and enhance social network composition. As with other forms of linkage, the roles and expectations of each participant, along with the extent and limits of confidentiality, must be made clear ahead of time. Many communities have a centralized program, such as the United Way Volunteer Bank, which accepts referrals for volunteer services, provides the match, and monitors the ensuing volunteer-client relationship over time. Other volunteer programs are targeted for a specific client population. For example, Compeer, which has been replicated in many states, matches community volunteers with persons with mental illness for the purpose of friendship, modeling of coping skills, and assisting with adaptation to community living (Skirboll & Pavelsky 1984). Other examples include Big/Little

Table 5.1.   Teaching Reciprocity Skills*

For those disproportionately giving, one or more of the following might be
    appropriate skills to teach:
Assertive skills, especially how to say no or ask for help
Self-care skills, such as self-reinforcement, pleasant events, taking time for
    yourself
Teaching "I" messages, especially how to confront
Time management skills, such as prioritizing tasks, organizing, scheduling activ-
    ities, and time off
Cognitive restructuring, such as RET, through-stopping, affirmations
Accepting and giving constructive feedback

For those disproportionately taking, one or more of the following might be
    appropriate to teach:
Social reinforcement, such as saying Thank you
The concept of returning favors, helping the client to identify his/her own personal
    strengths and resources that can be exchanged (for example, one mother
    allowed neighbors to use her washer/dryer in exchange for child care)
Active listening
"I" messages, especially how to disclose feelings (e.g., "I appreciate that")
How to balance requests for assistance so that one individual is not overloaded
    (this may include helping the client to identify other resources for help)

---

* An earlier version of this material was developed as part of the Family Support Project
(Whittaker et al. 1989).

Brothers and Sisters for at-risk children, mentoring programs for potential school dropouts, and volunteer visiting programs for children hospi-
talized with chronic illnesses or women who have had mastectomies.
Germain and Gittermain (1996) found that successful volunteer programs provide opportunities for useful and personally rewarding service, earn staff respect, and have the potential to lead to experiences
relevant for future career advancement.

A variant of the volunteer program involves matching consumers
with one another, e.g., consumers of mental health services and other
consumers, to assist in gaining access to community resources or to
provide specific services like transportation (Mowbray, Wellwood, &
Chamberlain 1988). Often, consumers of services are in the best position
to show others how to negotiate complex service delivery systems. In
addition, groups of consumers can advocate for needed system changes,
as the following example illustrates.

A social worker providing services to parents of children with disabilities
heard the same complaint from one parent after another. The complaint
was that the city's public transportation system did not recognize the

child's adaptive equipment as eligible for wheelchair seating. Consequently, the bus driver would not lower the wheelchair lift, and the parent
had to physically remove the child from his or her stroller, fold the equipment, and carry both the child and the stroller onto the bus. By getting the
parents together as a group and discussing each individual's experiences,
both the social worker and the parents reached a better understanding of
how to proceed. Ultimately, the group was able to effect a policy change, get
a wheelchair accessible sticker for a category of adaptive equipment, and
was instrumental in a training program for bus drivers on the new policy.

Such peer support approaches are discussed more fully in the next section.

Mutual Aid/Self-Help

Mutual-aid or self-help groups as they were formerly called, seek to
mobilize relationships among people who share common tasks, goals, or
problems, or among groups of people, as in support groups for rape
victims (Gitterman & Shulman 1986). Based on the helper therapy principle, they can also transform patterns of help-giving and receiving (Riessman 1965). Riessman (1990) recommended that since help-receiving is so
difficult in our society and help-giving has so many benefits, more opportunities should be developed for people to play the helping role. Programs based on mutual aid/self-help may take several forms: a support
group for a specific client population or locale, consumer-run programs or
drop-in centers, or volunteer matching of one consumer with another.
There are a number of advantages to these approaches:

- recognition and respect for clients as partners,
- ongoing source of support to clients, which typically extends beyond the boundaries of the worker-client relationship,
- positive contribution to recovery and maintenance for some client
  populations,
- ensuring that the program meets needs as perceived by the
  consumer,
- ability to empower clients, raise consciousness, and focus public
  attention and action on solutions to social problems (Whittaker
  & Tracy 1990).

A distinguishing feature of mutual-aid groups is their ability to support
people who have personal problems while at the same time advocating
for people who feel disenfranchised from the larger society (Mehr 1988).

Mutual-aid groups have been identified in four broad areas of need:
(a) physical or mental illness, (b) addictive behavior, (c) crises of transition, (d) coping by friends and relatives of individuals with specific

problems. There are literally hundreds of self-help organizations, many-organized nationwide, with chapters in every state. These groups reach out to consumers of services (e.g., Recovery Incorporated) and in some cases family members or concerned others (e.g., Alliance of the Mentally Ill; Alzheimer's Association). There are also a number of self-help clearinghouses and research centers (Powell 1995). In some areas of social work practice, such as community mental health or disabilities, consumer involvement approaches are the preferred mode of service delivery. Peer support is the underlying philosophy of the psychosocial rehabilitation or clubhouse models developed within the mental health community (Stroul 1986).

The relationship between professionals and self-help organizations has at times been fraught with tension. At one conference on partnerships between professionals and self-help groups, the comment was made from self-help group members that professionals should be "on tap, not on top" (see Table 5.2). Some professionals are reluctant to assume new roles vis-à-vis clients, or they have concerns about the quality of help provided via self-help groups. At times, the presence of self-help groups has been used to justify service reductions or to avoid responsibility for service. As in other social support interventions, the professional role is collaborative and clearly defined; although many self-help groups were initiated with professional involvement, some self-help groups fear being taken over or co-opted by professionals. For these reasons, some mutual-aid groups are jointly facilitated by a professional and "lay" leader; others have no provision for professional involvement whatsoever beyond that of referring potential new members.

Programs designed to organize and empower client groups represent a specialized form of peer support. Among the range of social network interventions, self-help strategies are uniquely suited to empowerment-based practice. Writing about practice strategies that promote empowerment, Parsons states:

> The primary principle for strategy selection is the education of and promotion of self-help in client systems. First and foremost, strategies suggested for empowerment include self-help groups, support groups, network building, education groups, social action groups. These strategies provide the opportunity for dialogue necessary for the development of critical thinking, knowledge and skill building, validation and support. They provide necessary linkage to larger systems which impinge upon the group and its defined problem. (1991, 13)

Self-help groups allow members to learn from one another and to expand their vision of their experience. People in a self-help group may realize for the first time that they are not alone and they are not fully responsible for their situation. Members can help each other sort out the

Table 5.2. Partnership: How to Get There

Working in small groups, participants generated several lists of "shoulds" and
 "should nots" for professionals and for self-help groups in working with
 professionals.

Professionals should
Listen to the expertise of self-help groups and respect their knowledge
Learn about and value self-help activities
Attend the group as a learner
Listen, listen, listen
Speak in plain, clear English
Be clear about what resources and skills they have to offer
Foster cooperation, not co-optation
Provide continuity and support
Be available
Provide a constructive focus
Help groups clarify the professional role
Be on tap, not on top
Respond to concrete, specific requests
Refer clients to self-help groups
Show respect for the client
Recognize volunteer credibility based on experience
Invite self-help groups to professional meetings
Attend combined self-help/profession functions

Professionals should not
Try to be all-knowing
View themselves as the experts
Dwell on professionalism
Use jargon
Take a leadership role
Go on an ego trip
Give advice
Overpower or try to control the group
Try to fix it if it isn't broken
Feel threatened by advocates
Use precanned material for teaching
Patronize or belittle clients

(continued)

Table 5.2.   Continued

What are some useful roles for professionals?
Provide information, resources, training
Help groups develop their own leadership
Offer empowerment
Refer clients to self-help groups and encourage them to attend
Facilitate the establishment and growth of self-help
Provide a link to other professionals
Facilitate access to self-help information for professional education
Learn when to let go

Self-help groups should
Educate the public, the professionals, and yourselves
Develop communication and public relations skills
Be open-minded
Give feedback about what you like and don't like
Be considerate; give plenty of notice when requesting services from professionals
Be clear about what you want from professionals; define roles and responsibilities
Speak to professional groups; reach out
Attend doctors' rounds; "tell your story"
Respect the professional's knowledge
Keep professionals up-to-date on your group (because groups evolve over time)
Meet with other self-help groups
Have an open-door policy
Have volunteers act as advocates for self-help group members
Gather information and record it
Define your goals and objectives; put them in writing and share them
Look for ways of evaluating your group
Foster relationships where constructive criticism is a possibility
Take responsibility for the continuation of your group

Self-help groups should not
Be intimidated by professionals
Exclude professionals
Overinvolve professionals and their expertise
Expect professionals to solve their problems
Be suspicious of professionals, or anticipate antagonism
Take on a victim stance
Lose control of their group

Source: United Way Self-Help Symposium, Vancouver, B.C., November 14–15, 1986.

personal aspects of their situation from the political aspects (Cox 1991). The group itself becomes a source for support for empowerment-oriented activities. A number of examples of empowerment- and environment-oriented groups can be found in the social work group work literature. Some examples include:

- elderly residents in a singe room occupancy hotel working on a wide range of social issues (e.g., differential rent rates, medical care, crime watch; Cox & Parsons 1994, 103–109),
- a self-help women's group for welfare recipients advocating for themselves with the social services department (Cox 1991),
- People First, a self-advocacy rights organization for people with mental retardation working toward greater self-determination and voice in decisions made (Shapiro 1994),
- African-American women systematically using their social support networks to resolve individual and community level problems in a network utilization project (Lewis & Ford 1991).

Self-help groups can be a significant force in work with people in impoverished communities. As a practice modality, community-building refers to activities that foster positive connections among individuals, groups, organizations, and neighborhoods (Weil 1996). Much of this work takes place at the grass roots level, organizing small groups of community members for the purposes of articulating shared values, developing skills, and working for social change (Homan 1994; Rubin & Rubin 1992). For example, the Cleveland Community Building Initiative has established "village councils" in four poor neighborhoods, operating on the philosophy that for the rebuilding of a community to occur, local communities must themselves be involved and people and families must directly experience strength and empowerment (Cleveland Foundation Commission on Poverty 1992). The underlying rationale is that economic development activities must be tied to neighborhood-level activities that rebuild the social fabric of the community. In a similar manner, recent public housing revitalization projects, such as the U.S. Department of Housing and Urban Development's HOPE VI, combine physical site reconstruction and modernization in the context of community; a designated portion of the funding to revitalize severely distressed urban housing projects is dedicated to people-based strategies, human services designed to rebuild a sense of community and self-sufficiency among the residents.

In underlining the value of these mesolevel community-building activities, we do not mean to neglect the fact that larger social/political changes may be needed, since many of the problems that poor neighborhoods face occur in the context of the wider social/structural issues (Halpern 1993). Nonetheless, we view mutual-aid groups in all of their diverse forms as both a critical means and a context for activating personal and social empowerment and change. Linked networks of informed consumers—drawing strength from one another—will be a critical political force in shaping the new human services environment.

Social Network Skills Training

Social network skills training, or social support skills training, teaches people ways of establishing and maintaining supportive interactions with others (Richey 1994). The purpose is to teach skills needed to initiate, maintain, and deepen relationships and to elicit support from others (Gambrill & Richey 1988) and, in a larger sense, to enable clients to gain better control over their environment. Based on models of life and social skills training, this approach assesses skill levels thought to be important to supportive relationships (such as problem-solving, communication skills, assertiveness) and provides systematic individual or group training in implementing a social network improvement plan. This intervention strategy draws upon a large body of work on the use of cognitive behavioral interventions to enhance interpersonal abilities to achieve personal goals (see Richey 1994, for a summary of studies) and on programs designed for at-risk families in need of social support (Kirkham, Schinke, Schilling, Meltzer, & Norelius 1986; Polansky, Gaudin, Ammons, & Davis 1985).

Social skills training encompasses the following implementation steps:

1. Identify and assess relevant skills (e.g., friendship skills for school age children or networking and advocacy skills for parents negotiating the special education system).
2. Instruct, model, and practice skills in groups, role-play simulations, or in real life.
3. Plan opportunities for generalization of the skills acquired.
4. Implement a step-by-step social network improvement plan.
5. Coordinate, consult, and train with network members as needed.
6. Monitor and evaluate the plan (Whittaker & Tracy 1990).

It may be difficult to determine precisely which skills are most relevant to obtaining social support or changing support systems in each situation. The skills selected for training depend largely on the client population and the nature of the presenting concern. Richey (1994) proposes four cognitive and five behavioral competencies as important content for social network skills training. The *cognitive competencies* are basic knowledge about relationships, perceptual skills to accurately decode others' communications, decision-making skills for choosing when and how to begin social interactions, and cognitive restructuring skills to alter distorted thoughts and beliefs that interfere with satisfying relationships (e.g., I'm the dumbest person here). The *behavioral competencies* are self-presentation skills, social initiation skills, basic conversational skills, maintenance skills, and conflict resolution skills. Individualized assessments are recommended as a means to identify the specific choice and focus for skills training.

In general, social network improvement plans involve change either in the structure of the network or in the skill level of the client or network members. In some cases both types of change are desired or needed. Some examples of *structural change:*

- Increase or decrease the size of the network.
- Change the composition of the social network, as in increasing the number of friends.
- Increase or decrease frequency of contact with particular social network members.

Some examples of *skill-enhancing* interventions:

- Develop or increase skills in making friends.
- Decrease negative beliefs about self (if this is a barrier to developing/maintaining supportive relationships); increase positive self-statements and increase ability to identify personal strengths.
- Develop strategies for handling criticism from others.
- Improve assertiveness skills (if this is a barrier to developing or maintaining supportive relationships).
- Improve communication skills (if this is a barrier to developing or maintaining supportive relationships).
- Learn reciprocity skills (if this is a barrier to developing or maintaining supportive relationships).
- Develop a plan to reach out to others during a crisis period (Whittaker et al. 1989).

One advantage of social network skills training is its consistency with an empowerment model of practice. Control of the intervention is fully in the hands of the client and is directed toward securing needed resources, building coalitions, overcoming organizational barriers, and forming new networks (Hopps et al. 1995). Outcomes of a successful social skills training program include (a) a skilled support system for a client (individual or family) and (b) a client with the competency to use that support system effectively. Competencies may take the form of recognizing stress and fatigue before they get out of hand, mobilizing network members in times of stress, knowing how to ask for and receive help, being able to negotiate formal services on their own behalf, and anticipating times when help will be needed. In short, the client is better able to meet his or her needs and is in charge of available resources. Training curricula for two social network skills training projects, one with Head Start parents (Giving and Getting Help from Others) and the other with child protective services clients (The Friendship Group), are described later in this chapter.

Unless significant environmental constraints and pressures are addressed, however, it is unlikely that social skills training alone will be of much use to clients. Used indiscriminately, skills-training approaches can assume a "blame the victim" attitude, implying that if only the clients possessed more skills, they could handle or adapt to an inadequate or impoverished environment. In some cases, skills deficits are a causal factor leading to low social support, but they may also be a consequence of lack of support or be related to other features of the external environment that interfere with the development of supportive relationships. Richey (1994) points out that geographic isolation, lack of safe and reliable transportation, restricted personal freedom, and prejudice and discrimination all hinder the development and maintenance of supportive social networks. For example, some young children do not have much opportunity to develop peer networks because their parents do not find the immediate environment surrounding their home to be a safe place to play. O'Brien (1995) provides an excellent description of the experience of living in public housing and the ways in which that environment limits and defines social relationships. The availability of time, income, and housing has also been cited as a factor to consider when assessing social support obstacles.

Fortunately, social network skills-training approaches can be put to larger purposes than individual interpersonal skill enhancement. For example, a social worker offering a training program for parents on Working with Special Education or Your Child's IEP can do much more than merely increase parental skills and enhance personal social networks. This type of training has the potential to change the educational system by producing more informed, involved, and assertive parents, who are now in a position to advocate for wider system changes. If training is also provided to the teaching and administrative staff on Enhancing Parent Involvement in Special Education, then an even more powerful push can be made toward organizational change. Used in this manner, social-skills-training approaches can be important components of wider organizational reforms and community-building efforts.

GENERAL CONSIDERATIONS FOR IMPLEMENTING ENVIRONMENTAL INTERVENTIONS

Social support interventions are best implemented by workers who are willing to share power with clients, to shift back and forth between practice roles, to respect and appreciate differences, and to work at both the individual and community level. Our experience also suggests that social network interventions require support and knowledge at all levels of the agency or sponsoring organization (Whittaker et al. 1994). Generally, the social network interventions described above are offered in some combination, e.g., skills training as part of network facilitation. Table 5.3 offers some additional guidelines, in the form of do's and don't's for those who implement social network interventions.

Social Network Interventions and Diversity Issues

Social network interventions need to be grounded in the principles of culturally competent practice, including respect and appreciation for differential values, beliefs, and behaviors regarding help-giving and help-seeking. This requires the ability to distinguish one's own way of thinking and behaving from that of the client (Hodges 1991). The practitioner working toward social network changes with a client must also possess some knowledge of specific cultural influences on social networks; depending on the cultural group, these might include such factors as social network composition, reciprocity across generations, and types of support exchanged (Devore & Schlesinger 1996; Green 1995; Lum 1996). While it is beyond the scope of this text to explore social support and culture fully, Table 5.4 lists practice guidelines to consider when working with families of color.

As one specific application, Lewis and Suarez (1995) cite a number of uses of natural-helping networks among various populations of color. Powell (1990) also describes self-help experiences across a number of racial and cultural groups. Other important knowledge areas to acquire include helping networks within specific client groups, e.g., children (Nestman & Hurrelmann 1994), substance abusers (Hawkins & Fraser

Table 5.3.   Dos and Don'ts for Social Network Interventions

Don't assume that more is better.

> *Do* remember that there is no perfect network. Small networks are not necessarily bad. Some people have networks that are too big. They are literally "spread too thin."

Don't assume that the network you see is the network experienced by the client.

> *Do* listen to the client's subjective experience of support. The perception of support is just as, if not more, important than the objective reality.

Don't equate social support interventions solely with increasing network size.

> *Do* remember that social skills and cognitive interventions may be used to achieve social support goals. People may need to learn to deal with network members differently or think about their social networks differently.

Don't create or encourage unequal relationships, with the client always on the receiving end.

> *Do* remember the importance of reciprocity in informational relationships. Try to build opportunities for reciprocal relationships to develop if the intervention is designed to enlarge the social network.

Don't forget to assess the types of support exchanged within the network.

> *Do* assess concrete, emotional, and informational support needs. Do the types of support available to the client match his or her needs?

Don't forget about the stress of caregiving.

> *Do* assess the capabilities of the network. Are they overworked or overburdened? Is it realistic to rely on their help or resources?

Don't assume that all families have the same social support needs.

> *Do* assess and plan for each family on an individual basis.

Don't become discouraged if people are not receptive.

> *Do* remember that timing is the key to introducing social support.

---

* An earlier version of this material was developed as part of the Family Support Project (Whittaker et al. 1989).

1983, 1985), and specific communities of identity such as the gay and lesbian communities (Hollander 1989) or the deaf community (Leuy, Glass, & Elliot 1996).

Social Environment in Relation to Other Levels of Environment

Our experience has been that the social network map provides a baseline of environmental information on all levels of the environment: physical, perceived, social/interactional, institutional/organizational, and social/political/cultural. From the perspective of an individual client or client

Table 5.4. Social Networks and Families of Color Practice Guidelines

1. Remember, the network you see may not be the network as experienced by the family. Make an effort to understand the family's social network as they perceive and experience it.
2. Social networks of ethnic minority families tend to have large extended families, which may contain both kin and fictive kin members. Allow the clients to define their families.
3. Social networks of ethnic minority families are likely to include members that are physically distant from one another, for example, relatives that live in another state or country. Remember that even though people may be geographically separated, family attachments and connections can be quite strong. Phone calls or letters to these distant family members may be needed.
4. The sense of mutual helping and obligation may be strongly reinforced by cultural beliefs and values, such as expressed by the notion of filial duty. Try to understand the family's values about help-seeking.
5. Respect for elders may be an important factor. It may be helpful to include elders in intervention plans, or to solicit their opinions on important matters.
6. Rules about help-seeking and help-giving are often culturally determined. Consider what constitutes helpful behavior, who should help whom, and how help should be requested.
7. Extended families of ethnic minority families typically provide a wide range of concrete, emotional, and informational supports to one another. Giving and getting support may extend across generations, as in the child care provided by grandparents.
8. For some ethnic minority families, the church is an important source of support and a major form of coping with life's problems. Church activities, ministers and other religious leaders, relationships with congregational members, and prayer may all be important sources of support.
9. Ethnic minority families, like most families, often rely "on their own" first before turning to outside sources of information and support. In addition, due to cultural, language, and class differences, they may be reluctant to use certain formal helping services, such as parenting classes or groups. It is important to be knowledgeable of and make use of services in the ethnic community, for example, a neighborhood center or tribal social service center.
10. Use an empowerment approach in working with ethnic minority families. The goal of intervention should be to empower the family to gain access to and make use of its own resources.

---

* An earlier version of this material was developed as part of the Family Support Project (Whittaker et al. 1989).

family, the social network map provides critical information on the individual, family, group, and neighborhood. This baseline assessment information informs the development and implementation of environmental interventions at various levels of the environment.

The social network strategies described in this chapter may be equally applicable to producing changes (both intended and unintended) in other levels of the environment. The social environment is often linked to and serves as a powerful indicator of the status of other environmental levels, such as the physical environment and immediate neighborhood or community environment, since these are the sites of social interaction and informal helping (Germain & Gitterman 1996). Froland et al. (1981) present a typology of interventions with informal helping networks across levels of the environment (Table 5.5).

Even though many interventions are carried out at the level of the personal or family network, the continuum of interventions reaches beyond the personal network to community-level empowerment strategies. For example, a mutual-aid group may mobilize and press for changes in the physical setting of an agency's waiting room in order to create a more familylike setting that is more conducive to social interaction. The connections between the physical and social environment are often so close that producing change in one frequently requires producing change in the other; this is particularly true for client populations who are most dependent on their immediate physical environment, e.g., those who rely on public transportation, the home-bound elderly, those who are physically challenged, infants, and young children.

Practice strategies in relation to physical environments include responding to the client's spatial needs, arranging professional office space, arranging agency space, coordinating spatial access and use, encouraging and teaching clients to use the built and natural environment, and using animals to provide companionship (Germain and Gitterman 1996; Resnick & Jaffee 1982). The arrangement of physical space within an agency setting to support therapeutic goals, to convey a welcoming attitude to clients, and to recognize and value diversity in all its forms is a particularly important consideration for social work practitioners (Gutheil 1996; Seabury 1971). Breton (1984) provides a clear example of promoting competence through the deliberate use of physical space in a drop-in program for transient women. Whittaker ([1979] 1997) likewise discusses the importance of physical structures in designing a therapeutic milieu for emotionally disturbed children.

Interventions directed toward other levels of the environment and other social work purposes may also hold implications for the social environment. For example, many of the techniques typically associated with locality community development and community liaison work—

Table 5.5. A Typology of Program Strategies

Strategies	Objectives	Informal Helping Networks	Relationship
Personal network	Consult with client's significant others, supporting existing efforts. Convene network of providers and family, friends, and others to resolve problems. Expand client's range of social ties.	Family members, friends, neighbors, service providers.	Primarily collegial.
Volunteer linking	Provide lay therapists for counseling. Establish companionate relationships. Recruit and link volunteer advocates to client.	Citizen volunteers. People with skills, interests relevant to client's needs. People with similar experience.	Primarily directive.
Mutual aid networks	Establish peer support groups. Consult with existing groups and support activities.	Local church associates. Clients with similar problems. People with shared concerns.	More collegial with existing network. Either directive or coordinative for created networks.
Neighborhood helpers	Establish consultative arrangement with neighbor to monitor problems. Convene neighbors to promote local helping.	Neighbors. Clerks, managers in local businesses. Religious leaders.	More collegial but may be coordinative.
Community empowerment	Establish local task forces for meeting community needs. Provide for community forums to have input into local policies.	Opinion leaders in local business, religious institutions. Members of local voluntary associations. Neighborhood leaders.	Primarily coordinative.

Source: Froland, C., et al. (1981). Reprinted by permission of Sage Publications.

advocacy, brokerage, mediation, and negotiation—may lead to a greater sense of community connection, identity, and purpose (Kemp 1995) and thus produce social and perceptual, along with physical changes in a community. Social work practitioners who work collaboratively with communities, conduct needs and strengths assessments, design services and programs responsive to community interests, coordinate community services and resources, and help community residents take control and action within their community rely on social network interventions in one form or another. A number of community practice models make use of or rely upon natural helping networks, self-help groups, and the creation of new connections and new supportive services (Weil 1996)

Focus of Intervention

Environmental interventions may be the sole focus for professional intervention, as in community-building practice (ibid.); in other situations, environmental interventions may serve as a supplement to other, person-oriented interventions, as in forming a support group within an agency or program setting. The explicit focus of the intervention is an important consideration because the focus holds implications for the manner in which the intervention is delivered. For example, if the environmental change effort is conceived solely in terms of a support for individual change, then factors related to client empowerment and collective action, such as client participation, critical reflection, and consumer input into evaluation, may receive less attention.

Some practitioners may also see environmental interventions as relevant only to the needs of poor families or families of color, an assumption that tends to marginalize and devalue both environmental interventions and the recipients of environmental helping. Certainly those living in poverty face more environmental stressors than those with more economic resources (Hopps et al. 1995; see also Chapter 6). It does not follow, however, that environmental intervention is of no benefit to more affluent clients. If we adopt a multidimensional definition of environment (Chapter 3), then environmental practice is relevant for all client groups, and both people- and environment-changing interventions are a legitimate part of direct social work practice.

Recent social work theorists have suggested that exploring the way in which people construct their environmental experience, or the meaning they apply to it, offers opportunities to incorporate the environment in direct practice (Berlin 1996; Saari 1992). The understanding that people internalize their experiences in the outside world and then use this framework to interpret other experiences enables the practitioner to enter into a dialogue with the client about the meaning of the environment (Granvold 1996). Take, for example, evidence that many young teenage mothers have chosen pregnancy because their environmental experiences have provided them with no vision of a different or better future (Franklin 1988). Practice that investigates this world view will look very different from that which assumes that the pregnancy is related to psychological, behavioral, or informational deficits. The worker then can be supportive of the environmental change efforts that may emerge from this reflective process. We need to reexamine the assumption that environmental intervention refers only to changes in the environment, and cannot be approached through work with the person.

Choice of Intervention

Ideally, interventions should be selected that are congruent with assessment information, compatible with client preferences and learning style, culturally responsive, and supported by empirical data: in short, the choice would represent the best possible selection given the client and the intended goals. In reality, interventive choices frequently are partly if not largely dictated by worker skills and preference, agency practices, time and resource limitations, and funding restrictions. Just as there are few clear empirically supported guidelines for choosing which social network intervention should be applied under what conditions in which situations, practitioners face similar dilemmas in implementing other environmental interventions.

While no certainty exists, a number of guidelines are helpful. The foremost is to base the choice of interventions upon a careful analysis and discussion with the client of the assessment information. While we have not focused in this text on "involuntary clients," "resistance," or "motivation," environmental assessment and intervention is based upon an explicit working relationship between client(s) and worker(s) and in situations where this type of relationship cannot be generated, the social work task will be that much more difficult or impossible. In our experience, it is sometimes easier to reach a working relationship around environmental change goals with clients, because the environment is a known entity to the client and producing concrete changes is perceived as stress reducing and helpful. Clearly, though, knowledge of engagement strategies with involuntary clients is a prerequisite to environmental assessment and intervention (Hepworth 1993; Rooney 1992; Schlosberg & Kagan 1988). With regard to social support, for example, the first guideline is to establish clearly that the client desires changes in social support, as opposed to other changes, environmental or otherwise. Social support is only one way of coping with stressful or threatening life conditions and transitions (Thoits 1986; Lazarus & Folkman 1984). The client's preferred coping strategies and orientation to involving network resources (Vaux, Burda, & Stewart 1986) must inform the decision to intervene with the social network. Following this decision, the most crucial next step is to arrive at some understanding, if only a hypothesis, of what factor or factors contribute to low or nonexistent social support. This involves frank consideration of barriers, whether they are situational or environmental, cognitive, psychological, or physiological (Richey 1994). For example, social network skills training is an option when the client's interpersonal competencies block or inhibit supportive exchanges. As Richey points out, an individual who is truly socially phobic may not benefit from skills training per se.

A final guideline is to consider and base choices on the presence of strengths and resources. An individual with strong social skills but who lacks a strong social network would be a candidate for network facilitation. An individual with a strong personal social network but who lacks social contacts for dealing with a specific life demand (such as raising twins) or life transition (such as becoming unemployed or widowed) would be a candidate for mutual-aid groups. Similarly, if a community assessment identifies strengths and resources that could be shared with others, then natural-helper as well as self-help/mutual-aid interventions may be indicated.

Issues of Time

Given the current moves toward managed care across a range of fields of practice, it is important to consider the issue of time in relation to environmental changes. A number of possible time-related dimensions to environmental practice are relevant. One is the professional or agency time in which to implement environmental interventions. Another is time as experienced from the client's point of view, e.g., when services are offered and the time required for participation. Another is the timing of outcomes: When can one determine that the intervention has been successful?

On one hand, environmental interventions are typically not limited to a prescribed number of sessions of equal length. Indeed, the process of linkage inherent in environmental intervention dictates a more flexible use of worker, agency, and client time. Likewise, the outcomes of environmental interventions may not be immediately apparent but may take some time to develop from the linkages established, necessitating follow-up measures over a period of time. For example, in an examination of women's groups for mutual support and collective action, Home (1991) points out, "It is sometimes necessary to slow down social change efforts, to ensure members function well enough to work together" (p. 162).

Environmental interventions may allow for more effective use of professional time, extending professional interventions over longer time periods than usual (e.g., twenty-four hour availability, seven days a week) and over longer durations of change. We may also find that "booster" shots of some environmental interventions at set time intervals may extend duration of change and prevent relapse (e.g., an alumnae group for women in recovery).

In many ways, use of time is a reflection of the choice of practice model together with the client and worker roles adopted. Strategic use of time may contribute to a more collaborative relationship between worker and client. The home-based services/family preservation movement is an example of a service strategy that defines the use of time in a clear and convincing manner (see Tracy 1995, for an overview of home-based services). The fact that home-based workers meet according to the family's schedule as often as the family needs contact conveys an important message to the participating families about the worker-client relationship. The way in which time is used is also reflected in the types of goals established and interventions employed. Dunst (1994) demonstrated the "added" benefits that flow from both family support programs and family-centered practices in terms of participants' self-efficacy. His study showed the relationship between help-giving models used by different types of human services programs—of which time is one important element—and the extent to which participants rated the service as effective and empowering.

SUMMARY:
WAYS TO BE ENVIRONMENTALLY ORIENTED

We have argued that, in order for social workers to embrace environmental interventions on a footing equal to person-oriented interventions, social workers will need to think differently about their clients and their work. A number of strategies are available that may help social workers maintain an environmental focus. One is to use ecosystemic assessment measures, such as the ecomap, community asset mapping, or the social network map (see Chapter 4). We would argue that assessments of the social environment should be carried out with all clients because of the central role of social support in achieving and maintaining other intervention gains and the critical role of social support in contributing to well-being and quality of life. In Chapter 4 we provided detailed information on the use of the social network map and supplemental material on a wide range of tools for assessing various levels of the environment. Environmental interventions that are based on an accurate, ecologically valid assessment of environmental influences on current functioning may need to be applied at several levels of environment.

Another method for maintaining a focus on the environment is to finds means for regular involvement in the daily lives of our clients, through home visiting, home- or neighborhood-based services, or active participation in the community (Brieland 1990). The family support/ home-based services movement has shown that the most effective practice with at-risk families is situated in agencies that are located in and responsive to the communities they serve (Schorr 1989).

The current political and economic climate calls for new or renewed practice approaches that incorporate various levels of the environment more fully and focus on "consumer-determined, long-term family and community capacity building" (Freeman 1996, 529). As we have tried to demonstrate in this chapter, environmental interventions at the level of the social environment can play a key role in transforming traditional service delivery models and changing community conditions.

A final method for keeping the environment in focus is to ensure that consumers of service participate in the planning, delivery, and monitoring of services. This translates into the client's active involvement in assessment, goal-setting, intervention, and evaluation, as articulated by feminist practice principles (Van Den Bergh 1995). It also means consumer input to agency structures and services, with participant action research in community development efforts (Rivera & Erlich 1992). Teaching people to conduct their own evaluations of programs and services has become an important component of empowerment practice (Fetterman 1994). In program development and community-building practice, participatory research and evaluation models (Whitmore 1991), coinquiry teams (Bailey 1992; Bailey & Koney 1995), and collaborative action research (Oja & Smulyan 1989) have resulted in increased self-sufficiency and capacity-building among traditionally disempowered client populations. The results of these approaches should be research focused from the consumers' point of view on topics and areas that are vitally important to and defined by consumers (Rapp, Shera, & Kisthardt 1993).

In the remaining chapters of this book, two important perspectives are offered. Chapter 6 deals with issues of diversity and the environ-

Table 5.6. Environmental Intervention: Selected Strategies

	Perceived Environment	Physical Environment	Social/Interactional	Institutional/Organizational	Social/Political/Cultural Environment
Individual	Interviewing for client strengths. Empowerment. Critical reflection/dialogue.	Brokerage and concrete services.	Network facilitation. Skills training.	Service coordination/case management.	Mediation. Advocacy.
Family	Use of narrative. Empowerment. Critical reflection/dialogue.	Home-based interventions. Family development programs. Concrete services.	Family education and support programs. Support groups and programs.	Consultation with larger systems. Family group conferencing.	Social action/advocacy groups.
Group	Empowerment group.	Therapeutic milieu.	Mutual aid/self-help/support groups.	Program development.	Social action groups.
Neighborhood	Community capacity awareness. Empowerment.	Locality development. Investment.	Community building. Natural helpers.	Social planning. Program development. Community liaison.	Grassroots groups.
Overall Goal	Interventions designed to transform perceptions of the environment.	Interventions in the natural and built worlds.	Interventions to mobilize social support.	Interventions to mobilize resources/services.	Interventions for social and political change.

ment, with particular emphasis on the way in which the environment is perceived and experienced based on individual differences and socially based classifications. Further implications for the future and current constraints and challenges to environmental practice are discussed in Chapter 7.

As in the preceding chapter on environmental assessment, we end this chapter with a summary table on environmental intervention across levels of the environment and client groups of different sizes (see Table 5.6). Our aim is to illustrate representative examples of environmentally oriented interventions across the various levels of environment and client systems that have formed the basis of this book. Our choices are neither comprehensive nor in every instance precise. For example, many of the interventions overlap both on the level of the client and the level of the environment. Many additional examples of environmental interventions exist in theory and practice and some that are cited may be conceptually understood in terms other than environmental intervention as we have defined it. In fact, particular applications may require modification to meet the test of the building blocks and key features of person-environment practice offered in Chapter 1. We offer this list as representative and illustrative of the fact that much exists in the current armament of social work and human services practice that meets or approximates what we here call environmental intervention. We intend this list as a beginning guide: to be modified, adapted in its various parts, and used as a springboard to the development of new forms of environmental intervention.

THE SOCIAL NETWORK INTERVENTION PROJECT

The Social Network Intervention Project (Gaudin et al. 1990/1991), implemented in both urban and rural areas of Georgia, sought to determine the effectiveness of a social network intervention model with a population of very low income neglectful families. A wide range of social network interventions was used in conjunction with intensive casework, case management, and advocacy: personal networking, mutual-aid groups, volunteer linking, neighborhood (natural) helpers, and social skills training. The project reported that these interventions in combination produced significant improvements in two measures of parenting adequacy and social network size and supportiveness as compared with a control group receiving usual casework services, although the stability of these changes over time was not determined. The project found that several issues need careful attention in implementing social network interventions, especially in rural settings. One issue was the protection of confidentiality when natural helpers were used; a contract was developed for use with natural helpers that clarified their role and their access to information about the client family. Another issue was the critical role of social skills training to enable families to relate effectively with a broad base of support. In most cases, family members needed training in basic social skills, e.g., starting a conversation, ways to say hello, expressing feelings. The project also found that successful implementation of the model was dependent upon small caseloads of fifteen or less and well-trained workers. For further information regarding social network interventions and child maltreatment see Thompson (1995).

References

Gaudin, J. M., Wodarski, J. S., Arkinson, M. K., & Avery, L. S. (1990/1991). Remedying child neglect: Effectiveness of social network interventions. *Journal of Applied Social Sciences 15*, 97–123.

Thompson, R. A. (1995). *Preventing child maltreatment through social support: A critical analysis*. Thousand Oaks, CA: Sage.

THE FAMILY GROUP DECISION-MAKING PROJECT

The Family Group Decision-Making Project is being carried out in the Canadian province of Newfoundland. Three culturally diverse sites are involved: Nain, located near the Labrador coast, with a predominantly Inuit population; Port au Port Peninsula, with people of English, French, and Micmac ancestry; and St. John's, the provincial capital, largely settled by immigrants from England and Ireland. Patterned after the "family group conferencing" model developed in New Zealand (Angus 1991; Atkin 1991; Ban 1993; Zalenski 1994), the model used in this project brings together the referred family with their extended family and other significant social support resources to work out a plan to stop abuse or neglect. Each family group's plan must be approved by the referring authority, which then supports its enactment. This model emphasizes the family group as a decision-making body.

The family group decision-making model flows from a statement of philosophy regarding the core components of effective interventions in situations of family violence: building support networks, allowing people a voice in decisions affecting their lives, providing needed protections and resources, tapping into strengths of families and communities, and being culturally responsive.

The first phase of the project involved the convening of a total of thirty-seven family group conferences. Outcome evaluation findings from a one-year follow-up study of the conferencing group and a comparison group of control families are forthcoming. However, several interesting conclusions can be drawn from the implementation process itself. While the model does not substitute for existing mandated authorities and takes time to coordinate and implement, it is no more costly than existing interventions and in some cases cost reductions are realized. The majority of invited family members come to the conference, and most families develop a satisfactory plan that does not place abused persons at greater risk of reabuse than other interventions. The results of the conference are an immediate mobilization of resources within the family and the community. This occurs regardless of whether or not the plan includes child placement.

Family group conferences are held in three stages: preparing for the conference, holding the conference, and approving the plan. In preparing for the conference, the conference coordinator contacts family members, consults with them about whom to invite and not to invite, and arranges practical matters such as travel, food, and translation. During this stage, an adaptation of the social network map (Tracy & Whittaker 1990) is used to identify support persons to invite to the meeting. Holding the conference involves greetings and openings conducted in a manner congruent with the family background (e.g., a prayer by a pastor or words from an elder), presentation by the professionals involved of the concerns that need to be addressed by the family plan, deliberation in private by the family group, and finalization of the plan with the coordinator. The plan is considered complete when it is approved by the referring worker and costs to implement are approved. Length of conferences and number of participants depend on the culture of the community and situational factors; in this project, conferences last on average six hours and are attended by thirteen or fourteen people.

The project report and implementation guide contain useful information for those interested in pursuing this model (Burford & Pennell 1995; Pennell & Burford 1995a, 1995b). Of particular importance are the role and training of the coordinator, flexible funding arrangements, local ownership, opening the conference in culturally appropriate ways, safety issues, and writing plans in clear language with contingencies clearly specified.

References

Agus, J. H. (1991). The Act: One year perspective on the Children, Young Persons and Their Families Act of 1989. *Social Work Review 3*, 5–6.

Atkin, B. (1991). New Zealand: Let the family decide. The new approach to family problems. *Journal of Family Law 29*(2), 387–397.

Ban, P. (1993). Family decision making: The model as practiced in New Zealand and its relevance in Australia. *Australian Social Work 46*(3), 23–93.

Burford, G., & Pennell, J. (1995). *Family group decision-making project: Implementation report summary.* Available from Memorial University of Newfoundland, School of Social Work, St. John's, Newfoundland, Canada A1C 5S7.

Pennell, J., & Burford, G. (1995a). *Family group decision making project: Implementation Report. Volume I.* St. John's, Newfoundland, Canada: Memorial University of Newfoundland, School of Social Work.

Pennell, J., & Burford, G. (1995b). *Family group decision making project: Implementation Report. Volume II. Research/Evaluation Instruments.* St. John's, Newfoundland, Canada: Memorial University of Newfoundland, School of Social Work.

Zalenski, J. (1994). A new/old practice to care for children: New Zealand's family decision making model. *Prevention Report* (spring), 11–14.

THE FRIENDSHIP GROUP

The Friendship Group was a social support skills training program offered through agency auspices to families referred from child protective services as being at high risk for child maltreatment. The program, offered in a group format and conducted both in Canadian and American settings, concentrated on key interpersonal skills for mobilizing, developing, and sustaining more supportive relationships. Training content included information, modeling, and behavioral rehearsal in the following areas: stages of relationships, danger signs in relationships, self-protection skills, pro-social activities, basic conversational skills, assertive skills, community support resources and endings and new beginnings. The need for training in these areas became apparent to the model developers after an initial six-month parenting and social support group yielded few changes in the participants' (mothers') social networks and social interactions with other group members. The parents appeared to lack basic communications and conflict resolution skills required for supportive exchanges with others. Based on this observation, subsequent groups focused primarily on developing and improving adult friendships—hence the name of the group. One innovative feature of the training that is included in the training manual is an allegorical Relationship Roadmap to illustrate normative stages of relationship development. Friendship development was represented visually by a road with five towns: Acquaintanceville, Buddy-borough, Friendly City, Personal Friendsville, and Partnersburg. Other training materials available include several videotapes demonstrating increasingly more complex social situations, e.g., changing the topic of conversation, starting a conversation with a stranger, handling criticism from another group member. A unique component of the program was post-training of ongoing case managers, whose role was to help group members maintain the social network goals established in the group over a three-month follow-up period. For further information about this program see Lovell and Richey (1991), Richey, Lovell, and Reid (1991), Lovell and Hawkins (1988), Lovell (1991).

References

Lovell, M. L. (1991). *The friendship group: Learning the skills to create social support. A manual for group leaders.* Vancouver: University of British Columbia, School of Social Work.

Lovell, M. L., & Hawkins, J. D. (1988). An evaluation of a group intervention to increase the personal social networks of abusive mothers. *Children and Youth Services Review 10,* 175–188.

Lovell, M. L., & Richey, C. A. (1991). Implementing agency-based social support skill training. *Families in Society 72,* 563–571.

Richey, C. A., Lovell, M., & Reid, K. (1991). Interpersonal skill training to enhance social support among women at risk for child maltreatment. *Children and Youth Services Review 13,* 41–59.

GIVING AND GETTING HELP FROM OTHERS

"Giving and Getting Help from Others" is a social support/social network training module that was delivered to parents of children in Head Start early childhood education programs in the State of Ohio. The module was delivered as one session of a twelve-week "Parenting Plus" program designed to address issues of social isolation, stress management, and parenting practices. The parenting program itself had been implemented in some format to parents of children in day care, homeless parents, parents of children with Attention Deficit Hyperactivity Disorder, parents of children with Oppositional Defiant Disorder, migrant farmworker parents, and middle-class working parents. The original pilot of the program, including the social support/social network module (Tracy & Abell 1994), was with low-income parents of Head Start children residing in Cleveland's inner city housing projects or subsidized living units. Subsequent use has been made of the module with teen parents and parents of children with chronic illnesses. Goals of the social support/social network module, as stated to the participants, were (a) understanding everybody's need for support (b) identifying who is in your social network, (c) identifying social support needs, and (d) learning ways of mobilizing social support. A significant component of the module was having each participant complete their own social network map and then in small groups discuss their map in terms of what they learned about their social network, types of support they received, and types of support they provided to network members, among others. In this way, participants were able to identify their social network and assess its strengths and capabilities. One interesting discussion point was the relationship between support provided to children and the issue of reciprocity. Most parents provided a great deal of support to their children and did not hold expectations that their children would give back the same amount. Group leaders reported that some parents, however, did hold inappropriate and troublesome expectations of support they expected from children. To address this issue, a large group discussion of what children can "give back" to parents appropriately at each age level (infants/toddlers, preschoolers, school age) was included. Participants also were involved in brainstorm session with a practice example. Following the practice example, all participants generated their own personal change goal, by completing a Worksheet for Getting More Support. The worksheet asked for written information in the following areas: strengths of my network, what I want to change (my goal), barriers to consider, and steps to reach my goal. A simplified menu of intervention plans was provided to the group to facilitate action. These strategies included linking up with new people or groups, working on changing relationships, getting needed skills or experiences, reestablishing old relationship if positive, and asking others for help. A unique component of the parenting program was the use of a parent partner, a volunteer, or other program participant who met and talked periodically with the participant for the purposes of ongoing support. Participants were then able to develop and share their plan with their parent partner in subsequent weeks of the training. Further information about the program can be obtained from Rebekah L. Dorman, Ph.D., Research and Training Department, The Guidance Centers, 2525 E. 22nd Street, Cleveland, Ohio 44115.

References

Ferguson, S. A., Tracy, E. M. & Simonnelli, D. (1992). *Parent Network Project Manual: Training Head Start Parent Advisors to Strengthen the Social Support Systems of Low-Income Parents*. Center for Practice Innovations, Mandel School of Applied Social Sciences.

Tracy, E. M., & Abell, N. (1994). The social network map: Some further refinements on administration. *Social Work Research 18*, 56–60.

6

The Diversity of Environmental Experience

While a concern with diversity has moved steadily from the margins of social work discourse to its center, the environmental dimensions of difference remain largely unexplored. In this chapter we make a beginning contribution to what we hope will become a deeper and more nuanced awareness of the intricate and potent relationships between diversity and environmental contexts. As we have explored the growing literature in other disciplines addressing the rich variability of environmental experience, we have become even more certain that a sophisticated understanding of context and its implications is essential to the empowering, strengths-based, culturally competent practice we and many others see as essential to effective social work.

Consistent, critical attention to the environmental dimensions of diversity is central to contemporary practice for several reasons:

1. An understanding of persons-in-context is fundamental to a full appreciation of the meaning of diversity.

2. As we noted in Chapter 3, neither the strengths perspective nor empowerment practice as yet includes a well-developed theory of environment. The lens of diversity both highlights this gap and underscores the importance of understanding the differential impacts of environments on the life opportunities of individuals, groups, and communities.

3. At the level of everyday practice, a lack of environmental sophistication limits the critical appraisal of environmental resources and constraints that lies at the core of an empowerment-strengths approach to practice. In Chapter 3, for example, we argued that critically reflective dialogue between client and worker is essential to a more informed and complex view of environmental barriers and assets. This assumes, how-

ever, a discussion fueled not only by the direct experiences of the client or client system, but also by the substantive environmental knowledge of the worker. Since the literature that currently funds social work knowledge of environments and their impacts is relatively limited, we are less than confident that social workers have access to the level of environmental knowledge that would fully support such a dialogical process.

Consider, for example, the everyday experiences of gays and lesbians. A growing body of literature suggests that the life experiences of sexual minorities are profoundly shaped by interactions with a series of environmental contexts, some of which are defined by heterosexual norms and some of which are not. The process of critical reflection with a gay or lesbian client should ideally include exploration of the impact of these various environments, for good and ill, on his or her well-being. Without substantive knowledge to guide such a discussion, however, workers will find it difficult to move beyond the client's subjective experience to contextual analysis and reflection. Indeed, the worker may have no idea about how to open up such a contextualized conversation.

We offer the material in this chapter both as a stimulus to a deeper awareness of the environmental dimensions of difference and as a set of prompts for a more informed and engaged exploration of the diverse environmental experiences of clients and consumers. In a generative spiral, these conversations will themselves expand worker understandings and perspectives of the everyday life experiences of clients and client systems, and thus further enrich the environmental knowledge base of the profession.

We have chosen to illustrate the potential of an environmental perspective on diversity by focusing on six axes of social experience: race, class, gender, age, sexual orientation, and physical and intellectual ability. We fully recognize that there are other relevant domains—for example, culture, ethnicity, mental capacity, and experiences of displacement (such as homelessness, immigrants and refugees, or children in out-of-home placement)—and that our discussions here tap only a small portion of the increasingly rich interdisciplinary literatures available in the areas we explore.

Conventional scholarship on the environment tends to assume that most people's experiences of the environment conform to dominant cultural norms and perspectives. A growing body of recent work, however, searches out and reveals the many ways in which environmental experience varies. This diverse literature is particularly informative in its focus on what has been termed the "geography of everyday experience" (Rollinson 1990). Descriptive material on the everyday interactions of people with different experiences of their environmental contexts is an important and useful adjunct to aggregate and cross-sectional research data, for it brings to life the immediate implications of larger social and cultural arrangements, and thus is directly applicable in practice.

RACE, CLASS, AND ENVIRONMENT

The deep, intricate linkages between race, class, and environmental context can be seen in the ways that spatial segregation and surveillance reinforce wider social patterns of power, privilege, and access to resources. In gated communities and buffered suburbs, or in racially "hypersegregated communities," such as Chicago, Minneapolis, or Seattle, for example, geographic boundaries maintain race and class distinctions.

Everyday lived experiences of racism are intensely spatial in nature, regardless of class or income. Despite the Civil Rights Act (1964) and three decades of civil rights activism, middle-class blacks still describe a sustained pattern of discrimination in public places: they are shadowed by security guards in department stores, ignored by cab drivers, given poor service in restaurants and hotels, harassed by the police, and denied access to housing in elite white neighborhoods (Feagin & Sikes 1994). In a recent editorial in the *New York Times*, eminent journalist Brent Staples describes his own experiences:

> One of my first assignments as a reporter was to interview a cartoonist who lived on Chicago's Gold Coast, a sliver of affluence set between Lake Michigan and a nasty housing project. Killing time before the interview, I stopped at a jeweler and asked the price of a watch in the window. The manager ducked into a storeroom and led out an enormous Doberman, straining on its leash. With a snarl that matched the dog's, she said, "Now may I help you?" The cartoonist was not much better. She opened the door a crack and then slammed it in my face. . . . [T]o be presumed a criminal is a punishing experience, one that even African American millionaires know well. (Staples 1996)

Low-income blacks are even more vulnerable to discrimination, hostility, and surveillance, not only in public places clearly defined as white, but also in their own communities and neighborhoods. For residents of housing projects, for example, ongoing oversight by police, security guards, and representatives of various social service agencies undermines independence and fuels hostility and perceptions of differential treatment (Murray 1995). Working-class black adults report high levels of workplace stress and discrimination, leading to increased risk of hypertension (Staples 1996). In social work agencies, African-American social workers experience their supervisory relationships as less empowering and more undermining than their white counterparts (Nagda 1996).

Less obvious but equally salient is the growing evidence that environmental risks concentrate disproportionately in low-income and minority communities. Outside social work there is a ground swell of interest in environmental justice and environmental racism (Bryant & Mohai 1990; Bullard 1990, 1994; Cutter 1995; Goldman 1996; Heiman 1996; Hofrichter 1993). Within the profession, however, just a trickle of articles has attempted to alert social workers to the growing evidence that racial minority and low-income groups bear a disproportionate burden of environmental risks (Epstein 1995; Rogge 1993, 1995; Soine 1987). Gross environmental disparities exist between white communities and communities of color, and between affluent and low-income communities, in the location of a range of environmental threats, including garbage dumps, recycling plants, toxic waste dumps, landfills, and increased exposure to toxic chemicals (Bryant & Mohai 1990; Bullard 1990, 1994; Cutter 1995). Despite uncertainty as to the exact effects of environmental toxins, the weight of evidence points to significant negative impacts on health, mental health, and economic outcomes. Such negative effects are potentiated in "hypersusceptible" communities, such as low-income neighborhoods—those in which a concentration of risk factors already exists (Rogge 1993, 1995).

Low-income communities of color, including African-American and Latino neighborhoods and American Indian reservations, are significantly (indeed increasingly) more likely to be sites for toxic waste disposal than are affluent white communities. Bullard reports, for example, that in Altgeld Gardens, a relatively small neighborhood on Chicago's Southeast Side that is 70 percent African American and 11 percent Latino, there are "50 active or closed commercial hazardous waste landfills, 100 factories (including seven chemical plants and five steel mills), and 103 abandoned toxic waste dumps" (1994, 14). Such disproportionality reflects the current and historical inability of low-income and minority neighborhoods to resist effectively either the siting of polluting facilities or the economic "sweeteners," in terms of jobs and taxes, that typically accompany them. Also, as Benjamin Goldman (1996) argues, it is one among several indicators that mark a wider trend of increasing inequality in American society, others being the increasing gap between rich and poor, the concentration of crime in poor neighborhoods, educational inequalities, and gross disparities in health risks and life expectancy.

The "landscape of risk" (Cutter 1995) in poor and minority communities has other, more insidious aspects. Less visible, but equally noxious, are the effects of freeways that bisect poor urban neighborhoods, the multiple biopsychosocial impacts of deteriorated, unsafe housing, and the siting in low-income communities of facilities that no one else wants, such as prisons and refuse treatment plants. Lead poisoning, which results from a combination of ingestion of lead paint, exhaust fumes, and manufacturing pollution, is thus much more prevalent among poor children of color (2 percent of white children, 12 percent of black children, and 19 percent of inner-city black children have lead levels high enough to warrant treatment; Rifai et al. 1993). High incidence rates of childhood asthma in poor minority communities can similarly be linked to the environmental quality of the neighborhood. Poor neighborhoods are less safe for children: violence, deteriorated housing, inadequate adult supervision, run-down playgrounds, and a whole range of environmental hazards, from heavy traffic to unfenced building sites, take their toll on child health and well-being. In rural settings, regular exposure to unacceptably high levels of toxic agricultural chemicals by migrant farm workers and their families adds a significant dimension of risk to lives that are already precarious. In all of these instances, the children and families concerned have little option but to live their lives as best they can despite the environmental hazards they confront. Faced with environmental conditions that threaten their health or quality of the life, families with more financial and social resources can make a "flight to health." The choice to flee from unsafe environments is significantly less available to the poor.

It is particularly important that social workers understand the "silent" and incremental effects of environmental toxins and hazards, for these can easily be interpreted as evidence of child, family, and neighborhood pathology. Lead poisoning, for example, results in patterns of child behavior that mirror developmental delays and child behavior problems. Similarly, the impacts of agricultural chemicals on migrant families are difficult to disentangle from the intersecting effects of poverty, high mobility, and inadequate health care. Given the relative lack of attention accorded to such environmental impacts in the training of social service professionals, there is a significant chance that the effects of noxious environmental conditions will be overlooked in assessment and intervention planning (Rogge 1993). In Chapter 4, we have thus included environmental hazards as a core domain of a comprehensive environmental assessment.

The growing recognition that communities of color and low-income neighborhoods bear an inequitable burden of environmental risk has stimulated increased environmental activism among lower-income and minority groups (Epstein 1995; Goldman 1996). In communities of color, this activism frequently builds on concerns and energies mobilized by the civil rights movement. Nationally, however, the new environmental movement draws on a remarkably diverse base that includes linkages across gender, race, and class lines. For social workers concerned about questions of environmental racism and environmental justice, significant opportunities exist to align with and support efforts to enhance environmental equity, not only by communities of color, but also by these more broadly based coalitions. Indeed, it may be important to shift attention from communities of color (who continually are given responsibility for addressing issues that are the responsibility of society as a whole) to include a focus on mobilizing the environmental self-interest of affluent communities and the "alienated" white working class.

WOMEN AND ENVIRONMENT

Although women's experiences in their everyday environments—as parents, caregivers, domestic partners, single mothers, welfare recipients, residents of housing projects, elderly women, and workers, to name but a few—are central to large expanses of social work practice, to date there has been little in the social work literature that explores the environment from a gendered perspective. The robust literature that informs social work thinking about women's experiences from a macro, or policy perspective—for example, the feminization of poverty (Lord 1993) or the social construction of domestic violence (Davis 1991)—tells workers little about the transactions between women and their daily environments. The clinical practice literature, on the other hand, has typically focused more on the gendered construction of women's relational experiences than on the everyday contexts of women's experience. To bridge this gap for direct practice, social workers must look outside the profession, to disciplines as diverse as geography, architecture, history, women's studies, and environmental psychology (see, for example, Altman & Churchman 1994; Michelson 1994).

Feminist scholarship on women's experiences of the environment has focused particularly on the spatiality of women's lives, the many ways in which women's experiences of space and place differ from men's, and the links between the use of space and gendered power relationships (Katz & Monk 1993; Rose 1993; Seager 1993; Spain 1992; Weisman 1992). Authors highlight, for example, the separation of public from private space (at least in Western culture) and the accompanying tendency to associate women and their roles with domestic spaces (Spain 1992). Whether symbolic or actual, this relegation of women to the "separate sphere" of home and family intensifies power and status differentials, since in capitalist society domestic life is typically separated from the more valued domains of production and culture. Though frequently invisible, assumptions about women's (and thus men's) "proper place" are deeply embedded in social and cultural arrangements. Surveying a range of spatial structures, both public and private, Joni Seager (1993) described them as "blueprints for inequality," and urged an increased awareness of the "imperatives of space" and their impact on women's lives. In a study of the spatial experiences of single women, who by definition do not conform to traditional expectations for women, Chasteen concludes, for example, that physical spaces are "bearers of meanings" about what "real 'women' and 'men' do, where, and with whom" (1994, 310). The unmarried women in Chasteen's study vividly describe the unique disadvantages they experience negotiating a social and physical landscape designed for women with partners. A whole array of environmental features, such as housing, public transportation, and conventions around the use of public space, assume that the women who use them will primarily be accompanied by or living with a man.

Many experiences that fall disproportionately on women—such as rape, domestic violence, and street harassment—have a significant environmental dimension. Personal safety, for example, is much more an issue for women than for men (Gardner 1990; Pain 1991; Valentine 1989), to the extent that Katz (1993) suggests that "fear of personal injury or violation may be the purdah of the industrialized West, effectively curtailing girls' and women's access to public space" (p. 89). De facto, women operate under a spatial curfew that determines when and how they can safely use public spaces. These spatial limits are defined not only by women's fears, but also by social attitudes. Media coverage of cases where women are raped or murdered when jogging alone at "inappropriate" times or in "inappropriate" places indicates, for example, the power of social judgments about what constitutes appropriate spatial behavior for women.

Such judgments have a considerable impact on the ways in which women interpret and use the environment. Chasteen (1994) suggests that "women do not restrict their movements, their housing opportunities, and their leisure activities because they are assaulted when they do not do so, but rather because engaging in certain activities 'in the wrong place' at a 'bad' time so violates standards of 'appropriate' behavior for women that they are afraid of what could happen as a result. . . . [W]omen see the world around them through a lens of socialized fear" (p. 326). This "geography of fear" is a constant counterpoint to and constraint on the decisions women make about where to go, at what times, and with whom. Paradoxically, women are in fact more at risk of violence in the "safety" of their own homes than they are in "dangerous" public places (Valentine 1989). In this context, since neither public nor private space is truly safe, shelters for battered women have been typically been constructed as hidden spaces, located outside male systems of control and domination.

The differential developmental experiences of boys and girls reinforce social and cultural messages about the environment. Feminist theorists suggest, for example, that boys and girls differ in their experiences and expectations around the use of space. Weisman concludes that boys are raised to be spatially dominant:

> [T]hey are encouraged to be adventurous, to discover and explore their surroundings, and to experience a wide range of environmental settings. Girls, on the other hand, tend to have less autonomy, a smaller spatial range, and less encouragement to explore and manipulate their environment: They are taught to occupy but not to control space. (1992, 24)

Some of this difference can be explained, Weisman suggests, by parental and societal evaluations of the relative "dangerousness" of the environment for boys and girls, and related assumptions about what thus constitutes appropriate behavior.

Feminist geographers also highlight the ways in which women's experiences in their environments shift and change over the life course. Katz and Monk (1993), for example, note the interconnections between women's environments and their caregiving roles. Women with young children (or those caring for older relatives) who also work outside the home spend enormous amounts of time and energy juggling responsibilities and tasks. These are simplified or made significantly more complex by spatial issues such as distance between home and workplace, location of child care, form of transportation, and the availability of other environmental supports and resources. Class and socioeconomic issues further compound the demands on many women. In a recent article in the *New York Times* (DeParle 1994), for example, a woman who was formerly a welfare recipient and is now employed describes her morning routine. To get to work by 7 A.M., she must wake her children at 5 A.M. and then take multiple buses, first to get the children to her mother's house, and then to get herself to work. For her, as for other poor women, spatial realities profoundly complicate her efforts to become self-sufficient, yet these realities rarely surface in discussions of welfare dependency or welfare reform. Nor are they addressed adequately in direct practice. Indeed, as Schnitzer (1996) points out, workers may be more likely to blame and pathologize poor families who do not follow through with services or keep appointments than to ask what else is going on in their lives. Yet, as she notes,

> [T]here are reasons other than irresponsibility that explain why appointments are not kept, for "the lives of those who consult [us] are far more richly detailed than their misfortune suggests" (Hunter, 1991, p. 173, citing Sherlock Holmes). (p. 574)

These few examples point to the need to move beyond universalistic assumptions about environmental experience, not only those that equate women's experience with that of men, but also those that obscure the rich variety of environmental experience among women. The importance of a developmental framework is also apparent, not only in relation to the differential experience of boys and girls, but also with regard to shifts in women's environmental experience across the life cycle.

SEXUALITY AND SPACE

The growing body of scholarship that explores the relationships between sexuality and environment (see, for example, Bell & Valentine 1995; Colomina 1992) contains within it a rich subgenre focused on the role of space and place in the lives of gays, lesbians, and bisexuals (Adler & Brenner 1992; Bell 1991; Bell, Vinnie, Cream, & Valentine 1994; Valentine 1993a, 1993b, 1994, 1995; Wolfe 1992). Geographer Gill Valentine (1994) points out that for sexual minorities, as for other minority groups, the environment is a source of both liberation and oppression. In the "gay ghettoes" of large cities such as San Francisco and New York, for example, the environment supports open expression and celebration of sexual identities and provides significant opportunities for sexual dissidence. More commonly, however, public spaces are defined in heterosexual terms: "Most spaces, from neighborhoods to workplaces and restaurants, are organized for, and appropriated and controlled by, heterosexual people" (ibid., 8). The daily lives of gays and lesbians thus tend to be an ongoing balancing act, involving continuous negotiations between openness and concealment, depending on how the current environment is defined and the extent to which it is perceived as hostile, dangerous, or stigmatizing.

These varying spatialities result in multiple sexual identities, in the sense that in different places at different times gays and lesbians may be more or less open about their sexual orientation. Many gays and lesbians are out in their social and recreational lives, for example, but closeted at work, and perhaps also with their families. In the course of a day, for example, a gay man may be out in the privacy of his own home, conceal his gay identity at work, be openly gay if he meets gay friends for a drink after work, or remain closeted if he has a business dinner or a social commitment involving people who do not know his sexual orientation. At any time, in any of these situations, he may be faced with the dilemma of whether to reveal or to hide his sexual identity, since in both gay or heterosexual environments he many encounter people who know him in his other persona.

Unlike heterosexuals, who may claim this identity at all times and in all places, gays can frequently be open about their sexual identity only in particular places. Very often, their lives and identities are thus profoundly shaped by their experiences in a series of exclusionary and oppressive spaces. The significant personal, psychological, and interpersonal costs of "passing," or constantly monitoring and negotiating one's identity (Brown 1991), as well as the need to constantly scan the environment for potential threats, are evidenced by the relatively high rates among gays and lesbians of suicide and suicidality (particularly among gay and lesbian teens), drug and alcohol use, and use of mental health services (Bradford, Ryan, & Rothblum 1994; Hammelman 1993; Proctor & Groze 1994; Shifren & Solis 1992).

Given the pressures to conform to heterosexual norms in most public spaces, gay environments are of central importance in affirming identity and relieving stress. These sequestered social spaces, to borrow Scott's (1990) term, or "free places," as Evans and Boyte (1986) describe them, provide gays, lesbians, and bisexuals with opportunities to connect with one another away from heterosexual society and the impact of dominant social norms. Gay bars, clubs, community programs, and cultural activities offer recreation, community, and support. Yet many of the transgressive, "free" environments at the heart of gay social life are not without their price. The "pleasure-geographies" (Bell et al. 1994) of gay males center, in many instances, around alcohol, drugs, and sexual experimentation. Drug and alcohol abuse, along with the ever-present specter of HIV/AIDS, are thus significant risks in this particular social milieu (Bradford et al. 1994).

For lesbians, a different set of issues emerges, related to the relatively invisible landscape of the lesbian community (Valentine 1995). Unlike many gay male neighborhoods, residential neighborhoods that attract lesbians are rarely marked by lesbian services and cultural institutions. The lesbian community is less a material, built environment than it is a relational one—an "imagined" community defined primarily by friendships, social networks, and a sense of shared identity and solidarity (ibid.). Those lesbian-identified spaces that do exist are often transient:

"Unlike many gay men's venues . . . lesbian spaces are often time-specific, that is they are only gay on one night a week or one night a month" (Valentine 1994, 9). It has been said that where gay men "subvert" straight space, lesbians merely cohabit in it (Bell et al. 1994). As Valentine notes, "There are no public expressions of lesbian sexualities; no mark on the landscape that 'lesbians live here.' It is a lesbian space only to those in the know" (1995, 99).

In part, the loose structure of the lesbian "scene" is a reflection of the constraints on income and leisure opportunities that lesbians have in common with other women, both as mothers and in the workplace (Adler & Brennan 1992; Wolfe 1992). Lesbians are also likely to have more concerns about personal safety than gay men, and to be more reluctant to expose themselves in public to the potential of antigay violence (Adler & Brennan 1992). The lack of overt structure in the lesbian community conceals, however, a rich relational community, characterized by dense, almost familial social networks and overlapping relationships. The formal and informal supports provided by this community are particularly important:

> [S]upport groups run by lesbians for lesbians are important sites around which "communities" are imagined (and contested). They provide emotional support for women "coming out"; and information about the timing and location of lesbian events, gay rights, artificial insemination, and about employers, businesses . . . and landlords sympathetic to sexual outlaws. . . . As sites of resistance, such groups can also unintentionally act as consciousness-raising groups. (Valentine 1995, 102)

Like social networks in the population at large, lesbian networks can be a source of tension and conflict as well as support. In her study of lesbian community life in England, for example, Valentine (1995) noted the degree to which this community can be both tolerant and controlling, supportive and expectant, particularly in relation to what constitutes an "appropriate" lesbian identity (dress, children, and bisexuality are examples of issues that have been sources of tension within the lesbian community). As a relatively small and integrated network, shifts in personal relationships, whether sexual or otherwise, tend also to have more of an impact than they would in a more diffuse community. In addition, the invisibility and fluidity of the "structured" lesbian community can be problematic for women seeking to make connections with other lesbians (particularly older lesbians, who frequently are totally closeted about their sexual identity).

The literature on the environmental experiences of sexual minorities—particularly gays, lesbians, and bisexuals, but also prostitutes and transgendered persons—enhances our understanding not only of the fundamental links between environments and oppression, but also of the dangers that lie in assuming that all sexual minorities experience the social and physical environment in the same way. Clearly, lesbians and gays have experiences that are similar but many that are different. Likewise, there are both similarities and differences in the ways that lesbians and heterosexual women negotiate their everyday realities. This variability within social categories or groupings underlines the importance of seeking out the particular ways in which individuals and groups experience aspects of their environments. In this context, as in others, the environment is interpreted and experienced in multiple and fluid ways—"the process of imagining, contesting, reworking, redefining, and the challenging of sexual identities, community identities and the reshaping of landscapes of desire continues" (ibid., 109).

THE CONTEXTS OF DISABILITY

The relationship between disability and surrounding environments is one of the better-explored areas of diversity and the environment. Not only are the environmental challenges facing physically disabled persons relatively obvious, they have been a significant focus of advocacy efforts and legislative reform. At this point, thanks to the disability movement (Shapiro 1993) and the provisions of the Americans with Disabilities Act (ADA; 1990), there is heightened awareness of the need for institutional and built environments, such as social service agencies, educational institutions, and shopping malls, to be accessible and user-friendly for people of all abilities.

Less widely available, but of central importance for social work practice, is information on the varied experience of disabled persons within their everyday environments or life-space. To illustrate the value of attention to this variability, we present information from three studies that examine different aspects of the transactions between persons with disabilities and their environments.

In a study of women with multiple sclerosis, a progressively debilitating and disabling chronic illness, Dyck explored the "complex ways in which gender, physical impairment and space intersect" in the lives of these women as they "respond to changes in the physical and social capacity of their body" (1995, 309). In particular, Dyck addressed the ways the women progressively "remap" and restructure the physical spaces of home and neighborhood in response to their illness. She describes a growing experience of disempowerment and social isolation as declining physical capacity constricted the women's ability first to work outside the home and then to meet demands within their homes. Essentially, these relatively young women experienced changes in their activities and ability to use their environments that would usually have occurred in old age. Shifts occurred not only in women's participation in work and at home, but also in their social networks and use of home and public space.

Significant changes in the women's environments included residential moves, a reordering of social relationships, and marked shifts in both patterns of use and in the meaning of neighborhood and city spaces. A majority of the women in Dyck's study had moved or were planning to move because of increased needs for accessibility in their homes and in their neighborhoods. For most this meant a move to a new neighborhood, with a resultant struggle to maintain existing social ties and supports as well as to build new ones. For a number this move was related also to separation or divorce from their partner, so the physical move was cross-cut with emotional and economic issues. In addition to the larger issue of moving house, the women were faced also with significant reorganization within their homes to accommodate their progressive physical deterioration, including, for some, a transitional period of using home as workplace when they could no longer work outside.

Given the nature of multiple sclerosis, however, not even the most profound changes in life-space and life-style can prevent a pattern of deepening dependency on others and progressive constriction of mobility and use of space. Unable to work, many of the women spent most of their time at home, punctuated only by trips for necessary activities such as shopping or medical appointments: "A sense of entrapment was voiced by several women. Concern about safety in negotiating the physical environment, attempts to follow medical advice to rest, and the unpredictability of symptoms acted to restrict women's use of the environment" (Dyck 1995, 315). The built environment, once readily accessible and full of resources, presented ever-increasing layers of constraint, and caused the women to constantly redefine their relationship to resources and sources of support.

Entwined with the external changes in women's lives, Dyck points out, was a shift in the ways that the women interpreted their experience and their sense of self. She describes a process of "biographical disruption" that is "profoundly social and inherently spatial" (ibid., 318). No longer the women they were or the women they anticipated being, women with multiple sclerosis must reconstruct their lives to accommodate their physical limitations and a surrounding environment that is increasingly limiting and that largely signifies dependency. To understand and fully respond to this experience requires multiple layers of awareness, including an understanding of the role of environment in the personal redefinitions that accompany chronic illness.

The salience of the environment in the "lived experience" of disability is also poignantly illustrated by Scott Andrews (1995), who describes the life of John, a young man with Down's syndrome, following his family's move from North Hollywood to Mendocino. This much smaller community embraces John and becomes a "safe space" in which he lives a life of increasing independence, full of new connections and experiences. In North Hollywood, John had few contacts outside his home, family, and the world of the developmentally disabled. In Mendocino, he was fully engaged in the life of the township:

> By the end of John's first year in Mendocino he was holding down two part-time jobs (sweeping in front of the local general store on Saturdays, and sweeping and cleaning at a local cafe on Fridays); taking weekly voice, art, and guitar lessons; attending aerobic lessons five mornings a week; occasionally reading stories to kids at the local preschool; helping his mother teach a class on self-esteem to a group of troubled adolescents; making daily visiting "rounds" in the community; and going out to dance or listen to music at least five nights a week. He had numerous friends and acquaintances, and he was daily growing more verbal and assertive. (p. 108)

In Mendocino, John became a part of a series of natural networks, integrated into the mainstream of daily life in the community. No longer identified primarily by his diagnostic label, he was able both to give and to receive, becoming in the process a full member of the town community. In Chapter 3, we described the importance of sense of place in terms of membership, sense of belonging, and identity. John's story vividly illustrates the impact of place on well-being, particularly for persons whose life opportunities are deeply influenced by the responsiveness or otherwise of the people and places of their lives.

The richness of John's life stands in contrast both to his previous life in North Hollywood, and to the life experiences of many disabled persons, who frequently are constricted in numbers and range of personal and social connections (Lutfiyya 1991). As Walker points out, "Nowadays, people with disabilities spend much more time in the community, but in many ways they are not part of the community" (1995, 175). In an ethnographic study of the social geography of three disabled women, Walker concludes that they had

> ample opportunity to develop both an identity based on disability and an affiliation and relationships with others who have disabilities. However, the types of places that they have gone that include people without disabilities, outside of family, have given them little opportunity to develop social connections with others. (ibid., 179)

The women in Walker's study spent a lot of time in places that were homogeneous based on disability—special schools, separate classrooms, segregated workplaces and residential settings, segregated recreational activities, and human service agencies. Their involvement in nonsegregated environments tended toward a predominant use of large, public places, such as stores, restaurants, movie theaters, and malls, that offer few opportunities for the development of new personal connections and indeed are relatively anonymous. Involvements in private spaces were primarily through family. Not surprisingly, Walker notes, "none of the informants participates in the private social worlds of peers without disabilities" (ibid., 180). Although the women in the study spent varying amounts of time out and about in their local neighborhoods, Walker describes them as drawn to their neighborhoods by convenience and familiarity rather than strong social connections. For these three, the social geography of their lives was determined largely by others, and limited in range to connections made through family or through helping agencies.

Walker's account points up the many ways in which environmental experiences underline and perpetuate social divisions between the able and the disabled. Inadvertently, families and human service agencies may contribute to these social dislocations if they fail to encourage everyday opportunities for the development of social connections and personal social networks outside as well as within the disabled community. In Mendocino, John became an integral and accepted part of the stream of daily life in the community. His family's move was a natural environmental intervention that profoundly restructured his experience as a disabled person. This "natural experiment" highlights the critical need for more careful attention to the environmental context as both resource and constraint, particularly for groups such as the disabled whose environmental experiences interact so profoundly with their access to wider life opportunities.

ENVIRONMENTS AT THE BEGINNING
AND END OF LIFE

Children and Environments

For children, the immediate environment, both physical and social, is a primary medium for learning and development (Altman & Wohlwill 1978; Weinstein & David 1987; Wolfe & Rivlin 1987). Through their interactions with and manipulation of the environment, children develop a sense of who they are in the world, what kind of everyday world they inhabit, and to what extent they can impact their external environment. From their earliest years, children build places for themselves in the larger spaces of their lives—play houses, tree forts, castles, snow tunnels, hideaways under beds and in closets—and in them experiment with social relationships, act out their fantasies, and project themselves into adult roles and responsibilities. Adolescents challenge and manipulate the environment through the personalization of private space: indeed psychologists have suggested that college students who do *not* decorate their dorm rooms signal an identity crisis that may be predictive of other problems, such as academic failure (Hansen & Altman 1976). Social workers and therapists build on children's natural spatial tendencies through modalities such as play therapy, including the "small worlds" technique, where the child uses an array of models and figures in a sand tray to recreate the inner and outer landscapes of his or her life.

Children's activities in shaping and transforming their environments contribute to the development of "environmental competence," or the knowledge, skill, and confidence to use the environment to meet personal and collective goals and enrich one's experience (Saegert & Hart 1978). Geographer Cindi Katz (1993) links findings on the spatial behavior of boys and girls with evidence from developmental psychology that suggests a relationship between autonomous environmental experience and the development of certain analytical skills, such as the acquisition of "cognitive maps" and associated spatial abilities. For girls, she suggests, restrictions in experience result in "lost spaces of knowing"— cognitive and experiential deficits that contribute to a decreased sense of efficacy and autonomy. Similarly, children who spend their after-school and summer hours sequestered in urban apartments, because their parents are at work or afraid to let them play outside, may lose important opportunities for physical, social, and cognitive development. As Katz notes, "Fear, danger, and children's safety rattle around at the root of children's geographies in urban settings" (1993, 102). Indeed, contemporary children of all classes are more spatially restricted than those of previous generations, raising questions about the impact of these constraints on children's confidence and competence in the external world.

Environmental competency in children is assumed to be linked developmentally to later beliefs that as adults they can have an impact on the external world. Researchers have hypothesized that efforts to involve children in creating and reconstructing environments will have positive impacts on their degree of citizenship and community participation as adults. Baldassari, Lehman, and Wolfe involved children from three New York neighborhood schools in a participatory action research project designed to provide the opportunity for children to imagine, plan for, and be involved in the creation of neighborhood change. While the project resulted in limited actual change at the community level, it had significant impacts on the children:

> The community research process allowed each of them to listen to one another and to listen to neighbors, family members, and community workers in a new way, as experts to be taken seriously. They began to connect their own experiences in their households and communities with what they were learning about the history and processes of neighborhood change. This validated their own cultures and everyday lives. . . . The vague they of their initial images became specific, as they began to envision a role for themselves in the process of change. (1987, 263)

Children experience their environments with great immediacy. Cobb (1977) has said that children use their "whole bodily self" in their interactions with the world around them. The impact of environments on children is both direct and symbolic (David & Weinstein 1987; Hart 1979). Built environments, for example, communicate much about adult power over children and about also adult expectations, intentions, and values (the gendered nature of children's bedrooms being a prime example). Discrepancies between the direct and indirect messages communicated by environments may be particularly profound in institutional settings. After a long period studying children in institutions of various kinds, including partial institutions such as schools and day care centers, Wolfe and Rivlin noted:

> Every institution that we have studied is striking in the routinization of daily life and lack of variety and change in both physical qualities and activities. . . . [D]aily life is an unvarying series of events taking place in an endless repetition of similar spaces, built into an unvarying time schedule, all defined by some outside power. . . . Little time or space belongs to the child. (1987, 101–102)

Adults typically control the environment: few spaces are designed especially for children, even those that will primarily be used by them. School classrooms, for example, are often designed more to enhance control by teachers than to promote student-centered learning. Likewise, residential gardens in suburban housing developments often lack the kinds of unconstructed and uncontrolled spaces in which children most delight. Children gravitate to long grass, woods, and materials that they can use to construct fantasy worlds—but adults impose order, manicured lawns, and neat edges. Residential institutions, agency waiting rooms, social work offices—frequently these physical environments send clear and often bleak messages to children about their lack of centrality and importance in an adult world. Indeed, children's environments tend to be saturated with the structures and symbols of control and surveillance. Opportunities for "serendipity" and "spontaneity" (Wolfe & Rivlin 1987) are limited, along with those for privacy, choice, independence, and self-determination. In such environments, Wolfe and Rivlin suggest, children learn "individualism rather than individuality, . . . conformity rather than community" (p. 107).

Effective environments for children foster personal identity, encourage the development of competence, provide opportunities for growth and enrichment, promote a sense of security and trust, allow both social interaction and privacy, and provide opportunities for play (David & Weinstein 1987). When environments are carefully constructed with children in mind, children respond with immediacy, pleasure, and a sense of ownership. In Seattle, for example, Children's Hospital is a series of colorful, child-friendly spaces, organized and decorated with children's needs and interests obviously as a first priority. For the child patient, the messages emanating from this environment suggest that, despite all the negative associations hospitals evoke, this is a place that cares about kids and is responsive to them.

In Chapter 3, we described the intricate relationships between the developing child, his or her immediate environmental contexts, and health and well-being over the life course. In everyday settings—home, school, the local neighborhood—children learn fundamental and lasting lessons about self-in-environment. Secure attachments to people, places, and objects, familiar daily routines in predictable settings, and explorations and experiences in a relatively safe and consistent external world provide the scaffolding for optimal development (Bradley 1995). Environments that are unsafe, chaotic, and unpredictable undermine resilience and derail the healthy coping mechanisms of the developing child. Psychologist James Garbarino (1993) describes, for example, how children growing up in violent and unsafe inner-city neighborhoods learn brutal truths: that violence is pervasive and human life inherently fragile; and that their parents and community lack the power to protect them from danger. These violations of fundamental developmental needs for safety, protection, and recognition set the stage, Garbarino suggests, for later behaviors, such as vigilantism and aggression by young men, that can be interpreted as distorted attempts to create safety and meaning in an environment that is experienced as profoundly meaningless, unmanageable, and incomprehensible (Antonovsky 1979, 1987). In his essay review, "Children on the Edge," Robert Halpern (1995a) describes these coping strategies as "fatally flawed" and intrinsically self-defeating, since they fail to meet core developmental needs, further undermine family and community stability, and very often result in injury, death, or incarceration.

In their work with children and their families in a multitude of public and private spaces, social workers have many opportunities for thoughtful attention to the interaction between children and their everyday environments. Given the exquisite responsiveness of children to environmental change, a small and apparently simple environmental intervention can be highly effective. Berenson (1967), for example, found a significant positive change in the appearance and behavior of adolescent girls in residential treatment when a mirror was placed by their beds. For social workers, the challenge is to better imagine and incorporate the "landscapes of childhood" into practice: to envision the environment as perceived and experienced from the child's perspective, and to involve children more fully in assessing and changing their everyday worlds.

Environments and the Elderly

Ward, LaGory, and Sherman point out that "aging is a contextual process: the nature and consequences of aging depend on the environment within which it occurs" (1988, 201). This is not at all to say that the elderly are entirely at the mercy of their environments. Indeed, as Elder and other developmental psychologists have demonstrated (Elder 1985; Moen et al. 1995), at all points the life course is both transactional and contextual. Evidence suggests, however, both that there are differences in the environmental experiences and perceptions of the elderly and that the elderly may be more sensitive to aspects of their environments than younger adults (Howell 1994; Ward et al. 1988). For example, while elders become at once more dependent on the surrounding environment and progressively constricted within it, it seems that some compensation for this is found in more extensive reliance on memory, fantasy, and imagination (Rowles 1978). What the old lose in actual experiences in the environment they make up for vicariously—watching TV, reading, observing others, and through reminiscence and story, including the memories evoked by familiar and treasured objects (Howell 1980). Hence, as Howell (1983) points out, place and its elements—people, photographs, mementos, the family china cabinet or grandfather clock—are central to the identity and thus well-being of the elderly.

Further, for the elderly as at other points in the life course, experiences and meanings of home, neighborhood, and community shift and transform with the ebb and flow of different life experiences and situations. To illustrate the rich and varying transactions between elders and their environments, we present two qualitative studies that offer very different perspectives on the experiences and contexts of aging.

In an ethnographic study of elderly occupants of Single Room Occupancy hotels (SROs) in Chicago, Rollinson (1990) vividly portrays the everyday experiences of vulnerable elderly within these settings. Located in the inner city in an impoverished, rundown neighborhood, the SROs were seedy and decrepit, and housed mixed populations of the elderly, the chronic mentally ill, and transient adults. Many of the non-elderly tenants were actively involved with drugs and alcohol. In this study, Rollinson depicts a cadre of the elderly who live essentially out of the public gaze: seemingly independent but in fact highly isolated, trapped inside their hotels by declining physical capabilities and the constraints of the hotel and neighborhood environments:

> Any ties that did exist were, out of fear and necessity, very limited and ephemeral. The mean journey beyond the hotel extended to a mere three city blocks. Major roads in the study neighborhood were significant barriers to movement. . . . Crime was omnipresent in the neighborhood and these men and women were very vulnerable to attack and robbery. Stories of the danger on the street ran rampant throughout the hotels, causing the elderly tenants to restrict movement even further, thus exacerbating their geographic and social isolation. (ibid., 203)

Proud and fiercely self-reliant, many of the elders in Rollinson's study did not reach out to much-needed social and medical services for fear of losing their independence. Social services, on the other hand, tend to respond only to those who seek help. The gap between the real needs of these elders and external perceptions of these needs was thus significant. As Rollinson observed, "The elderly tenants were overlooked by social scientists, social service providers, and planners because the majority were trapped inside their hotels and not visible to the wider society. This isolation should not be confused with independence" (ibid., 203). In the midst of a highly populated urban area, in an bustling environment rich in social resources despite its many constraints, these elderly SRO occupants were essentially alone, "victims of the barriers they had erected to protect themselves from an uncertain, uncaring, and often hostile environment" (ibid., 204).

In contrast, a study of rural Appalachian elderly (Rowles 1983), who were equally poor and by objective criteria (income, housing quality, health status) equally in need of assistance, paints a very different picture. In a three-year participant observation study of the elderly residents of a declining town in rural Appalachia, Rowles explored the environmental experience of this community of the old and found them to be embedded in rich indigenous support networks that significantly compensated for other aspects of their lives. Unlike the elderly in Rollinson's (1990) study, these elders had mostly lived out their lives in this one place and had a deep affinity with it. Rowles describes three levels of "insideness" that come from this long-term involvement: (a) physical familiarity with the local environment; (b) social integration with the local community; and (c) autobiographical insideness, stemming from the links between place and personal history. This multilayered insideness provided the foundation for "an array of social supports harnessed by the Colton elderly" (Rowles 1983, 115), most of which were informal and indigenous: family, friends, neighbors, and "fellow members of the society of the old" (ibid.).

Digging further into the spatial dimensions of these social supports, Rowles identified a "hierarchy of environmental spaces," each of which offered different kinds and levels of support. Beyond the home, which offered the most immediate level of support, Rowles identified an immediate surveillance zone, or the area visible from the windows of an elderly person's house. He describes this as critical space, particularly for the home-bound, within which the elderly watch out for one another, monitor the community, and maintain a sense of social involvement:

> Within the surveillance zone a watchful reciprocity is apparent, particularly among elderly neighbors, which frequently includes the scheduled exchange of visual signals—such as drawing the curtain or switching on the porch light to signal that all is well. In times of crisis support from within this zone is particularly important. (p. 120)

Moving out from the surveillance zone, the next level of environment is the vicinity, or the immediate local neighborhood. People who live within close proximity also look out for one another: "Within the vicinity, family members and close friends provide frequent functional support" (ibid.). 120). In this zone, Rowles reports, old people who have known one another a long time coalesce into a subcommunity of the old, defined as much by shared memories and experiences as by shared needs.

Beyond the vicinity lies the community. Rowles observed that for the elderly in his sample, most functional linkages and relationships were confined within a two-mile radius. While people who lived further apart than this kept in touch by telephone, these interactions lacked the immediate, daily quality of those in the proximate geographic area. These more diffuse linkages, while important, were overshadowed by those in the immediate environment.

In Rowles's study, ties to persons and place were highly significant elements of a spatial pattern of support and reciprocity. Together, these constitute, Rowles suggests, a "dynamic sociospatial support system with distinctive geographical characteristics" (ibid.).

Careful consideration of the environments of aging points up the importance of a multilayered appreciation of the relationships between older persons and their everyday contexts. Implications for practice include the need for heightened awareness of the core importance of natural networks and supports to the well-being of the elderly; greater appreciation for the multiple textures of the sociospatial environment, both in physical terms and as a function of proximity or distance; and the need for greater attention to what Rowles has elsewhere called the "neighborhood of the mind" (1978, 201), or the subjective ties of the elderly to the people and places of the past as well as the present.

CONCLUSION

The materials in this chapter illustrate the many and richly varied ways that environments are experienced and interpreted. The scholarship we have presented brings to life our observation that people differ in their experiences of the environment, in the ways that they are impacted by environmental factors, and in the meanings environments have for them. In earlier chapters, particularly those on assessment and intervention, we have stressed the importance of understanding and responding to the client's view of his or her impinging environment. The importance of "ecological validity"—or the extent to which there is consistency between our assessments of the environment and the environmental experience of clients—is underlined by the information here, such as that on gays and lesbians, or the elderly, which points up the absolute necessity of cross-checking our assumptions against the "local knowledge" of clients and communities. The perspectives in this chapter both emphasize this point and provide the foundation for more richly detailed and critically informed dialogues between workers and clients.

The examples in this chapter likewise underscore the many ways in which personal and group experience is mediated and shaped by larger social and structural forces. The lens of diversity heightens our awareness of the extent to which environments are sites of liberation and resistance but also of oppression; sources of nourishment and strength but also of constraint and conflict. This more complex view is central, as we argued earlier, to the full realization of an empowering, strengths-based approach in practice.

Much work remains to be done to fully develop the social work knowledge base on the environmental dimensions of diversity. Consider, for example, the wonderful variability in environmental experience as a function of cultural and ethnic background, or shifts in environmental experience across the whole span of the life course. The materials presented here are at least a starting point: a stimulus, we hope, both for further scholarship and for enriched attention to the contexts of difference in social work education and practice.

7

Current Issues and Future Challenges for Person-Environment Practice

Throughout this book, we have attempted to sketch the essential features of an environmentally oriented approach to interpersonal helping, which we call person-environment practice. Central to this approach are the twin strategies of environmental assessment and intervention. As scholars of practice, we have no illusion that the widespread adoption of either the general approach or the specific strategies will be easily accomplished. In Chapter 1, we identified some particular barriers to person-environment practice at the professional, client-community, and organizational-institutional levels. Specific examples are provided later in this chapter and throughout the book. We view these and related issues as part of three larger and often intertwined challenges: to develop knowledge for professional practice; to disseminate this knowledge through professional education and training; and to address professional issues and the organizational and political contexts in which practice is carried out. In this last chapter, we focus on the meaning of these challenges for environmentally oriented practice.

THE CHALLENGE OF KNOWLEDGE DEVELOPMENT

As a recent volume on child development research suggests, Bronfenbrenner's theoretical paradigm, the ecology of human development, has transformed the way many social and behavioral scientists think about and study human beings and their environments: "Urie was the quintessential person for spurring psychologists to look up and realize

199

that interpersonal relationships did not exist in a social vacuum but were imbedded in the larger social structures of community, society, economics and politics" (Kohn, quoted in Moen 1995, 1). The impressive corpus of empirical research on development-in-context does not, however, easily translate into practice technology, although the implications for intervention appear considerable (McCubbin, Thompson, Thompson, & Fromer 1994; McCubbin, Thompson, Thompson, & Futrell 1995; Moen et al. 1995). This reflects the different missions of social science and social work: understanding how something works and understanding how to change it. The translation function is missing in the social arena—what industry calls research and development (R&D). Rothman's observation of some years ago with respect to the physical sciences and applied technology remains apt:

> It is as though a theoretical physicist at Princeton were expected to state his propositions and theorems in a form that could be put to use immediately by the factory foreman in Bayonne. (1980, 9)

In point of fact, Rothman, Thomas, and others have labored long and hard to develop models for what has variously been called: "social R&D" (Rothman 1980), "developmental research and utilization" (Thomas 1978), and, most recently, "intervention design and development" (Rothman & Thomas 1994). In a recent and richly detailed volume, the authors and their contributors define and expand the construct of "intervention research" and present a refined phase model of intervention design and development that builds upon but considerably extends their earlier formulations. Six phases of activity are identified: (a) problem analysis and project planning, (b) information gathering and synthesis, (c) design, (d) early development and pilot testing, (e) evaluation and advanced development, and (f) dissemination. The process typically makes use of multiple data sources ranging from social science research findings to practice wisdom. Each phase is explicated in detailed examples, and recent projects suggest promise for identifying interventions among vulnerable populations (Rothman 1994). Despite these impressive accomplishments, social R&D capacity—as an organized, coherent, and *institutional* component of social work practice—continues to suffer from failure to thrive. As Patti (1981) pointed out in an early and prescient critical review, this probably has something to do with the characteristic of many social science findings (often a key data source for intervention design) to contain the possibility of alternative interpretations and thus generate multiple and sometimes contradictory implications for practice. Given the relatively low priority that social work as a profession places on research and knowledge development generally, it seems unlikely that there will be a ground swell of support for a high-profile social R&D capacity any time in the near future. Thus, the prospects are slim for any significant increases in environmentally oriented practice knowledge, without either a powerful stimulus external to the profession or some fundamental rethinking of the nature of interpersonal practice.

From our perspective, one ray of hope can be found in the growing trend to view client-consumers as stakeholders and partners—not only in practice design and implementation but in practice research formulation, design, and execution. A recent multiauthored contribution on "values-based multi-cultural research" (Uehara et al. 1996) captures the essence of what is typically called "participatory-action research." The authors state:

> We believe that too many models of social science research replay and reinforce the theme of disenfranchisement, providing little opportunity for community members to shape research questions, claim ownership of data, develop findings and implications for action, and hone their critical inquiry skills. (ibid.)

The authors propose three general criteria for research in a multicultural context: (a) The researcher should constantly reflect privately and publicly on collaboration issues critically ranging from how the researcher's own biases and motives affect the research process to the impact of the larger political economy on disadvantaged groups. (b) The context should democratize the research process through continuous community collaboration rather than token representation of community members in limited advisory roles. (c) Research objectives should be linked to goals of community empowerment, social justice, and social transformation (Uehara et al. 1996).[1]

This values-based multicultural orientation to knowledge development is consistent with person-environment practice and the ecological-systems paradigm from which it is derived. In particular, the approach to participatory-action research suggested by these authors and others provides a means of ensuring application of Bronfenbrenner's original notions of "ecological validity" (the extent to which the environment experienced by the subjects in a social experiment actually has the properties the researcher supposes or assumes it to have), and it is consistent with what he termed the "transforming experiment":

> A transforming experiment involves the systematic alteration and restructuring of existing ecological systems in ways that challenge the forms of social organization, belief systems, and lifestyles prevailing in a particular culture or subculture. (1979, 41)

The notion of the transforming experiment extends our earlier formulation of "mission-oriented research" (Whittaker & Tracy 1989) and exemplifies the critical link between individual and collective empowerment needs in person-environment practice (Chapter 1). Just as P.E.P. requires a collegial relationship between practitioner and client with respect to assessment and intervention, so also this partnership extends to research and evaluation activities. Such partnership activities can be fairly small, simple, and straightforward, or complex and multifaceted. For example, Higginson (1990) describes multiple pathways for consumer involvement in a "family centre" situated on a housing estate in the United Kingdom. A regularly scheduled "users' meeting" provided key feedback on the mix of services/activities offered and identified avenues for future initiatives. On a larger scale, Cohen and Lavach (1995) described the Ventura (California) Children's Demonstration Project (Jordan & Hernandez 1990), which sought to create individually tailored, family-centered, community-based services for families with seriously emotionally handicapped children. This communitywide project brought together teams of professionals, representing the wide spectrum of services utilized by children with serious emotional handicaps, and parents, who bring their own particular expertise as full-time caregivers. Such projects illustrate the richness of environmental knowledge that is gained through full consumer participation. As Bernheim (1990; personal communication, 1992) notes, professionals, whatever the depth of their expertise, "know" emotionally disturbed children cross-sectionally through the aggregation of many clinical exchanges and through the accumulation of research studies. Parents, on the other hand, know one "big thing": their own child with emotional disturbance as seen through the prism of the most mundane aspects of daily life over the course of a lifetime. Successful interventions—with an individual or an entire community as in the Ventura project—will be those that seek to merge and blend these perspectives in all phases of intervention/evaluation design and implementation. It is no small leap to move from a view of parents as "empty vessels" (Weiss 1985), waiting to be filled with the latest child development information, to parents as possessors of a very special expertise essential to ecologically valid research and intervention.

Partnership, whether in participatory-action research or practice, will be difficult to achieve. Leaving aside the problems of potential compromises to research validity and reliability as well as the inevitable conflicts of power sharing, the idea of participatory-action research as suggested by Uehara and colleagues (1996) appears incredibly complex and time-consuming, including such "nontraditional" research activities as mutual consciousness-raising, empowerment, and historical analysis of problems. Many of these activities will likely fall outside the scope (and funding) of the grant or contract that stimulated the evaluation study. Nonetheless, we believe the goal of full and joint ownership of the knowledge development process should be pursued and that it ought to be seen as a specific exemplar of a more general move toward collaborative practice. For us, the demands of culturally competent and ecologically valid practice and research come together in the concept of the practitioner as personal scientist: engaged in continuous dialogue with the client to discover the meaning of environmental supports and challenges and working to extract hypotheses and insights to inform an ongoing research and evaluation process. We believe that the critical nature of this confluence of research and action cannot be overstated. Stokols (1995), a leading contemporary environmental psychologist, concluded his "author's response" to his earlier and comprehensive review of that field's body of research as follows:

> By encouraging theory development in the context of purposeful efforts to resolve social and environmental problems—epitomizing Lewin's (1946) notion of "action research"—environmental psychology will continue to generate novel theoretical and applied contributions and strengthen its distinctive identity and coherence in the 21st century. (1996, 1188)

In our quest to understand person-environment interaction, we encounter the truth of Dearborn's observation made years ago: "If you want to understand how something works, try and change it" (cited in Bronfenbrenner 1979, 40). Actions taken collaboratively with client-consumers to effect change and empowerment provide the crucible within which new insights on fundamental processes of human adaptation and change emerge. In a similar vein, we view each practitioner and each client as contributors to an ever-expanding knowledge base for P.E.P. and the corpus of theory and empirical research that supports it. In this we agree with Lewin and Dearborn and our more contemporary environmental psychology research colleagues. We believe that elevation of knowledge development activities generally, through collaborative models of research, is a necessary condition for increasing the volume of ecologically valid environmental knowledge and practice technology available to social workers. Knowledge development of itself, however, will not be sufficient to change practice. We also need a thorough, critical evaluation of the way we teach practice in professional social work education and the relationship between professional education and staff training in the overall continuum of knowledge dissemination.

THE CHALLENGE OF KNOWLEDGE DISSEMINATION

Some years ago, Bernard Neugeboren, professor of social work at Rutgers University, suggested in a letter to the editor of *Social Work* (1990) that clinical social work, with its emphasis on client-changing, may be inappropriate for the social problems confronted in public child welfare practice. Needed, he said, was a model of nonclinical practice that maximizes environmental supports through coordination of resources from both formal and informal community networks. This service delivery model would require skills in the arenas of politics, law, and negotiation where, the author speculated, clinically educated social workers had a "trained incapacity" to work. In a subsequent and richly illustrated text, Neugeboren (1996)—echoing Specht and Courtney (1994) among many others—calls for social work to return to its historic mission of environmental change. Neugeboren recognized the potential for integration of person-environment content in generalist models of practice. However, he cautioned that a rush to adopt generic practice approaches might blur key differences between micro- and macropractice. This, he felt, could actually retard the integration of environmental content into the knowledge base for practice because of the disproportionate influence of the more fully developed individual change models (1996, 10).

We share Neugeboren's concern about premature integration of micro-,meso-, and macropractice models, particularly as they are rendered in current generalist approaches. We have long argued that it is a large enough task to put the "social" back into social work practice with individuals, families, and small groups without *necessarily* linking that task with the development of an overall generalist practice formulation (Whittaker 1974; Whittaker & Tracy 1989). Moreover, we believe it is useful to discriminate between environmental lacunae in *some* approaches to "clinical practice" and what might be viewed as inherent limitations to incorporating environmental knowledge and skills in *any* direct or clinical practice approaches. As we have argued throughout this volume, our view of "environment" and "environmental intervention" is complex and intricately involved with individual and shared perceptions. Successful environmental interventions will involve much more than resource mobilization, linkage, and structural changes, important as these activities are. They will include, as well, perception shifts and

skillful individual work in "meaning making." They will require enhanced competence in teaching clients how to review their immediate
and more distal environments accurately and to shape them to meet
their needs.

Our work in social support and social network assessment with primary caregivers in high-risk families has strengthened our conviction
that work with client perceptions of environmental demands and resources is a critical element of environmental practice skill (Tracy &
Whittaker 1990; Tracy et al. 1994; Whittaker et al. 1994; see also Wahler
1990). In our view, it is misplaced concreteness to argue, as some have
done, that what clinical practice needs is a major transplant of meso- and
macropractice knowledge and skill to become more environmentally robust. We agree rather with the environmental practice skills formulation
laid out by Neugeboren (1996) ranging from micro to macro. As he
approaches the task from the perspective of organizational and
community-level practice, we work from a grounding in interpersonal
practice. Both traditions, in our judgment, will contribute to the final
development of a comprehensive body of knowledge of environmental
assessment and intervention relevant for all of social work practice.

What implications does the foregoing have for the way in which social
work practice is taught today? In our view, the increasing dominance of
generalist approaches to practice at the undergraduate and beginning
graduate level offers both opportunity and challenge for those who wish
to see a more environmentally oriented practice. Certainly, the early
introduction of a systemic perspective closely linked with a broad view
of multilevel practice protects against identifying the professional social
work role as either a narrowly clinical or solely a macropractice activity.
Moreover, the almost complete identification of entry-level bachelor's
practice with a generalist approach helps ensure that the foundation for
more advanced and specialized practice sequences—for example, in interpersonal practice—offers perspectives beyond the microlevel.

As practice teachers with considerable experience at both B.A.S.W.
and M.S.W. levels, we note that what is easy to affirm in principle is
often difficult to implement in practice. The challenge of presenting a
coherent, procedurally specific and helpful generalist course sequence
while avoiding the pitfalls of reductionism and superficiality continues
to concern us. As noted earlier, generalist practice formulations, for all
their attempts to broaden the scope of practice, often actually define it
disproportionately as direct service. We also observe that a generalist
formulation is neither a necessary nor a sufficient condition to ensure
the presence of relevant content on environmental assessment and intervention at any level. For example, a review of three representative generalist texts reveals that neither "environment" nor "environmental

intervention" appears in the index, and the treatment given to what might possibly be construed as environmental helping is either superficial or extremely limited. We realize that many forces shape the generalist/specialist debate within the profession. We believe the ascendancy of the generalist approach as a framework for introductory practice in social work has had some limited utility in expanding students' understanding of the scope of practice. We are concerned, however, about its uncritical expansion. We tend to agree with a British faculty colleague who, commenting on the similar stampede to generic practice in the United Kingdom, commented:

> Before any social work course is validated, the Central Council [akin to our Council on Social Work Education] must receive evidence that it is providing education across the full range of social work methods . . . in relation to a comprehensive range of client groups and needs. In practice, the majority of courses are not doing what is expected of them. . . . Nevertheless, they are being pressed to cram more and more into their courses and it is this pressure, more than anything else, that leads to the proliferation of curriculum papers, the prolongation of inspections and the intrusion of largely spurious educational theorising into social work teaching. (Pinker 1990, 9)

The author concludes:

> If I ever meet a truly "generic" social worker, I am sure I will feel like Oliver Goldsmith's village rustics, contemplating their schoolmaster. They:
>> " . . . ranged around;
>> And still they gazed, and still the wonder grew.
>> That one small head could carry all he knew."
>> (ibid., 10)

A profession clearly and rightly identified with multilevel, generalist practice in its whole should nonetheless allow for specialization in its parts. The work begun in this volume from the perspective of interpersonal practice and that undertaken by Neugeboren (1996) from the vantage point of macropractice needs to be refined and extended to derive a body of knowledge and skills for environmentally oriented practice spanning the continuum from micro to macro. Both traditions have something rich and distinctive to offer to such a knowledge base. As scholars of practice, we ought to resist the temptation to prematurely homogenize or otherwise simplify the diverse forms of environmental practice until we fully understand their meanings and purposes.

Finally, however well conceived, B.A.S.W. or M.S.W. education provides only a beginning base for practice. Lifelong learning is essential with the emergence of critical knowledge areas, such as AIDS and sub-stance abuse, and practice trends, such as the growth and impact of managed care. This means not only creating an expanded menu of train-ing materials in environmentally oriented practice, but elevating training as the primary postgraduate support for practitioners.

Much work remains to be done in translating the general principles and strategies of P.E.P. for use within the diverse methods and models of contemporary social work practice. For example, how will practice within a task-centered approach or a brief solution-focused approach vary the content and emphasis of environmental assessment and inter-vention? In some of our previous work in family preservation, for exam-ple, we found that differential rationales for examining social networks and social support were needed for workers operating from different theoretical orientations. For example, those operating from a cognitive-behavioral base saw the utility of social support identification in terms of maintenance of treatment objectives, whereas those operating from more structural perspectives saw the utility of the same material primari-ly in terms of understanding family boundaries.

As we have said, our goal in this initial volume on P.E.P. is to view interpersonal helping through the prism of environment and illustrate, selectively, some strategies for environmental assessment and interven-tion. We see a next phase of activity both for ourselves and the field as expanding our repertoire of environmental assessment and intervention skills and customizing them to fit the myriad of models and methods that make up contemporary social work practice. Continued work in practice theory development and innovative approaches to core and advanced social work practice education, together with high-quality staff training are, in our view, critical to move the field toward greater acceptance of environmental helping.

PROFESSIONAL, ORGANIZATIONAL, AND POLITICAL CHALLENGES FOR PERSON-ENVIRONMENT PRACTICE

Early in the family preservation debate in the United States, a very senior clinical social work practitioner, commenting on the mix of "con-crete" and "clinical" tasks within the intervention, observed that, al-though areas of ambiguity existed, at the very least it was evident that one thing graduate level social workers did *not* do was "clean ovens." A recent graduate replied, "I did just that only yesterday!" (P. Forsythe, personal communication, 1988). Indeed, the boundary-spanning nature of interventions like family preservation in terms of both the loci and foci of specific practice activity challenges traditional conceptions of professional role. Key questions are raised (Kinney et al. 1991; Whittaker et al. 1990):

- How is "partnership" achieved and maintained?
- How is "mutuality" made manifest?
- What are acceptable levels of client dependence?
- How is "reciprocity" carried out in a helping relationship?
- How is "confidentiality" operationalized?

In what we have earlier referred to as situated practice, the question of confidentiality poses interesting challenges as worker and client meet, not in the privacy of a secluded office, but in the hub of the client's living space—often with family members, friends, and neighbors present. On a somewhat broader level, what does the involvement of more gatekeepers and informal helpers in service provision signify for the client's right to privacy and confidentiality?

To a certain degree, the parameters of acceptable professional behavior and issues like confidentiality will be conditioned by the extent to which the practitioner is identified with the community he or she serves. The much studied "patch" approach from the United Kingdom offers one model for reducing the differences between the helpers and the helped in a human services context. Adams and Krauth describe the overall approach as a community-centered model of service delivery, wherein a locally based team of human service workers serves a limited geographical area (the "patch") with "accessible, flexible and holistic services based on their knowledge of the local cultural and physical environment and on the formal and informal partnerships they develop" (1995, 87). As the authors point out, patch came into being as a response to a national report (Seebohm 1968) critical of the fragmented and overspecialized social services system then present in Britain. It was further stimulated by the call in a second national report (Barclay Report 1982) for a new focus on "community social work," to replace the more narrowly drawn psychotherapeutic professional models (Hadley & McGrath 1984; Hadley & Young 1990). From the outset, patch and the closely related community social work have been controversial in Britain. Robert Pinker, who holds the chair of social work studies at the London School of Economics and Political Science and is a member of the original Barclay Working Party, argued several points strongly in a minority response to the working party's main report: first, that the clinical or "counselling" functions of social work should not be divorced from those having to do with more basic social care; second, that there were serious questions about prospects for local community-based social work teams without the political infrastructure to support them; and third, Pinker came down squarely on the side of specialist over generalist practice: Because of the enormous complexity, variety and range of needs calling for social work intervention, the case for specialization is self-evident (Pinker 1982).

Evaluations of the adaptation of the patch approach to U.S. social services (Adams & Krauth 1995) and other U.K.-based attempts to merge individual- and community-level practice (Smale 1995) are expected to shed light on the prospects of models of service organization compatible with environmentally oriented practice. The renewed interest in neighborhood as both a locus and focus for social work intervention (Baldwin 1993; Fisher 1994; Halpern 1995a, 1995b; Henderson & Thomas 1980; Naparstek, Biegel, & Spiro 1982; Neugeboren 1996; Payne 1995; Weil 1996) is welcome. The related family support movement provides excellent programmatic examples of both partnership and neighborhood-based environmentally oriented service delivery (Lightburn & Kemp 1994; Dunst, Trivette, & Deal 1994).

Overshadowing the professional debate over generalist vs. specialist practice, or alternative models of service organization, however, are the present realities of declining social service budgets and the growth of managed care initiatives. A director of a large urban local authority social services department in Britain observes that social service interests and social work interests are not necessarily the same thing. Citing an earlier critical work on the personal social services, the author notes:

> [S]ociety and the social work profession have different objectives and different interests. "The task allocated to the personal social services and to social work is primarily that of *exercising social control and providing a service of last resort—at a manageable cost* [emphasis added]. The objective is that of allowing decent citizens to sleep safely at night with easy consciences." (Webb & Wistrow 1987, 205, quoted in Bamford 1990, 160)

Bamford notes with some concern the trend both toward a "mixed economy" of service provision with multiple vendors and the uncoupling of professional social work from social service delivery—spurred in part by yet another commissioned report on social and health services in Britain (Griffiths Report 1988). Noting the resilience of the social work profession in the face of both declining resources and public outrage, he nonetheless expresses a deep concern about the future of public sector social service departments:

> If social work itself is in good heart it is difficult to be so sanguine about social services departments. Politically out of tune with the times, located in a sector of public service which is being progressively stripped of influence and power, and the subject of populist feeling about incompetence and interference, the departments increasingly resemble beached whales threshing about but ultimately doomed. (p. 166)

In our own (U.S.) context, one only need look at the recent backlash against family preservation services in particular, or child protection investigations in general to hear similar strains (Gelles 1996). We are greatly concerned by the confluence of a social service sector increasingly oriented toward managed care, with its irresistible tendencies toward problemization and medicalization, and the yet-to-be felt impact of recent welfare and social service recisions on the most vulnerable of clients. We fear both the effects of benefit cuts on needy clients and the identification of environmentally oriented, largely informally delivered "service" provision as a sort of panacea. To repeat what we strongly stated in the introduction to this volume, social services in any form are no substitute for the basics of adequate income, housing, health, and public safety. Within the area of service provision, we are enthusiastic proponents of informal helping and the use of volunteers and paraprofessionals. However, we in no sense view their contribution as a substitute for competent, high-quality professionally delivered services. Environmental intervention often requires the kind of sophisticated direct practice skill associated with a graduate-level social work or related human services professional. In an era of rapid change in virtually all aspects of social services—funding, organizational auspices, and diagnostic and interventive formulary—we must be vigilant against efforts to provide services "on the cheap" and be wary of any interpretation of "environmental helping" as a replacement for professionally delivered services.

In sum, we are aware that creating or restoring an environmental focus to interpersonal practice involves challenges on many different levels. At the client level, we need to distill the fruits of existing research and to create new knowledge to understand the diverse array of client groups whom social work serves and the multiplicity of environmental niches they inhabit. At the professional level, serious work is needed to ascertain and refine the precise nature of environmental intervention within the social work practice arena with its many models and methods. At the organizational level, supervisory and accountability structures in synchrony with P.E.P. are needed to nurture and support environmentally oriented practice. At the political level, individual practitioners and their professional associations must be vigilant against attempts to yoke a renewed focus on environmental helping with either budgetary recisions or antiprofessional initiatives. Finally, at the broadest level of societal values, social work must rethink its fundamental assumptions about client-worker relationships. As we move into what appears to be an era stressing responsibilities over rights and entitlements, we must distinguish between those responsibilities which are purely personal and those which are communal. The previously cited British social welfare theorist, Richard Titmuss (1968, 1974) believed it to be the objective of social policy to build the identity of a person around some community with which he or she is associated (Reisman 1977). Thus:

> [S]ocial policy accordingly ought to be seen as being concerned not simply with the relief of individual needs but with the furtherance of a sense of common citizenship (which necessitates common facilities and equality of access as of right and without the socially divisive stigma of a means test). (Reisman 1977, 69)

We wonder how many practitioners of social work today would view their role as furthering a "sense of common citizenship" as opposed to relieving pain or remediating social pathology. The present political climate seems far from supporting equality of access or universalist services (witness the recent fate of health care reform). We believe there is, however, a growing recognition that we must reduce social isolation and rethink such cherished cultural values as "privacy," if we are seriously to address critical problems such as domestic violence or child maltreatment.

We are unclear about the precise role of direct social work practice in achieving that end. Nevertheless, we remain as certain as Mary Richmond at the turn of the last century that we have a function to fulfill in achieving social integration that is complementary to and not subsumed by broad-scale, communitywide social reform efforts.

As we near the century's end, the very nature of citizenship in the post–cold war, postindustrial society is ripe for debate and redefinition. As usual, it is those at the margins of society—the poor and the vulnerable—who will provide the test of whatever social guarantees will carry forward into the next century. As usual, the issues and cleavages appear sharpest at the core of our great cities, although other disparities—for example, between the very old and the very young— transcend rural-urban boundaries. Bold initiatives for broad-scale reform are sorely needed and in short supply: the penetrating urban analysis and encompassing proposals of William Julius Wilson come to mind as an immediate exception to the general rule of limited expectations and satisfaction with changes at the margins (1980, 1987, 1996). As at the end of the previous century, we now stand at a critical juncture with respect to social provision of all kinds.

A POSTSCRIPT ON DIRECT PRACTICE

We wish to end this brief volume with a resounding affirmation of direct social work practice. We salute its many practitioners, who:

- minister daily to victims of abuse, neglect and family violence,
- bring hope and needed services to frail homebound elders,
- offer treatment to those suffering from major depression and other serious disorders,
- provide crisis intervention, life skills teaching, and concrete help to families at the brink of dissolution,
- help give voice to those suffering from oppression, discrimination, and marginalization in society,
- bring comfort, healing, and skillful intervention to those afflicted with cancer, AIDS, and other debilitating diseases,
- work in family support and other prevention initiatives, in concert with fellow professionals, to bring opportunity and hope to the very young and their families.

Taken together, these heroic individual efforts are, with the broad-scale reform efforts noted previously, what the social welfare historian, Clarke Chambers, refers to as "overlapping phases of a common enterprise" (1980, 20). They are, in fact, the "retail" side of social reform identified nearly a century ago by Mary Richmond, who saw, as she did so many other things, the critical link between what we would call today micro- and macropractice:

> The time has arrived . . . to put our young people to school at such retail methods of social service as will lead to fruitful generalizations later on and so back to their retail method of working out. The process must be got into their muscles early [and] include a thorough drill in doing small things well, for our present generation is drunk with big figures, and their instructors must understand the relation of small things to large. (1930, 220)

As teachers and scholars of direct practice, we accept the criticism that parts of direct practice have become overly identified with individual over social pathology (Specht & Courtney 1994). Indeed, that recognition was one of our primary stimuli to developing this present conception of person-environment practice. Our reading of the history of social work suggests that reformulations and midcourse corrections are integral to the direct practice tradition. We vehemently reject, however, attempts to stereotype all of direct service or its practitioners as "narrow," "overly clinical," or interested only in accommodation and adjustment at the expense of social transformation and environmental change. That is neither our reading of what direct practice is nor is it consistent with the views of the great architects of practice whose considerable earlier efforts have shaped our present work. We believe in our bones, as did Richmond and others who followed, not only that direct practice is a vital, life-sustaining and socially integrative activity of itself, but that it offers a critical and necessary ingredient in broad-scale social reform: it helps us to understand the relationship of "small things to large." Direct practice, properly recalibrated to focus on environments as well as the people who construct and inhabit them and those parts of social work identified with broader reform and change are for us distinctive yet integrally related parts of the whole.

For our part, we will continue to labor at "doing small things well."

NOTE

1. For a fuller explication of "participatory-action research," see Elden and Chisholm (1993), Greenwood, White, and Harkavy (1993), Simonson and Bushaw (1993), and Park (1992). These are from an annotated bibliography prepared by Susan A. Comerford and Oscar Carter (1993), available from the author. See also the subject bibliography prepared by Armstead and Cancian (1990), Freire (1970), and Lewin (1946).

References

Abbott, A. D. (1982). *The emergence of American psychiatry, 1880–1930*. Unpublished doctoral dissertation, University of Chicago.

Adams, P., & Krauth, K. (1995). Working with families and communities: The Patch approach. In P. Adams & K. Nelson (Eds.), *Reinventing human services: Community and family centered practice* (pp. 87–109). Hawthorne, NY: Aldine de Gruyter.

Adler, S., & Brenner, J. (1992). Gender and space: Lesbians and gay men in the city. *International Journal of Urban and Regional Research 16*, 24–34.

Agnew, J., & Duncan, R. (1989). *The power of place: Bringing together geographical and sociological imaginations*. Winchester, MA: Unwin Hyman.

Altman, I., & Christensen, K. (Eds.) (1990). *Environment and behavior studies: Emergence of intellectual traditions*. New York: Plenum.

Altman, I., & Churchman, A. (Eds.) (1994). *Women and the environment*. New York: Plenum.

Altman, I., & Wohlwill, J. F. (Eds.) (1978). *Children and the environment*. New York: Plenum.

Andrews, S. S. (1995). Life in Mendocino: A young man with Down Syndrome in a small town in northern California. In S. J. Taylor, R. Bogdan, & Z. M. Lutfiyya (Eds.), *The variety of community experience: Qualitative studies of family and community life* (pp. 101–192). Baltimore: Paul Brookes.

Angus, J. H. (1991). The Act: One year perspective on the Children, Young Persons and Their Families Act of 1989. *Social Work Review 3*, 5–6.

Antonovsky, A. (1979). *Health, stress, and coping*. San Francisco: Jossey-Bass.

Antonovsky, A. (1987). *Unraveling the mystery of health: How people manage stress and stay well*. San Francisco: Jossey-Bass,

Antonovsky, A. (1994). The sense of coherence: An historical and future perspective. In H. I. McCubbin, E. A. Thompson, A. I. Thompson, & J. E. Fromer (Eds.), *Sense of coherence and resiliency: Stress coping and health* (pp. 3–21). Madison: University of Wisconsin System.

Armstead, C., & Cancian, F. M. (1990). *A short annotated bibliography on participatory action research*. Department of Sociology, University of California at Irvine.

Atkin, B. (1991). New Zealand: Let the family decide. The new approach to family problems. *Journal of Family Law 29*(2), 387–397.

Auerswald, E. H. (1968). Interdisciplinary vs. ecological approach. *Family Process 7*(2), 202–215.

Austin, L. M. (1948). Trends in differential treatment in social casework. *Social Casework 29*(6), 203–211.

Bailey, D. (1992). Organizational change in a public school system: The synergism of two approaches. *Social Work in Education 14*, 94–105.

Bailey, D., & Koney, K. M. (1995). An integrative framework for the evaluation of community-based consortia. *Evaluation and Program Planning 18*, 245–252.

Baker, A., Barthelemy, K., & Kurdek, L. (1993). The relation between fifth and sixth graders' peer-related classroom social status and their perceptions of family and neighborhood factors. *Journal of Applied Developmental Psychology 14*, 547–556.

Baldassari, C., Lehman, S., & Wolfe, M. (1987). Imagining and creating alternative environments with children. In C. S. Weinstein & T. G. David (Eds.), *Spaces for children: The built environment and child development* (pp. 241–268). New York: Plenum.

Baldwin, S. (1993). *The myth of community care: An alternative neighborhood model of care.* London: Chapman & Hall.

Bamford, T. (1990). *The future of social work.* London: Macmillan.

Ban, P. (1993). Family decision making: The model as practiced in New Zealand and its relevance in Australia. *Australian Social Work 46*(3), 23–93.

Bannister, R. C. (1987). *Sociology and scientism: The American quest for objectivity, 1880–1940.* Chapel Hill: University of North Carolina Press.

Barclay Report: Social workers: Their roles and tasks. (1982). London: Bedford Square.

Barnard, R. E., Hammond, M., Mitchell, S. K., Booth, C. L., Speitz, A., Snyder, C., & Elsas, T. (1985). Caring for high risk infants and their families. In M. Green (Ed.), *The psychosocial aspects of the family* (pp. 245–266). Lexington, MA: D. C. Heath.

Barrera, M. (1988). Models of social support and life stress: Beyond the buffering hypothesis. In L. H. Cohen (Ed.), *Life events and psychological functioning: Theoretical and methodological issues* (pp. 211–236). Newbury Park: Sage.

Barsh, E. T., Moore, J. A., & Hamerlynck, L. A. (1983). The foster extended family: A support network for handicapped foster children. *Child Welfare 62*, 349–359.

Bartlett, H. M. (1970). *The common base of social work practice.* Washington, DC: National Association of Social Workers.

Beardslee, W. R. (1989). The role of self-understanding in resilient individuals: The development of a perspective. *American Journal of Orthopsychiatry 59*, 266–278.

Bechtel, R. B. (1986). Choice, control and Japanese and American responses to the environment. In W. H. Ittlelson, M. Asai, & M. Ker (Eds.). *Cross cultural research in environment and behavior* (pp. 29–49). Tucson: University of Arizona.

Bell, D. J. (1991). Insignificant others: Lesbian and gay geographies. *Area 23*, 323–329.

Bell, D. J., & Valentine, G. (Eds.) (1995). *Mapping desire: Geographies of sexualities.* New York: Routledge.

Bell, D. J., Vinnie, J., Cream, J., & Valentine, G. (1994). All hyped up and no place to go. *Gender, Place and Culture 1*(1), 31–47.

Belle, D. E. (1982). The impact of poverty on social networks and supports. *Marriage and Family Review 5*, 89–103.

Benard, B. (1993). Resiliency requires changing hearts and minds. *Western Center News 6*, 42–44.

Berenson, B. (1967). Considerations for behavioral research in architecture. In C. W. Taylor, R. Bailey, & C. H. H. Branc (Eds.), *Second National Conference on Architectural Psychology* (pp. 91–98). Salt Lake City: University of Utah.

Berger, P. L., & Luckmann, T. (1967). *The social construction of reality: A treatise in the sociology of knowledge.* New York: Anchor.

Berlin, R., & Davis, R. (1989). Children from alcoholic families: Vulnerability and resilience. In T. Dugan & R. Coles, (Eds.), *The child in our times: Studies in the development of resiliency* (pp. 81–105). New York: Brunner/Mazel.

Berlin, S. B. (1996). Constructivism and the environment: A cognitive-integrative perspective for social work practice. *Families in Society 77*, 326–335.

Berman-Rossi, T., & Miller, I. (1994). African-Americans and the settlements during the late nineteenth and early twentieth centuries. *Social Work with Groups 3*, 77–96.

Bernheim, K. F. (1989). Psychologists and families of the severely mentally ill: The role of family consultation. *American Psychologist 44*, 561–564.

Bernheim, K. F. (1990). Principles of professional and family collaboration. *Hospital and Community Psychiatry 41*, 1353–1355.

Biegel, D. E. (1987). Neighborhoods. In A. Minahan (Ed.), *Encyclopedia of social work* (vol. I, pp. 182–197). Silver Spring, MD: National Association of Social Workers.

Biegel, D. E., Shore, B. K., & Gordon, E. (1984). *Building support networks of the elderly: Theory and applications.* Newbury Park, CA: Sage.

Biegel, D., & Tracy, E. (1993). *Natural supports project.* Final Report to the Cuyahoga County Community Mental Health Board, Center for Practice Innovations, Mandel School of Applied Social Sciences, Case Western Reserve University, Cleveland.

Biegel, D., Tracy, E. M., & Corvo, K. N. (1994). Strengthening social networks: Intervention strategies for mental health case managers. *Health and Social Work 19*, 207–216

Biegel, D. E., Tracy, E. M., & Song, L. (1995). Barriers to social network interventions with persons with severe and persistent mental illness: A survey of mental health case managers. *Community Mental Health Journal 31*, 335–349.

Billingsley, A., & Giovannoni, J. (1972). *Children of the storm.* New York: Harcourt Brace.

Birt, C. J. (1956). Family-Centered Project of St. Paul. *Social Work 1*, 41–47.

Bisno, H. (1956). How social will social work be? *Social Work 1*, 12–18.

Black, W, G. (1991). Social work in World War I: A method lost. *Social Service Review 65*(3), 379–402.

Blunt, A., & Rose, G. (Eds.) (1994). *Writing women and space: Colonial and post-colonial geographies.* New York: Guilford.

Bohm, D. (1980). *On dialogue.* Ojai, CA: David Bohm Seminars.

Bondi, L., & Domosh, M. (1992). Other figures in other places: On feminism, postmodernism and geography. *Environment and Planning D: Society and Space 10,* 199–213.

Bonecutter, F. J., & Gleeson, J. P. (in press). Broadening our view: Lessons from kinship foster care. *Journal of Multicultural Social Work.*

Boyd, C., & Mast, D. (1983). Addicted women and their relationships with men. *Focus on Women: Journal of Addictions and Health 3,* 106–117.

Boyer, P. (1978). *Urban masses and moral order in America, 1829–1920.* Cambridge, MA: Harvard University Press.

Bradford, J., Ryan, C., & Rothblum, E. D. (1994). National Lesbian Health Care Survey: Implications for mental health care. *Journal of Consulting and Clinical Psychology 62*(2), 228–242.

Bradley, R. H. (1995). Environment and parenting. In M. H. Bornstein (Ed.), *Handbook of parenting* (vol. 2, pp. 235–261). Mahwah, NJ: Lawrence Erlbaum Associates.

Bradshaw, C., Soifer, S., & Gutièrrez, L. (1994). Toward a hybrid model for effective organizing in communities of color. *Journal of Community Practice 1,* 25–41.

Brager, G., & Holloway, S. (1978). *Changing human service organizations.* New York: Free Press.

Braziel, D. J. (Ed.) (1996). *Family-focused practice in out of home care: A handbook and resource directory.* Washington, DC: CWLA.

Breton, M. (1984). A drop-in program for transient women: Promoting competence through the environment. *Social Work 29,* 542–546.

Breton, M. (1994). Relating competence-promotion and empowerment, *Journal of Progressive Human Services 5,* 27–44.

Brewer, D. D., Hawkins, J. D., Catalano, R. F., & Neckerman, H. J. (1995). Preventing serious, violent, and chronic juvenile offending: A review of evaluations of selected strategies in childhood, adolescence, and the community. In J. C. Howell, B. Krisberg, J. D. Hawkins, & J. J. Wilson (Eds.) *Serious, violent, and chronic juvenile offenders* (pp. 61–141). Thousand Oaks, CA: Sage.

Briar, S. (1968). The casework predicament. *Social Work 13,* 5–11.

Briar, S., & Miller, H. (1971). *Problems and issues in social casework.* New York: Columbia University Press.

Brieland, D. (1990). The Hull-House tradition and the contemporary social worker: Was Jane Addams really a social worker? *Social Work 35,* 134–138.

Brodsky, A. E. (1996). Resilient single mothers in risky neighborhoods: Negative psychological sense of community. *Journal of Community Psychology 24*(4), 347–363.

Bronfenbrenner, U. (1977). Toward an experimental ecology of human development. *American Psychologist* (July), 513–531.

Bronfenbrenner, U. (1979). *The ecology of human development: Experiments by nature and design.* Cambridge, MA: Harvard University Press.

Bronfenbrenner, U. (1995). The bioecological model from a life course perspective: Reflections of a participant observer. In P. Moen, G. H. Elder, Jr., & K. Lüscher (Eds.), *Examining lives in context: Perspectives on the ecology of human development* (pp. 599–619). Washington, DC: American Psychological Association.

Brooks-Gunn, J., Duncan, G., Klebanov, P., & Sealand, N. (1993). Do neighborhoods influence child and adolescent development? *American Journal of Sociology 99*, 353–395.

Brown, K. S., & Ziefert, M. (1988). Crisis resolution, competence, and empowerment: A service model for women. *Journal of Primary Prevention 9*, 92–103.

Brown, P. (1991). Passing: Differences in our public and private self. *Journal of Multicultural Social Work 1*, 33–50.

Bruhn, J. G., & Philips, B. U. (1984). Measuring social support: A synthesis of current approaches. *Journal of Behavioral Medicine 7*, 151–167.

Bruner, J. (1990). *Acts of meaning.* Cambridge, MA: Harvard University Press.

Bryant, B., & Mohai, P. (1990). *Race and the incidence of environmental hazards: A time for discourse.* Boulder, CO: Westview.

Buell, J. B. (1922). Review of *What is social casework?. The Family 3*(3), 69–70.

Bullard, R. D. (Ed.) (1990). *Dumping in Dixie: Race, class, and environmental quality.* Boulder, CO: Westview.

Bullard, R. D. (1994). Environmental justice for all. In R. D. Bullard (Ed.). *Unequal protection: Environmental justice and communities of color* (pp. 3–22). San Francisco: Sierra Club Books.

Burford, G., & Pennell, J. (1995). *Family group decision-making project: Implementation report summary.* Available from Memorial University of Newfoundland, School of Social Work, St. John's, Newfoundland, Canada A1C 5S7.

Carling, P. J. (1995). *Return to community: Building support systems for people with psychiatric disabilities.* New York: Guilford.

Center for Urban Affairs and Policy Research. (1988). *Getting connected: How to find out about groups and organizations in your neighborhoods.* Evanston, IL: Author.

Chambers, C. (1980). Social service and social reform: A historical essay. In F. R. Bruel & S. J. Diner (Eds.), *Compassion and responsibility: Readings in the history of social welfare policy in the United States* (pp. 14–28). Chicago: University of Chicago Press.

Chasteen, A. L. (1994). "The world around me": The environment and single women. *Sex Roles 31*, 309–328.

Chavis, D., Hogge, J. H., McMillan, D. W., & Wandersman, A. (1986). Sense of community through Brunswik's lens: A first look. *American Journal of Community Psychology 14*, 24–40.

Chavis, D., & Wandersman, A. (1990). Sense of community in the urban environment: A catalyst for participation and community development. *American Journal of Community Psychology 14*, 24–40.

Cleveland Foundation Commission on Poverty (1992). *The Cleveland community building initiative.* Cleveland, OH: Mandel School of Applied Social Sciences.

Cloward, R., & Epstein, I. (1965). Private social welfare's disengagement from the poor: The case of the family adjustment agencies. In M. Zald (Ed.), *Social welfare institutions* (pp. 623–644). New York: John Wiley.

Cobb, E. (1977). *The ecology of imagination in childhood*. New York: Columbia University Press.

Cochran, M. M., & Brassard, J. A. (1979). Child development and personal social networks. *Child Development 50*, 601–616.

Cochran, M., & Niego, S. (1995). Parenting and social networks. In M. H. Bornstein (Ed.), *Handbook of parenting* (vol. 3, pp. 393–418). Mahwah, NJ: Lawrence Erlbaum Associates

Cohen, R., & Lavach, C. (1995). Strengthening partnerships between families and service providers. In P. Adams & K. Nelson (Eds.). *Reinventing Human Services: community and family centered practice* (pp. 261–277). Hawthorne, NY: Aldine de Gruyter.

Cohen, S., & Wills, T. A. (1985). Stress, social support and the buffering hypothesis. *Psychological Bulletin 98*, 310–357.

Collins, A. H. (1983). Rebuilding refugee networks. In D. L. Pancoast, P. Parker, & C. Froland (Eds.), *Rediscovering self-help: Its role in social care* (pp. 53–66). Beverly Hills: Sage.

Collins, A. H., & Pancoast, D. L. (1976). *Natural helping networks: A strategy for prevention*. Washington DC: National Association of Social Workers

Collins, P. H. (1986). Learning from the outsider within: The social significance of black feminist thought. *Social Problems 33*, 14–32.

Colomina, B. (Ed.) (1992). *Sexuality and space*. New York: Princeton Architectural.

Comerford, S., & Carter, O. (1993). *Annotated bibliography on participatory action research*. Mandel School of Applied Social Sciences, Case Western Reserve University, Cleveland, OH.

Congress, E. P. (1994). The use of culturalgrams to assess and empower culturally diverse families. *Families in Society 75*, 531–540.

Conti, G., Counter, J., & Paul, L. (1991). Transforming a community through research. *Convergence 24*, 3, 31–40.

Cook, D. A., & Fine, M. (1995). Motherwit : Childrearing lessons from African American mothers of low income. In B. B. Swadener & S. Lubeck (Eds.), *Children and families "at promise": Deconstructing the discourse of risk* (pp. 118–141). Albany: State University of New York Press.

Cormier, W. H., & Cormier, L. S. (1991). *Interviewing strategies for helpers: Fundamental skills and cognitive behavioral interventions* (3rd ed.). Pacific Grove, CA: Brooks/Cole.

Corrigan, E. M. (1991). Psychosocial factors in women's alcoholism. In N. Van Den Bergh (Ed.), *Feminist perspectives on addictions* (pp. 61–71). New York: Springer.

Coulton, C. J., Korbin, J. E., & Su, M. (1996). Measuring neighborhood context for young children in an urban area. *American Journal of Community Psychology 24*, 1, 5–32.

Coulton, C. J., Korbin, J. E., Su, M., & Chow, J. (1995). Community level factors and child maltreatment rates, *Child Development 66*, 1262–1276.

Coulton, C. J., Pandey, S., & Chow, J. (1990). Concentration of poverty and the changing ecology of low-income urban neighborhoods: An analysis of the Cleveland area. *Social Work Research and Abstracts 26*, 4, 5–16.

Courtney, M. (1992). Psychiatric social workers and the early days of private practice. *Social Service Review 66*, 199–214.

Cowen, E. L. (1994). The enhancement of psychological wellness: Challenges and opportunities. *American Journal of Community Psychology 22*, 149–179.

Cowen, E. L., Wyman, P. A., Work, W. C., & Parker, G. (1990). The Rochester Child Resiliency Project: Overview and summary of first year findings. *Development and Psychopathology 2*, 193–212.

Cowger, C. D. (1994). Assessing client strengths: Clinical assessment for client empowerment. *Social Work 39*, 262–268.

Cowger, C. D. (1996). Assessment of client strengths. In D. Saleebey (Ed.), *The strengths perspective in social work practice* (2nd. ed., pp. 59–73). New York: Longman.

Cox, E. O. (1991). The critical role of social action in empowerment-oriented groups. *Social Work with Groups 14*, 77–107.

Cox, E. O., & Parsons, R. J. (1994). *Empowerment-oriented social work practice with the elderly.* Pacific Grove, CA: Brooks/Cole.

Coyle, G. L. (1947). *Group experience and democratic values.* New York: Women's Press.

Crosby, C., & Barry, M. M. (1995). *Community care: Evaluation of the provision of mental health services.* Brookfield, VT: Avebury.

Cutler, D. L., & Tatum, E. (1983). Networks and the chronic patient. In D. L. Cutler (Ed.), *Effective aftercare for the 1980s.* (New directions for mental health services, No. 19, pp. 13–22). San Francisco: Jossey-Bass.

Cutter, S. (1995). Race, class and environmental justice. *Progress in Human Geography 19*, 111–122.

Daly, A., Jennings, J., Beckett, J. O., & Leashore, B. R. (1996). Effective coping strategies of African Americans. In P. L. Ewalt, E. M. Freeman, S. A. Kirk, & D. L. Poole (Eds.), *Multicultural issues in social work* (pp. 189–203). Washington DC: National Association of Social Workers.

David, T. G., & Weinstein, C. S. (1987). The built environment and children's development. In C. S. Weinstein & T. G. David (Eds.), *Spaces for children: The built environment and child development* (pp. 3–18). New York: Plenum.

Davis, A. F. (1967). *Spearheads for reform; the social settlements and the progressive movement, 1890–1914.* New York: Oxford University Press.

Davis, L. (1991). Violence and families. *Social Work 36*, 371–373.

Day, F. R. (1937). Changing practices in case work treatment. *Family 18*, 3–9.

DeJong, P., & Miller, S. D. (1995). How to interview for client strengths. *Social Work 40*, 729–736.

Delgado, M. (1996). Community asset assessments by Latino youths. *Social Work in Education 18*, 169–178.

DeParle, J. (1994). Better work than welfare: But what if there's neither? *New York Times Magazine* (December 18), 42–49, 56, 58, 74.

Devine, E. T. (1910). *Social forces.* New York: Charities Publication Committee.

Devore, W., & Schlesinger, E. G. (1996). *Ethnic-sensitive social work practice* (4th ed.). Boston: Allyn and Bacon.

Dodd, P., & Gutiérrez, L. (1990). Preparing students for the future: A power perspective on community practice. *Administration in Social Work 14*, 2, 63–78.

DuBois, B., & Miley, K. K. (1996). *Social work: An empowering profession*. Boston: Allyn and Bacon.

Dumas, J. E., & Wahler, R. G. (1983). Predictors of treatment outcome in parent skills training: Mother insularity and socioeconomic disadvantage. *Behavioral Assessment 5*, 301–313.

Dunn, P. L. (1995). Volunteer management. In *Encyclopedia of Social Work* (19th ed., Volume 3, pp. 2483–2490). Washington, DC: National Association of Social Workers.

Dunst, C. J. (1994). *Family-centered practice: Beyond rhetoric toward better operationalization*. Paper presented at the 11th Annual Smokey Mountain Winter Institute, Asheville, NC, March.

Dunst, C. J. & Trivette, C. M. (1986). Looking beyond the parent-child dyad for the determinants of maternal styles of interaction. *Infant Mental Health Journal 7*, 69–80.

Dunst, C. J., Trivette, C. M., & Deal, A. G. (1988). *Enabling and empowering families: Principles and guidelines for practice*. Cambridge: Brookline Books.

Dunst, C. J., Trivette, C. M., & Deal, A. G. (1994). *Supporting and strengthening families*. Cambridge: Brookline Books.

Dyck, I. (1995). Hidden geographies: The changing lifeworlds of women with multiple sclerosis. *Social Science and Medicine 40*, 3, 307–320.

D'Augelli, A. R., & Ehrlich, R. P. (1982). Evaluation of a community-based system of training for natural helpers. II. Effects of informal helping activities. *American Journal of Community Psychology 10*, 447–455.

Egan, T. (1995). Many seek security behind walls and guards of private community. *New York Times*, September 3, p. 1.

Ehrenreich, J. H. (1985). *The altruistic imagination: A history of social work and social policy in the United States*. Ithaca, NY: Cornell University Press.

Elden, M., & Chisholm, R. F. (1993). Emerging varieties of action research. *Human Relations 46*, 121–141.

Elder, G. H. (Ed.) (1985). *Life course dynamics: trajectories and transitions*. Ithaca, NY: Cornell University Press.

Elliot, D. S., Wilson, W. J., Huizinga, D., Sampson, R. J., Elliot, A., & Rankin, B. (1996). The effects of neighborhood disadvantage on adolescent development. *Journal of Research in Crime and Delinquency 33*(4), 389–426.

Ellis, S. J. (1994). *The volunteer recruitment book*. Philadelphia: Energize.

Epstein, B. (1995). *Grassroots environmentalism and strategies for social change*. Unpublished paper presented at the New Social Movements and Community Organizing Conference, University of Washington, Seattle.

Etzioni, A. (1993). *The spirit of community*. New York: Crown.

Evans, S. M., & Boyte, H. C. (1986). *Free spaces: The sources of democratic change in America*. Chicago: University of Chicago Press.

Fahlberg, V. I. (1991). *A child's journey through placement*. Indianapolis, IN: Perspectives.

Feagin, J. R., & Sikes, M. P. (1994). *Living with racism: The black middle-class experience*. Boston: Beacon.

Feldman, R. M., & Stall, S. (1994). The politics of space appropriation: A case study of women's struggles for homeplace in Chicago public housing. In I. Altman & A. Churchman (Eds.), *Women and environment* (pp. 167–199). New York: Plenum.

Ferguson, S. A., Tracy, E. M. & Simonnelli, D. (1992). *Parent Network Project Manual: Training Head Start Parent Advisors to Strengthen the Social Support Systems of Low-Income Parents*. Center for Practice Innovations, Mandel School of Applied Social Sciences.

Fetterman, D. M. (1994). Steps of empowerment evaluation: From California to Cape Town. *Evaluation and Program Planning 17*, 305–313.

Finkelstein, N., Duncan, S. A., Derman, L., & Smeltz, J. (1990). *Getting sober, getting well: A treatment guide for caregivers who work with women*. Cambridge, MA: The Women's Alcoholism Program of CASPAR.

Finn, J. (1994). The promise of participatory research. *Journal of Progressive Human Services 5*, 25–42.

Fischer, C. S. (1982). *To dwell among friends: Personal networks in Town and City*. Chicago: University of Chicago Press.

Fischer, J. (1973a). Is casework effective? A review. *Social Work 18*, 5–20.

Fischer, J. (1973b). Has mighty casework struck out? *Social Work 18*, 107–109.

Fischer, J. (1975). *The effectiveness of social casework*. Springfield, IL: Charles C. Thomas.

Fisher, R. (1994). *Let the people decide: Neighborhood organizing in America*. New York: Twayne.

Flexner, A. (1915). Is social work a profession? *Proceedings of the National Conference of Charities and Correction* (pp. 576–590). Chicago: Hildemann.

Foucault, M. (1980). *Power/knowledge: Selected interviews and other writings*. New York: Pantheon.

Franklin, C., & Jordan, C. (1992). Teaching students to perform assessments. *Journal of Social Work Education 28*, 222–241.

Franklin, C., & Nurius, P. S. (1996). Constructivist therapy: New directions in social work practice. *Families in Society 77*, 323–325.

Franklin, D. L. (1988). Race, class and adolescent pregnancy: An ecological analysis. *American Journal of Orthopsychiatry 58*, 339–354.

Franklin, D. L. (1990). The cycles of social work practice: Social action vs. individual interest. *Journal of Progressive Human Services 1*, 59–81.

Fraser, M. W., & Hawkins, J. D. (1984). The social networks of opioid abusers. *International Journal of Addictions 19*, 903–917.

Fraser, M. W., Pecora, P. J., & Haapala, D. (1991). *Families in crisis: The impact of intensive family preservation services*. Hawthorne, NY: Aldine de Gruyter.

Freedberg, S. (1984). *Bertha Capen Reynolds: A woman struggling in her times*. Unpublished doctoral dissertation, Columbia University School of Social Work, New York.

Freeman, E. M. (1996). Welfare reforms and services for children and families: Setting a new practice, research, and policy agenda. *Social Work 41*, 521–532.

Freire, P. (1970). *Pedagogy of the oppressed*. New York: Seabury.

Freire, P. (1973). *Education for critical consciousness*. New York: Seabury.

Friedland, R., & Boden, D. (Eds.) (1994). *NowHere: Space, time and modernity.* Berkeley, CA: University of California Press.

Froland, C., Pancoast, D., Chapman, N.. & Kimboko, P. (1981). *Helping networks and human services.* Beverly Hills, CA: Sage Publications.

Gambrill, E. (1990). *Critical thinking in clinical practice: Improving the accuracy of judgments and decisions about clients.* San Francisco, CA: Jossey-Bass.

Gambrill, E., & Richey, C. A. (1988). *Taking charge of your social life.* Berkeley, CA: Behavioral Options.

Garbarino, J. (1977). The price of privacy: An analysis of the social dynamics of child abuse. *Child Welfare 56,* 565–575.

Garbarino, J. (1981). *Children and families in the social environment.* New York: Aldine de Gruyter.

Garbarino, J. (1983). Social support networks: Rx for the helping professions. In J. K. Whittaker, J. Garbarino, & Associates, *Social support networks: Informal helping in the human services* (pp. 3–28). New York: Aldine de Gruyter.

Garbarino, J. (1993). Presentation at Columbia University School of Social Work, New York, May.

Garbarino, J., & Kostelny, K. (1993). Neighborhood and community influences on parenting. In T. Luster & L. Okagaki (Eds.), *Parenting: An ecological perspective* (pp. 203–226). Hillsdale, NJ: Erlbaum Associates.

Garbarino, J., Kostelny, K., & Dubrow, N. (1991). *No place to be a child: Growing up in a war zone.* Lexington, MA: Lexington Books.

Gardner, C. B. (1990). Safe conduct: Women, crime and self in public places. *Social Problems 37,* 311–328.

Garmezy, N. (1985). Stress-resistant children: The search for protective factors. In J. E. Stevenson (Ed.), *Journal of Child Psychology and Psychiatry: Recent research in developmental psychopathology* (Book Suppl. No. 4, 213–233). Oxford: Pergamon.

Garmezy, N. (1993). Children in poverty: Resilience despite risk. *Psychiatry 56,* 127–136.

Garmezy, N., & Masten, A. S. (1994). Chronic adversities. In M. Rutter, E. Taylor, & L. Hersov (Eds.), *Child and adolescent psychiatry.* Oxford: Blackwell.

Garvin, C. D. & Seabury, B. A. (1997). *Interpersonal practice in social work: Promoting competence and social justice* (2nd ed.). Boston: Allyn and Bacon.

Gaudin, J. M., & Polansky, N. (1986). Social distancing of the neglectful family: Sex, race, and social class influences. *Children and Youth Services Review 8,* 1–12.

Gaudin, J. M., Wodarski, J. S., Arkinson, M. K., & Avery, L. S. (1990/1991). Remedying child neglect: Effectiveness of social network interventions. *Journal of Applied Social Sciences 15,* 97–123.

Geertz, C. (1983). *Local knowledge: Further essays in interpretive anthropology.* New York: Basic Books.

Gelles, R. (1996). *Son of David.* New York: Holt, Rinehart, & Winston.

Germain, C. B. (1968). Social study: Past and future. *Social Casework 49,* 403–409.

Germain, C. B. (1971). Casework and science: An historical encounter. In R. W. Roberts, & R. H. Nee (Eds.), *Theories of social casework* (pp. 3–32). Chicago: University of Chicago Press.

Germain, C. B. (1976). Time: An ecological variable in social work practice. *Social Casework 57*, 419–426.

Germain, C. B. (1978). Space: An ecological variable in social work practice. *Social Casework 59*, 515–522.

Germain, C. B. (1979). Introduction: Ecology and social work. In C. B. Germain (Ed.), *Social work practice: People and environments* (pp. 103–124). New York: Free Press.

Germain, C. B. (1980). Social context of clinical social work. *Social Work 25*, 483–438.

Germain, C. B. (1981a). Teaching primary prevention in social work: An ecological perspective. *Journal of Education for Social Work 18*, 20–28.

Germain, C. B. (1981b). The physical environment in social work practice. In A. N. Maluccio (Ed.), *Promoting competence in clients: A new/old approach to social work practice* (pp. 103–124). New York: Free Press.

Germain, C. B. (1983). Using physical and social environments. In A. Rosenblatt & D. Waldfogel (Eds.), *Handbook of clinical social work* (pp. 110–133). San Francisco: Jossey-Bass.

Germain, C. B., & Gitterman, A. (1980). *The life model of social work practice*. New York: Columbia University Press.

Germain, C. B., & Gitterman, A. (1987). Ecological perspective. In A. Minahan (Ed.), *Encyclopedia of social work* (vol. 1, pp. 488–499). Silver Spring, MD: National Association of Social Workers.

Germain, C. B., & Gitterman, A. (1995). Ecological perspective. In R. L. Edwards & J. G. Hopps (Ed.), *Encyclopedia of social work* (pp. 816–824). Silver Spring, MD: National Association of Social Workers.

Germain, C. B., & Gitterman, A. (1996) *The life model of social work practice: Advances in theory and practice* (2nd ed.). New York: Columbia University Press.

Gesler, W. M. (1992). Therapeutic landscapes: Medical issues in light of the new cultural geography. *Social Science in Medicine 34*, 735–746.

Gibbs, L. E., & Gambrill, E. (1996). *Critical thinking for social workers: A workbook*. Thousand Oaks, CA: Pine Forge.

Gilgun, J. F. (1994). An ecosystemic approach to assessment. In B. A. Compton & B. Galaway (Eds.), *Social work processes* (pp. 380–394). Pacific Grove, CA: Brooks/Cole.

Gilgun, J. F., Daly, D., & Handel, G. (Eds.) (1992). *Qualitative methods in family research*. Newbury Park, CA: Sage.

Gitterman, A., & Germain, C. B. (1976). Social work practice: A life model. *Social Service Review 50*, 601–610.

Gitterman, A., & Shulman, L. (Eds.) (1986). *Mutual aid groups and the life cycle*. Itasca, IL: Peacock.

Glynn, T. J., (1986). Neighborhood and sense of community. *Journal of Community Psychology 14*, 341–352.

Goldman, B. (1996). What is the future of environmental justice? *Antipode 28*, 122–141.

Goldstein, E. G. (1984). Ego psychology and social work practice. New York: Free Press.

Gordon, W. E. (1969). Basic constructs for an integrative and generative conception of social work. In G. Hearn (Ed.), *The general systems approach: Contributions towards an holistic conception of social work.* New York: Council on Social Work Education.

Gottlieb, B. H. (1983). *Social support strategies.* Beverly Hills, CA: Sage.

Gottlieb, B. H. (1985). Social support and community mental health. In S. Cohen & S. L. Syme (Eds.), *Social support and health* (pp. 303–326). Orlando, FL: Academic.

Gottlieb, B. H., & Coppard, A. E. (1987). Using social network therapy to create support systems for the chronically mentally disabled. *Canadian Journal of Community Mental Health 6,* 117–131.

Gould, K. H. (1987). Life model vs. conflict model: A feminist perspective. *Social Work 32,* 346–351.

Graebner, W. (1991). *The age of doubt: American thought and culture in the 1940s.* Boston: Twayne Publishers.

Granvold, D. K. (1996). Constructivist psychotherapy. *Families in Society 77,* 345–357.

Grasso, A., & Epstein, I. (1992). *Research utilization in the human services.* New York: Haworth.

Green, J. W. (1995). Cultural awareness in the human services: A multi-ethnic approach (2nd ed.). Boston: Allyn and Bacon.

Green, J. W., & Leigh, J. W. (1989). Teaching ethnographic methods to social service workers. *Practicing Anthropology 11,* 8–10

Greenwood, D. J., White, W. F., & Harkavy, I. (1993). Participatory action research as a process and a goal. *Human Relations 46,* 175–192.

Greenwood, E. (1957). Attributes of a profession. *Social Work 2,* 45–55.

Gregory, D. (1994). *Geographical imaginations.* Cambridge, MA: Blackwell.

Greif, G. L., & Lynch, A. A. (1983). The eco-systems perspective. In C. H. Meyer (Ed.), *Clinical social work in the eco-systems perspective* (pp. 35–71). New York: Columbia University Press.

Griffiths report: Community care: Agenda for action. (1988). London: HMSO.

Grinnell, R. M. (1973). Environmental modification: Casework's concern or casework's neglect? *Social Service Review 47,* 208–220.

Grinnell, R. M., & Kyte, N. S. (1974). Modifying the environment. *Social Work 19,* 477–483.

Grinnell, R. M., & Kyte, N. S. (1975). Environmental modification: A study. *Social Work 20,* 313–318.

Groze, V. (1996). *Successful adoptive families: A longitudinal study of special needs adoption.* Westport, CT: Praeger.

Gutheil, I. A. (1992). Considering the physical environment: an essential component of good practice. *Social Work 37*(5), 391–396.

Gutheil, I. A. (1996). Using the agency's physical environment as a practice tool. *Smith College Studies in Social Work 66,* 185–199.

Gutiérrez, L. M. (1990). Working with women of color: An empowerment perspective. *Social Work 35,* 149–153.

Gutiérrez, L. M. (1996). Understanding the empowerment process: Does consciousness make a difference? In P. L. Ewalt, E. M. Freeman, S. A. Kirk, &

D. L. Poole (Eds.), *Multicultural Issues in Social Work* (pp. 43–59). Washington, DC: National Association of Social Workers.

Gutiérrez, L. M., DeLois, K. A., & GlenMaye, L. (1995). The organizational context of empowerment practice: Implications for social work administration. *Social Work 40*, 249–258.

Gutiérrez, L. M., & Lewis, E. (in press). *Empowering women of color.* New York: Columbia University Press.

Gutiérrez, L. M., & Ortega, R. (1991). Developing methods to empower Latinos: the importance of groups. *Social Work with Groups 14*, 23–43.

Hadley, R., & McGrath, M. (1984). *When social services are local: The Normanton experience.* London: George Allen & Unwin.

Hadley, R., & Young, K. (1984). *Crating a responsive public service.* Hemel Hempstead: Harvester Wheatsheaf.

Haggerty, R. J., Sherrod, L. R., Garmezy, N., & Rutter, M. (1994). Stress, risk, and resilience in children and adolescents. Cambridge: Cambridge University Press.

Hall, J. (1963). Status and social change. *Social Work 9*, 107–108.

Halpern, R. (1993). Neighborhood-based initiatives to address poverty: Lessons from experience. *Journal of Sociology and Social Welfare 20*, 111–135.

Halpern, R. (1995a). Children on the edge: an essay review. *Social Service Review* (March), 131–151.

Halpern, R. (1995b). Neighborhood-based services in low income neighborhoods: A brief history. In P. Adams & K. Nelson (Eds.), *Reinventing human services: Community and family-centered practice* (pp. 19–41). Hawthorne, NY: Aldine de Gruyter.

Halpern, R. (1995c). *Rebuilding the inner city: A history of neighborhood initiatives to address poverty in the United States.* New York: Columbia University Press.

Hamilton, G. (1940). *Theory and practice of social casework.* New York: Columbia University Press.

Hamilton, G. (1951). *Theory and practice of social casework* (2nd ed.). New York: Columbia University Press.

Hamilton, G. (1958). A theory of personality: Freud's contribution to social work. In H. G. Parad (Ed.), *Ego psychology and dynamic casework* (pp. 11–37). New York: Family Service Association of America.

Hammelman, T. L. (1993). Gay and lesbian youth: Contributing factors to serious considerations of suicide. *Journal of Gay and Lesbian Psychotherapy 2*, 77–89.

Hammer, M. (1981). Social supports, social networks, and schizophrenia. *Schizophrenia Bulletin 7*, 45–57.

Hansen, W. B., & Altman, I. (1976). Decorating personal places. *Environment and Behavior 8*, 491–504.

Haraway, D. (1988). Situated knowledges: The science question in feminism and the privilege of a partial perspective. *Feminist Studies 14*, 575–598.

Harding, S. (1986). *The science question in feminism.* Ithaca, NY: Cornell University Press.

Hardy, K. V., & Laszloffy, T. A. (1995). The cultural genogram: Key to training culturally competent family therapists. *Journal of Marital and Family Therapy 21*, 227–237.

Hart, M. U. (1990). Liberation through consciousness raising. In J. Mezirow & Associates (Eds.), *Fostering critical reflection in adulthood* (pp. 47–73). San Francisco: Jossey-Bass.

Hart, R. (1979). *Children's experiences of place*. New York: Irvington.

Hartman, A. (1970). To think about the unthinkable. *Social Casework 51*, 467–474.

Hartman, A. (1972). *Casework in crisis, 1932–1941*. Unpublished doctoral dissertation, Columbia University School of Social Work, New York.

Hartman, A. (1978). Diagrammatic assessment of family relationships. *Social Casework 59*, 465–476.

Hartman, A. (1992). In search of subjugated knowledge. *Social Work 37*, 483–484.

Hartman, A. (1994). Diagrammatic assessment of family relationships. In B. R. Compton & B. Galaway (Eds.), *Social work processes* (pp. 154–165). Pacific Grove, CA: Brooks/Cole.

Hartman, A., & Laird, J. (1983). *Family-centered social work practice*. New York: Free Press.

Hartmann, H. (1958). *Ego psychology and the problem of adaptation* (trans. D. Rapaport). New York: International Universities Press.

Harvey, D. (1989). *The condition of postmodernity*. Cambridge, MA: Basil Blackwell.

Hashimi, J. K. (1981). Environmental modification: Teaching social coping skills. *Social Work 26*, 323–326.

Hatfield, A. B. (1978). Psychological costs of schizophrenia to the family. *Social Work 23*, 355–359.

Hatfield, A. B. (Ed.) (1994). *Family interventions in mental illness*. San Francisco: Jossey-Bass.

Havassy, B. E., Hall, S. M., & Tschann, J. M. (1987). Social support and relapse to tobacco, alcohol and opiates. In *Problems of drug dependence* (NIDA Research Monograph No. 76). Rockville, MD: National Institute on Drug Abuse.

Hawkins, J. D., Catalano, R. F., & Miller, J. Y. (1992). Risk and protective factors for alcohol and other drug problems in adolescence and early adulthood: Implications for substance abuse prevention. *Psychological Bulletin 112*, 64–105.

Hawkins, J. D., & Fraser, M. W. (1983). Social support networks in treating drug abuse. In J. K. Whittaker & J. Garbarino (Eds.), *Social support networks: Informal helping in the human services* (pp. 357–380). Hawthorne, NY: Aldine de Gruyter.

Hawkins, J. D., & Fraser, M. W. (1985). The social networks of street drug users: A comparison of descriptive propositions from control and differential association theories. *Social Work Research and Abstracts 21*, 3–12.

Heiman, M. (1996). Race, waste and class: New perspectives on environmental justice. *Antipode 28*, 111–121.

Hekman, S. (1997). Truth and method: Feminist standpoint theory revisited. *Signs 22*(2), 341–365.

Heller, K., & Swindle, R. W. (1983). Social networks, perceived social support and coping with stress. In R. D. Felner, L. A. Jason, J. Moritsugu, & S. S. Farber (Eds.), *Preventive psychology: Theory, research and practice* (pp. 87–103). New York: Pergamon.

Henderson, P., & Thomas, D. N. (1980). *Skills in neighborhood work*. London: George Allen & Unwin.

Hepworth, D. H. (1993). Managing manipulative behavior in the helping relationship. *Social Work 38*(6), 674–684.

Hepworth, D. H., & Larsen, J. A. (1993). *Direct social work practice: Theory and skills* (4th ed.). Pacific Grove, CA: Brooks/Cole.

Herr, K. (1995). Action research as an empowering process. *Journal of Progressive Human Services 6*, 45–58.

Higginson, J. (1990). Partners not problems: Developing new roles for staff and consumers. In G. Darvill, G. Smale, A. Cooper, D. Eastham, J. Higginson, M. Howard, J. Griffin, T. Ross, J. Taylor, G. Croft, B. Lawson, I. Smith, & G. Tuson (Eds.), *Partners in empowerment: Networks of innovation in social work*. London: National Institute for Social Work.

Hodges, V. G. (1991). Providing culturally sensitive intensive family preservation services to ethnic minority families. In E. M. Tracy, D. A. Haapala, J. Kinney, & Pecora, P. J. (Eds.), *Intensive family preservation services: An instructional sourcebook* (pp. 95–116). Cleveland: Mandel School of Applied Social Sciences.

Hoff, M. D., & Rogge, M. E. (1996). Everything that rises must converge: Developing a social work response to environmental injustice. *Journal of Progressive Human Services 7*, 41–57.

Hofrichter, R. (1993). *Toxic struggles: The theory and practice of environmental justice*. Philadelphia: New Society.

Hofstadter, R. (1955). *The age of reform*. New York: Vintage.

Holahan, C. J., Wilcox, B. L., Spearly, J. L., & Campbell, M. D. (1979). The ecological perspective in community mental health. *Community Mental Health Review 4*, 1–9.

Hollander, J. (1989). Restructuring lesbian social networks: Evaluation of an intervention. *Journal of Gay and Lesbian Psychotherapy 1*, 63–71.

Hollis, F. (1949). The techniques of casework. *Social Casework 30*, 235–244.

Hollis, F. (1951). The relationship between psychosocial diagnosis and treatment. *Social Casework 32*, 67–74.

Homan, M. S. (1994). Promoting community change: Making it happen in the real world. Pacific Grove, CA: Brooks/Cole.

Home, A. M. (1991). Mobilizing women's strengths for social change: The group connection. In A. Vinik & M. Lewin (Eds.), *Social Action in Group Work* (pp. 153–173). New York: Haworth.

Hooks, B. (1990). *Yearning: race, gender, and cultural politics*. Boston: South End.

Hooyman, N. R., & Lustbader, W. (1986). *Taking care: Supporting older people and their families*. New York: Free Press.

Hopps, J. G., Pinderhughes, E., & Shankar, R. (1995). *The power to care: Clinical practice effectiveness with overwhelmed clients*. New York: Free Press.

Howell, S. C. (1980). *Designing for aging: Patterns of use*. Cambridge, MA: MIT Press.

Howell, S. C. (1983). The meaning of place in old age. In G. D. Rowles & R. J. Ohta (Eds.), *Aging and milieu: Environmental perspectives on growing old* (pp. 97–107). New York: Academic.

Howell, S. C. (1994). Environment and the aging woman: Domains of choice. In I. Altman & A. Churchman (Eds.), *Women and the environment* (pp. 105–132). New York: Plenum.

Husserl, E. (1970). *The crisis of European sciences and transcendental phenomenology.* Evanston, IL: Northwestern University Press.

Imber-Black, E. (1988). *Families and larger systems: A family therapist's guide through the labyrinth.* New York: Guilford.

Jackson, P. (1989). *Maps of meaning: An introduction to cultural geography.* London: Unwin Hyman.

Jacobsen, D. E. (1986). Types and timing of social support. *Journal of Health and Social Behavior 27,* 250–264.

Jeger, A. M., & Slotnick, R. S. (Eds.) (1982). *Community mental health and behavioral ecology: A handbook of theory, research, and practice.* New York: Plenum.

Jenson, J. M., Hawkins, J., & Catalano, R. (1986). Social support in aftercare services for troubled youth. *Children and Youth Services Review 8,* 323–347.

Jenson, J. M., & Whittaker, J. K. (1987). Parental involvement in children's residential treatment: From preplacement to aftercare. *Children and Youth Services Review 9,* 81–100.

Jezierski, L. (1991). Postmodern geographies (book review). *Socialist Review 21,* 177–185.

Johnson, L. C. (1995). Social work practice: A generalist approach (5th ed.). Boston: Allyn and Bacon

Jones, R. R., Weinrott, M. R., & Howard, J. R. (1981). *Impact of the teaching family model on troublesome youth: findings from the national evaluation* (NTIS #PB82-224353). Rockville, MD: National Institute of Mental Health.

Jordan, C., & Franklin, C. (1995). *Clinical assessment for social workers: Quantitative and qualitative methods.* Chicago: Lyceum.

Jordan, D. D., & Hernandez, M. (1990). The Ventura planning model: A proposal for mental health reform. *Journal of Mental Health Administration 17,* 26–47.

Josselyn, I. M. (1948). The caseworker as therapist. *Social Casework 29,* 351–355.

Kadushin, A. (1958). Prestige of social work: Facts and factors. In A. J. Kahn (Ed.), *Issues in American social work* (pp. 39–79). New York: Columbia University Press.

Kagan, S. L. (1996). America's family support movement: A moment of change. In E. F. Zigler, S. L. Kagan, & N. W. Hall (Eds.), *Children, families and government: Preparing for the twenty-first century* (pp. 156–170). Cambridge: Cambridge University Press.

Kagan, S. L., Powell, D., Weissbourd, B., & Zigler, E. (Eds.) (1987). *America's family support programs.* New Haven, CT: Yale University Press.

Kahn, R. L., & Antonucci, T. C. (1981). Convoys of social support: A life course approach. In S. B. Kiesler, J. N. Morgan, & V. C. Oppenheimer (Eds.), *Aging: Social change.* New York: Academic.

Kaplan, C. P., Turner, S., Norman, E., & Stillson, K. (1996). Promoting resilience strategies: A modified consultation model. *Social Work in Education 18,* 158–168.

Kaplan, L., & Girard, J. L. (1994). *Strengthening high-risk families: A handbook for practitioners.* New York: Lexington.

Karls, J. M., Lowery, C. T., Mattaini, M. A., & Wandrie, K. E. (1997). The use of the PIE (person-in-environment) system in social work education. *Journal of Social Work Education 33*(1), 49–58.

Karls, J. M., & Wandrie, K. E. (1992). PIE: A new language for social work. *Social Work 37*, 80–85.

Karls, J. M., & Wandrie, K. E. (1994). *Person-in-environment system: The PIE classification system for social functioning problems.* Washington, DC: National Association of Social Workers.

Karls, J. M., & Wandrie, K. E. (1995). Person-in-environment. In *Encyclopedia of Social Work* (vol. 3, pp. 1818–1827). Washington, DC: National Association of Social Workers.

Katz, C. (1993). Growing girls/closing circles: Limits on the space of knowing in rural Sudan and U.S. cities. In C. Katz & J. Monk (Eds.), *Full circles: Geographies of women over the life course* (pp. 88–106). New York: Routledge.

Katz, C., & Monk, J. (Eds.) (1993). *Full circles: Geographies of women over the life course.* New York: Routledge.

Keith, M., & Pile, S. (1993). *Place and the politics of identity.* London: Routledge.

Kemp, S. P. (1994). *Social work and systems of knowledge: The concept of environment in social casework theory, 1900–1983.* Unpublished doctoral dissertation, Columbia University School of Social Work, New York.

Kemp, S. P. (1995). Practice with communities. In C. H. Meyer & M. A. Mattaini (Eds.), *The foundations of social work practice: A graduate text* (pp. 176–204). Washington, DC: National Association of Social Workers.

Kieffer, C. (1984). Citizen empowerment: A developmental perspective. *Prevention in Human Services 3*, 9–35.

Kinney, J., Haapala, D., & Booth, C. (1991). *Keeping families together: The Homebuilders model.* Hawthorne, NY: Aldine de Gruyter.

Kirby, K. (1996). *Indifferent boundaries: Spatial concepts of human subjectivity.* New York: Guilford.

Kirkham, M. A., Schinke, S. P., Schilling, R. F., Meltzer, N. J., & Norelius, K. I. (1986). Cognitive-behavioral skills, social supports, and child abuse potential among mothers of handicapped children. *Journal of Family Violence 1*, 235–245.

Kirst-Ashman, K. K., & Hull, G. H. (1996). *Understanding generalist practice* (2nd ed.). Chicago: Nelson Hall.

Kisthardt, W. E. (1997). The strengths model of case management: Principles and helping functions. In D. Saleebey (Ed.), *The strengths perspective in social work practice* (2nd ed., pp. 97–113). New York: Longman.

Klein, P. (1968). *From philanthropy to social welfare: An American cultural perspective.* San Francisco: Jossey-Bass.

Kopp, J. (1993). Self-observation: An empowering strategy in assessment. In J. B. Rauch (Ed.), *Assessment: A sourcebook for social work practice* (pp. 255–268). Milwaukee: Families International.

Korbin, J. E., & Coulton, C. J. (in press). Understanding the neighborhood

context of children and families: Combining epidemiological and eth-
nographic approaches. In J. Brooks-Gunn, G. J. Cuncan, & J. L. Aber (Eds.).
Neighborhood poverty; Context and consequences for children. New York: Russell
Sage Foundation Press.

Koren, P. E., DeChillo, N., & Friesen, B. J. (1992). Measuring empowerment in
families whose children have emotional disabilities: A brief questionnaire.
Rehabilitation Psychology 37, 305–321.

Kretzmann, J. P., & McKnight, J. L. (1993). *Building communities from the inside out:
A path toward finding and mobilizing a community's assets.* Chicago, IL: ACTA.

Laird, J. (Ed.) (1994). *Revisioning social work education: A social constructionist approach.* New York: Haworth.

Larner, M., Halpern, R., & Harkavy, O. (1992). *Fair Start for Children: Lessons
learned from seven demonstration projects.* New Haven, CT: Yale University
Press.

Lazarus, R. S., & Folkman, S. (1984). *Stress, appraisal and coping.* New York:
Springer.

Leiby, J. (1978). *A history of social welfare and social work in the United States.* New
York: Columbia University Press.

Leonard, P. (1994). Knowledge/power and postmodernism: Implications for the
practice of a critical social work education. *Canadian Social Work Review 11,*
11–26.

Leonard, P. (1995). Postmodernism, socialism, and social welfare: *Journal of Progressive Human Services 6,* 3–19.

Leung, P., Cheung, K. M. & Stevenson, K. M. (1994). A strengths approach to
ethnically sensitive practice for child protective service workers. *Child Welfare 73,* 707–721.

Leuy, H. S., Glass, L., & Elliot, H. (1996). Hard of hearing or deaf: Issues of ears,
language, culture and identity. In P. L. Ewalt, E. M. Freeman, S. A. Kirk, &
D. L. Poole (Eds.), *Multicultural issues in social work* (pp. 282–292). Washington, DC: National Association of Social Workers.

Lewin, K. (1931). Environmental forces in child behavior and development. In
C. Murchison (Ed.), *A handbook of child psychology* (pp. 94–127). Worcester,
MA: Clark University Press.

Lewin, K. (1935). *A dynamic theory of personality.* New York: McGraw-Hill.

Lewin, K. (1936). *Principles of topological psychology.* New York: McGraw-Hill.

Lewin, K. (1946). Action research and social problems. *Journal of Social Issues 2,*
34–36.

Lewin, K. (1951). *Field theory in social science: Selected theoretical papers.* New York:
Harper.

Lewis, E. A., & Ford, B. (1991). The network utilization project: Incorporating
traditional strengths of African-American families into group work practice.
Social Work with Groups 13, 7–22.

Lewis, E. A., & Suarez, Z. E. (1995). Natural helping networks. In *Encyclopedia of
Social Work* (19th ed., vol. 2, pp. 1765–1772). Washington, DC: National
Association of Social Workers.

Lichtenberg, P. (1990). *Undoing the clinch of oppression.* New York: Peter Lang.

Lightburn, A. (1991). *Hall Neighborhood House Family Support Program: Pilot demon-*

stration report. Washington, DC: Office of Head Start, Department of Health and Human Services.

Lightburn, A., & Kemp, S. P. (1994). Family support programs: Opportunities for community-based social work practice. *Families in Society 75*, 16–26.

Lindblad-Goldberg, M., & Dukes, J. L. (1985). Social support in Black low income single parent families: Normative and dysfunctional patterns. *American Journal of Orthopsychiatry 55*, 42–58.

Longres, J. F. (1996). Is it feasible to teach HBSE from a strengths perspective, in contrast to one emphasizing limitations or weaknesses? No. In M. Bloom & W. C. Klein (Eds.), *Controversial issues in Human Behavior and the Social Environment* (pp. 16–32). Boston: Allyn & Bacon.

Longres, J. F., & McLeod, E. (1980). Consciousness raising and social work practice. *Social Casework 61*, 267–276.

Lord, S. A. (1993). *Social welfare and the feminization of poverty.* New York: Garland.

Lovell, M. L. (1986). *An evaluation of a parent training and social support group for mothers at risk to maltreat their children.* Ph.D. dissertation, University of Washington, Seattle.

Lovell, M. L. (1991). *The friendship group: Learning the skills to create social support. A manual for group leaders.* Vancouver: University of British Columbia, School of Social Work.

Lovell, M. L., & Hawkins, J. D. (1988). An evaluation of a group intervention to increase the personal social networks of abusive mothers. *Children and Youth Services Review 10*, 175–188.

Lovell, M. L., & Richey, C. A. (1991). Implementing agency-based social support skill training. *Families in Society 72*, 563–571.

Lubove, R. (1965). *The professional altruist: The emergence of social work as a career, 1880–1930.* Cambridge, MA: Harvard University Press.

Lum, D. (1996). *Social work practice and people of color: A process-stage approach* (3rd ed.). Pacific Grove, CA: Brooks/Cole.

Lutfiyya, Z. M. (Ed.) (1991). *Personal relationships and social networks: Facilitating the participation of individuals with disabilities in community life.* Syracuse, NY: Center on Human Policy.

Lynd, M. (1992). Creating knowledge through theater: A case study with developmentally disabled adults. *American Sociologist* (winter), 100–115.

MacDonald, J. G. (1987). Predictors of treatment outcome for alcoholic women. *International Journal of Addictions 22*, 235–248.

Maguire, P. (1987). *Doing feminist research: A participatory approach.* Amherst, MA: Center for International Education.

Maluccio, A. (1979). *Learning from clients: Interpersonal; helping as viewed by clients and social workers.* New York: Free Press.

Maluccio, A. (1981). *Promoting competence in clients: A new/old approach to social work practice.* New York: Free Press.

Maluccio, A. (1987). *Research perspectives on family support systems for children.* Unpublished paper, presented at Conference on Enhancing Direct Practice with Families, Mandel School of Applied Social Sciences, Case Western Reserve University, Cleveland, June 9.

Marrow, A. J. (1969). *The practical theorist: The life and work of Kurt Lewin.* New York: Basic Books.

Massey, D. (1994). *Space, place, and gender.* Minneapolis: University of Minnesota Press.

Masten, A. S., Best, K. M., & Garmezy, N. (1990). Resiliency and development: Contributions from the study of children who overcome adversity. *Development and Psychopathology 2,* 425–444.

Mattaini, M. A. (1990). Contextual behavior analysis in the assessment process. *Families in Society 71,* 236–245.

Mattaini, M. A. (1993). *More than a thousand words: Graphics for clinical practice.* Washington, DC: National Association of Social Workers.

McAdoo, H. P. (Ed.) (1988). *Black families* (2nd ed). Beverly Hills, CA: Sage.

McCubbin, H. I., Thompson, E. A., Thompson, A. I., & Fromer, J. E. (1994). *Sense of coherence and resiliency: Stress, coping and health.* Madison: University of Wisconsin System.

McCubbin, H. I., Thompson, E. A., Thompson, A. I., & Futrell, J. A. (1995). *Resiliency in ethnic minority families: African-American families.* Madison: University of Wisconsin System.

McFarlane, A. H., Norman, G. R., Streiner, D. L., & Roy, R. G. (1984). Characteristics and correlates of effective and ineffective social supports. *Journal of Psychosomatic Research 28,* 501–509.

McKnight. J. L., & Kretzmann, J. P. (1990). *Mapping community capacity.* Evanston, IL: Northwestern University, Center for Urban Affairs and Policy Research.

Mehr, J. (1988). *Human services: Concepts and intervention strategies* (4th ed.). Boston: Allyn and Bacon.

Merle, S. (1962). Some arguments against private practice. *Social Work 7,* 12–17.

Meyer, C. H. (1970). *Social work practice: A response to the urban crisis.* New York: Free Press.

Meyer, C. H. (1973a). Practice models: The new ideology. *Smith College Studies in Social Work 43*(2), 85–98.

Meyer, C. H. (1973b). Purposes and boundaries: Casework fifty years later. *Social Casework 54,* 268–275.

Meyer, C. H. (1979). What directions for direct practice? *Social Work 24,* 267–272.

Meyer, C. H. (1981). Social work purpose: Status by choice or coercion? *Social Work 26,* 69–75.

Meyer, C. H. (Ed.) (1983). *Clinical social work in the eco-systems perspective.* New York: Columbia University Press.

Meyer, C. H. (1989). Keynote address: Third oral history day. *Newsletter of the Alumni Association of the Columbia University School of Social Work.* New York: Columbia University.

Meyer, C. H. (1993). *Assessment in social work practice.* New York: Columbia University Press.

Meyer, C. H., & Mattaini, M. A. (Eds.) (1995). *The foundations of social work practice: A graduate text.* Washington, DC: National Association of Social Workers.

Michelson, W. (1994). Everyday life in contextual perspective. In I. Altman & A.

Churchman (Eds.), *Women and the environment* (pp. 17–42). New York: Plenum.

Millar, M. (1939). Modern use of older treatment methods. In F. Lowry (Ed.), *Readings in social casework, 1920–1938* (pp. 344–353). New York: Columbia University Press.

Mills, C. W. (1959). *The sociological imagination.* New York: Oxford University Press.

Minahan, A., & Briar, S. (1977). Introduction to special issue on conceptual frameworks. *Social Work 22,* 339.

Mishler, E. (1979). Meaning in context: Is there any other kind? *Harvard Educational Review 499*(1), 1–19.

Moen, P. (1995). Introduction. In P. Moen, G. H. Elder, & K. Lüscher (Eds.), *Examining lives in context: Perspectives on the ecology of human development* (pp. 1–15). Washington, DC: American Psychological Association.

Moen, P., Elder, G. H., & Lüscher, K., (Eds.) (1995). *Examining lives in context: Perspectives on the ecology of human development.* Washington, DC: American Psychological Association.

Moncher, F. J. (1995). Social isolation and child-abuse risk. *Families in Society 76,* 421–433.

Moore, J. A., Hamerlynck, L., Barsh, E. T., Spieker, S., & Jones, R. R. (1982). *Extending Family Resources: Final Project Report.* Seattle: Children's Clinic and Preschool.

Moos, R. H. (1996). Understanding environments: The key to improving social processes and program outcomes. *American Journal of Community Psychology 24*(1), 193–201.

Moreno, J. L., & Borgatta, E. F. (1951). An experiment with sociodrama and sociometry in industry. *Sociometry 14,* 71–103.

Morin, R. C., & Seidman, E. (1986). A social network approach and the revolving door patient. *Schizophrenia Bulletin 12,* 262–273.

Mowbray, C. T., Wellwood, R., & Chamberlain, P. (1988). Project Stay: A consumer-run support service. *Psychosocial Rehabilitation Journal 12,* 33–42.

Mullen, E. J., Dumpson, J. R., and Associates (Eds.) (1971). *Evaluation of social work intervention.* San Francisco: Jossey-Bass.

Murray, M. (1995). Correction at Cabrini-Green. *Environment and Planning D: Society and Space 13,* 311–327.

Murty, S. A., & Gillespie, D. F. (1995). Introducing network analysis into the social work curriculum. *Journal of Applied Social Analysis 19,* 107–119.

Nagda, B. A. (1996). *A social relationship approach to worker empowerment: Similarities and differences across race and gender.* Unpublished doctoral dissertation, University of Michigan, Ann Arbor.

Nagda, B. A., & Gutièrrez, M. (1996). *A praxis and research agenda for multicultural human service organizations.* Paper presented at the Second International Conference of the International Society for Third Sector Research, Mexico City, Mexico, July.

Naparstek, A. J., Beigel, D. E., & Spiro, H. R. (1982). *Neighborhood networks for human mental health care.* New York: Plenum.

National Association of Social Workers (1996). *Code of ethics.* Washington, DC: Author

Nestman, F., & Hurrelmann, K. (Eds.) (1994). *Social networks and social support in childhood and adolescence.* Hawthorne, NY: Aldine de Gruyter.

Netting, F. E., Kettner, P. M., & McMurtry, S. L. (1993). *Social work macro practice.* New York: Longman.

Neugeboren, B. (1990). Letter to the editor. *Social Work 35,* 373–374.

Neugeboren, B. (1996). *Environmental practice in the human services: Integration of micro and macro roles, skills and contexts.* New York: Haworth.

Norton, D. (1978). *The dual perspective.* New York: Council on Social Work Education.

Nurius, P. S., & Hudson, W. W. (1993). *Human services practice, evaluation and computers: A practical guide for today and beyond.* Pacific Grove, CA: Brooks/Cole.

O'Brien, D., & Ayidiya, S. (1991). Neighborhood community and life satisfaction. *Journal of the Community Development Society 22,* 32–37.

O'Brien, P. (1995). From surviving to thriving: The complex experience of living in public housing. *Affilia 10,* 155–178.

Oja, S. N., & Smulyan, L. (Eds.) (1989). *Collaborative action research.* Philadelphia: Falmer.

Olds, D. (1988). Common design and methodological problems encountered in evaluating family support services: Illustrations from the pre-natal/early infancy project. In H. B. Weiss & F. H. Jacobs (Eds.), *Evaluating family programs* (pp. 239–267). Hawthorne, NY: Aldine de Gruyter.

O'Melia, M., Dubois, B., & Miley, K. (1994). From problem-solving to empowerment-based social work practice. In L. Gutièrrez & P. Nurius (Eds.), *Education and research for empowerment practice* (pp. 161–169). Seattle: Center for Policy and Practice Research, School of Social Work, University of Washington.

Oritt, E. J., Paul, S. C., & Behrman, J. A. (1985). The perceived support network inventory. *American Journal of Community Psychology 13,* 565–582.

Pain, R. (1991). Space, sexual violence and social control: Integrating geographical and feminist analyses of women's fear of crime. *Progress in Human Geography 15,* 415–431.

Pancoast, D. L., Parker, P., & Froland, C. (1983). *Rediscovering self-help: Its role in social care.* Beverly Hills: Sage.

Park, P. (1992). The discovery of participatory research as a new scientific paradigm: Personal and intellectual accounts. *American Sociologist* (winter), 29–42.

Parsons, R. J. (1991). Empowerment: Purpose and practice principle in social work. *Social Work with Groups 14,* 7–21.

Patterson, S. L., Germain, C. B., Brennan, E. M., & Memmott, J. (1988). Effectiveness of rural natural helpers. *Social Casework, 69,* 272–279.

Patti, R. J. (1981). The prospects for social R&D: An essay review. *Social Work Research and Abstracts 17,* 45–63.

Payne, M. (1995). *Social work and community care.* London: Macmillan.

Perlman, H. H. (1968). Can casework work? *Social Service Review 42*(4), 435–447.

Pecora, P. J., & English, D. J. (1993). *Multi-cultural guidelines for assessing family strengths and risk factors in child protective services.* Seattle: Washington Risk Assessment Project, Office of Children's Administration Research.

Pennell, J., & Burford, G. (1995a). *Family group decision making project: Implementation Report. Volume I.* St. John's, Newfoundland, Canada: Memorial University of Newfoundland, School of Social Work.

Pennell, J., & Burford, G. (1995b). *Family group decision making project: Implementation Report. Volume II. Research/Evaluation Instruments.* St. John's, Newfoundland, Canada: Memorial University of Newfoundland, School of Social Work.

Perkins, F. (1929). Social seer. *Family 9,* 338–339.

Pierce, G. R., Sarason, B. R., & Sarason, I. G. (Eds.). (1996). *Handbook of social support and the family.* New York: Plenum.

Pincus, A., & Minahan, A. (1977). *Social work practice: Model and method.* Itasca, IL: Peacock.

Pine, B., Warsh, R., & Maluccio, A. N. (1993). *Together again: Family reunification in foster care.* Washington, DC: Child Welfare League of America.

Pinker, R. (1982). An alternative view. In *The Barclay Report: Social workers: Their roles and tasks* (pp. 236–263). London: Bedford Square.

Pinker, R. (1990). *Social work in an enterprise society.* London: Routledge.

Polansky, N. A., & Gaudin, J. M. (1983). Social distancing of the neglectful family. *Social Service Review 57,* 196–208.

Polansky, N. A., Gaudin, J. M., Ammons, P. W., & Davis, K. B. (1985). The psychological ecology of the neglectful mother. *Child Abuse and Neglect 9,* 263–275.

Poresky, R. H. (1987). Environmental Assessment Index: Reliability, stability and validity of the long and short forms. *Educational and Psychological Measurements 47,* 969–975.

Powell, D. R. (1979). Family-environment relations and early childrearing: The role of social networks and neighborhoods. *Journal of Research and Development in Education 13,* 1–11.

Powell, T. J. (Ed.) (1990). *Working with self-help.* Washington, DC: National Association of Social Workers.

Powell, T. J. (1995). Self-help groups. In *Encyclopedia of Social Work* (19th ed., vol. 3, pp. 2116–2123).

Pray, K. (1947). A restatement of the generic principles of social casework practice. *Social Casework 28,* 283–315.

Proctor, C. D., & Groze, V. K. (1994). Risk factors for suicide among gay,lesbian, and bisexual youths. *Social Work 39,* 504–514.

Proctor, E. K., & Davis, L. E. (1994). The challenge of racial difference: Skills for clinical practice. *Social Work 39,* 314–323.

Proctor, E. K., & Rosen, A. (1983). Problem formulation and its relation to treatment planning. *Social Work Research and Abstracts 19,* 22–28.

Proctor, E. K., Vosler, N. R., & Sirles, E. A. (1993). The social-environmental context of child clients: An empirical exploration. *Social Work 38,* 256–262.

Rank, M. R. (1994). *Living on the edge: The realities of welfare in America.* New York: Columbia University Press.

Rapp, C. A., Shera, W., & Kisthardt, W. (1993). Research strategies for consumer empowerment of people with severe mental illness. *Social Work 38*, 727–735.

Rappaport, J. (1987). Terms of empowerment/exemplars of prevention: Toward a theory for community psychology. *American Journal of Community Psychology 15*(2), 121–148.

Rappaport, J. (1990). Research methods and the empowerment agenda. In P. Tolan, C. Keys, F. Chertak, & L. Jason (Eds.), *Researching community psychology*. Washington, DC: American Psychological Association.

Reisman, D. A. (1977). *Richard Titmuss: Welfare and society*. London: Heinemann.

Resnick, H., & Jaffee, B. (1982). The physical environment and social welfare. *Social Casework 63*, 354–362.

Reynolds, B. C. (1933). Can social case work be interpreted to a community as a basic approach to human problems? *Family 13*, 336–342.

Reynolds, B. C. ([1934] 1982). *Between client and community: A study in responsibility in social case work*. Silver Spring, MD: National Association of Social Workers.

Reynolds, B. C. (1935). Whom do social workers serve? *Social Work Today 2*, 34.

Reynolds, B. C. (1938). Rethinking social casework—III. *Social Work Today 5*, 5–8.

Reynolds, B. C. (1942). *Learning and teaching in the practice of social work*. New York: Rhinehart.

Reynolds, B. C. (1951). *Social work and social living: Explorations in philosophy and practice*. (First NASW Classic Edition, 1975). Washington, DC: National Association of Social Workers.

Reynolds, B. C. (1963). *An uncharted journey: Fifty years of growth in social casework*. New York: Citadel.

Rich, R. C., Edelstein, M., Hallman, W. K., & Wandersman, A. H. (1995). Citizen participation and empowerment: The case of local environmental hazards. *American Journal of Community Psychology 23*, 657–676.

Richey, C. A. (1994). Social support skill training. In D. K. Granvold (Ed.), *Cognitive and behavioral treatment: Methods and applications* (pp. 299–338). Belmont, CA: Brooks/Cole.

Richey, C. A., Lovell, M., & Reid, K. (1991). Interpersonal skill training to enhance social support among women at risk for child maltreatment. *Children and Youth Services Review 13*, 41–59.

Richmond, M. (1899). *Friendly visiting among the poor*. New York: Macmillan.

Richmond, M. ([1906] 1930). The retail method of reform. In M. Richmond, *The long view* (pp. 214–221). New York: Russell Sage Foundation.

Richmond, M. E. (1917). *Social diagnosis*. New York: Russell Sage Foundation.

Richmond, M. E. (1922). *What is social casework?*. New York: Russell Sage Foundation.

Richmond, M. E. (1930). *The long view*. New York: Russell Sage Foundation.

Riessman, F. (1965). The "helper" therapy principle. *Social Work 10*, 27–32.

Riessman, F. (1990). Restructuring help: A human services paradigm for the 1990s. *American Journal of Community Psychology 18*, 221–230.

Rifai, N., Cohen, G., Wolf, M., Cohen, L., Faser, C., Savory, J., & Depalma, L. (1993). Incidence of lead poisoning in young children from inner-city, suburban, and rural communities. *Therapeutic Drug Monitor 15*, 71–74.

Riger, S. (1993). What's wrong with empowerment? *American Journal of Community Psychology 21*, 279–292.

Rivera, F., & Erlich, J. (Eds.) (1992). *Community organizing in a diverse society.* Boston: Allyn and Bacon.

Robinson, V. P. (1930). *A changing psychology in social case work.* Chapel Hill: University of North Carolina Press.

Rock, D. L., Green, K. E., Wise, B. K., & Rock, R. D. (1984). Social support and social network scales: A psychometric review. *Research in Nursing and Health 7*, 325–332.

Rogers-Warren, A., & Rogers-Warren, S. F. (Eds.) (1977). *Ecological perspectives in behavior analysis.* Baltimore: University Park Press.

Rogge, M. E. (1993). Social work, disenfranchised communities, and the natural environment: field education opportunities. *Journal of Social Work Education 29*, 111–120.

Rogge, M. E. (1995). Coordinating theory, evidence, and practice: toxic waste exposure in communities. *Journal of Community Practice 2*, 55–76.

Rollinson, P. A. (1990). The story of Edward: The everyday geography of elderly Single Room Occupancy (SRO) hotel tenants. *Journal of Contemporary Ethnography 19*, 188–206.

Rooney, R. H. (1992). *Strategies for work with involuntary clients.* New York: Columbia University Press.

Rose, G. (1993). *Feminism and geography: The limits of geographical knowledge.* Cambridge: Polity.

Rose, S. (1990). Advocacy/empowerment: An approach to clinical practice for social work. *Journal of Sociology and Social Welfare 17*, 41–51.

Rosen, A., & Levine, S. (1992). Personal versus environmental emphases in social workers' perceptions of client problems. *Social Service Review 66*, 85–96.

Ross, D. (1991). *The origins of American social science.* New York: Cambridge University Press.

Rothman, J. (1980). *Social R&D: Research and development in the human services.* Englewood Cliffs, NJ: Prentice-Hall.

Rothman, J. (1994). *Practice with highly vulnerable clients.* Englewood Cliffs, NJ: Prentice-Hall.

Rothman, J., & Thomas, E. J. (1994). *Intervention research: Design and development for human service.* New York: Haworth.

Rowles, G. D. (1978). *Prisoners of space: Exploring the geographical experience of older people.* Boulder, CO: Westview.

Rowles, G. D. (1983). Geographical dimensions of social support in rural Appalachia. In G. D. Rowles & R. J. Ohta (Eds.), *Aging and milieu: Environmental perspectives on growing old* (pp. 111–130). New York: Academic.

Rubin, H. J., & Rubin, I. S. (1992). *Community organizing and development* (2nd ed.). New York: Macmillan.

Rutter, M. (1979). Protective factors in children's responses to stress and disadvantage. In M. W. Kent & J. Rolf (Eds.), *Primary prevention of psychopathology: Vol. 3. Social competence in children* (pp. 49–74). Hanover, NH: University Press of New England.

Rutter, M. (1985). Resilience in the face of adversity: Protective factors and resistance to psychiatric disorder. *British Journal of Psychiatry 147*, 598–611.

Rutter, M. (1993). Resilience: Some conceptual considerations. *Journal of Adolescent Health 14*(8), 626–631.

Rutter, M., Champion, L., Quinton, D., Maughan, B., & Pickles, A. (1995). Understanding individual differences in environmental risk exposure. In P. Moen, G. H. Elder, & K. Lüscher (Eds.), *Examining lives in context: Perspectives on the ecology of human development* (pp. 61–97). Washington, DC: American Psychological Association.

Rzepnicki, T. L. (1991). Enhancing the durability of intervention gains: A challenge for the 1990s. *Social Service Review 65*(1), 92–111.

Saari, C. (1991). *The creation of meaning in clinical social work*. New York: Guilford.

Saari, C. (1992). Person-in-environment reconsidered: New theoretical bridges. *Child and Adolescent Social Work Journal 9*, 205–219.

Saegert, S., & Hart, R. (1978). The development of environmental competence in boys and girls. In M. Salter (Ed.), *Play: Anthropological perspectives*. Cornwall, NY: Leisure.

Saleebey, D. (1992). *The strengths perspective in social work practice*. New York: Longman.

Saleebey, D. (1994). Culture, theory, and narrative: The intersection of meanings in practice. *Social Work 39*, 351–359.

Saleebey, D. (1996). The strengths perspective in social work practice: Extensions and cautions. *Social Work 41*, 296–305.

Saleebey, D. (Ed.) (1997). *The strengths perspective in social work practice* (2nd ed.). New York: Longman.

Sameroff, A. J., & Seifer, R. (1995). Accumulation of environmental risk and child mental health. In H. E. Fitzgerald, B. M. Lester, & B. Zuckerman (Eds.), *Children of poverty: Research, health and policy issues* (pp. 233–258). New York: Garland.

Scheier, I. H. (1993). *Voluntarism and social work practice: A growing collaboration*. New York: University Press of America.

Schlesinger, A. M. (1986). *The cycles of American history*. Boston: Houghton Mifflin.

Schlosberg, S. B., & Kagan, R. M. (1988). Practice strategies for engaging chronic multiproblem families. *Social Casework 68*, 284–289.

Schnitzer, P. K. (1996). "They don't come in!" Stories told, lessons learned about poor families in therapy. *American Journal of Orthopsychiatry 66*(4), 572–582.

Schorr, A. L. (1959). The retreat to the technician. *Social Work 4*, 29–33.

Schorr, L. B. (1989). *Within our reach: Breaking the cycle of disadvantage*. New York: Anchor.

Scott, D. (1989). Meaning construction and social work practice. *Social Service Review 63*, 39–62.

Scott, J. C. (1990). *Domination and the art of resistance: Hidden transcripts*. New Haven, CT: Yale University Press.

Seabury, B. A. (1971). Arrangement of physical space in social work settings. *Social Work 16*, 43–49.

Seager, J. (1993). Blueprints for inequality. *Women's Review of Books 10*, 1.

Seamon, D. (1979). *A geography of the life world: movement, rest, and encounter.* New York: St. Martin's.

Seebohm Report (1968). *Report of the Committee on Local Authority and Allied Personal Social Services,* Cmnd. 3703. London: HMSO.

Seidman, E. (1991). Growing up the hard way: Pathways of urban adolescents. *American Journal of Community Psychology 19,* 173–207.

Seidman, E., Aber, J. L., Allen, L., & French, S. E. (1996). The impact of transition to high school on the self-system and perceived social context of poor urban youth. *American Journal of Community Psychology 24,* 489–517.

Seifer, R., Sameroff, A. J., Baldwin, C. P., & Baldwin, A. L. (1992). Child and family factors that ameliorate risk between 4 and 13 years of age. *Journal of the American Academy of Child and Adolescent Psychiatry 31,* 893–903.

Sheafor, B. W., Horejsi, C. R., & Horejsi, G. A. (1997). *Techniques and guidelines for social work practice* (4th ed.). Boston: Allyn and Bacon.

Shapiro, J. P. (1993). *No pity: People with disabilities forging a new civil rights movement.* New York: Times.

Sheffield, A. E. (1920). *The social case history: Its construction and content.* New York: Russell Sage Foundation.

Sheffield, A. E. (1931). The situation as the unit of family case study. *Social Forces 9*(4), 465–483.

Sheffield, A. E. (1937). *Social insight in case situations.* New York: D. Appleton Century.

Shifren, F., & Solis, M. (1992). Chemical dependency in gay and lesbian youth. *Journal of Chemical Dependency Treatment 5,* 67–76.

Shinn, M. (1996). Ecological assessment [Special issue]. *American Journal of Community Psychology 24.*

Shulman, L. (1992). *The skills of helping: Individuals, families, and groups* (3rd ed.). Itasca, IL: Peacock.

Simon, B. L. (1990). Rethinking empowerment. *Journal of Progressive Human Services 1,* 27–39.

Simon, B. L. (1994). *The empowerment tradition in American social work: A history.* New York: Columbia University Press.

Simonson, J., & Bushaw, V. A. (1993). Participatory-action research: Easier said than done. *American Sociologist* (spring), 27–37.

Siporin, M. (1970). Social treatment: A new-old helping method. *Social Work 15,* 13–26.

Siporin, M. (1972). Situational assessment and intervention. *Social Casework 53* (February), 91–109.

Siporin, M. (1975). *Introduction to social work practice.* New York: Macmillan.

Skirboll, B. W., & Pavelsky, P. K. (1984). The compeer program volunteers as friends of the mentally ill. *Hospital and Community Psychiatry 35,* 938–939.

Sklar, K. K. (1985). Hull House in the 1880s: A community of women reformers. *Signs 10,* 507–532.

Smale, G. G. (1995). Integrating community and individual practice: A new paradigm in practice. In P. Adams & K. Nelson (Eds.), *Reinventing Human Services: Community and family centered practice* (pp. 59–80). Hawthorne, NY: Aldine de Gruyter.

Smith, D. (1987). *The everyday world as problematic: A feminist sociology*. Boston: Northeastern University Press.

Soine, L. (1987). Expanding the environment in social work: The case for including environmental hazards content. *Journal of Social Work Education 23*, 40–46.

Soja, E. W. (1989). *Postmodern geographies: The reassertion of space in critical social theory*. New York: Verso.

Sokolove, R. L., & Trimble, D. (1986). Assessing support and stress in the social networks of chronic patients. *Hospital and Community Psychiatry 37*, 370–372.

Sohng, S. S. (in press). Research as an empowerment strategy. In R. Parson, E. Cox, & L. Gutièrrez (Eds.), *Empowerment social work practice: A source book*. Pacific Grove, CA: Brooks/Cole.

Spain, D. (1992). *Gendered spaces*. Chapel Hill: University of North Carolina Press.

Specht, H., & Courtney, M. E. (1994). *Unfaithful angels: How social work has abandoned its mission*. New York: Free Press.

Stack, C. (1974). *All our kin: Strategies for survival in a black community*. New York: Harper & Row.

Stadum, B. A. (1991). *Poor women and their families: Hard working charity cases, 1900–1930*. Albany: State University of New York.

Staples, B. (1996). Death by discrimination: Of prejudice and heart attacks. *New York Times*, November 24.

Stokols, D. (1995). The paradox of environmental psychology. *American Psychologist 50*, 821–837.

Stokols, D. (1996). Bridging the theoretical and applied facets of environmental psychology. *American Psychologist 51*, 1188.

Streeter, C. I. & Franklin, C. (1992). Defining and measuring social support: Guidelines for social work practitioners. *Research in Social Work Practice 2*, 81–98.

Stroul, B. A. (1986). *Models of community support services: Approaches to helping persons with long-term mental illness*. Boston: Center for Psychiatric Rehabilitation, Sargent College of Allied Health Professions, Boston University.

Sullivan, W. P. (1992a). Reclaiming the community: The strengths perspective and deinstitutionalization. *Social Work 37*, 204–209.

Sullivan, W. P. (1992b). Reconsidering the environment as a helping resource. In D. Saleebey (Ed.), *The strengths perspective in social work practice* (pp. 148–157). New York: Longman.

Sullivan, W. P., & Rapp, C. A. (1994). Breaking away: The potential and promise of a strengths-based approach to social work practice. In R. G. Meinert, J. T. Pardeck, & W. P. Sullivan (Eds.), *Issues in social work: A critical analysis* (pp. 83–104). Westport, CT: Auburn House.

Swadener, B. B., & Lubeck, S. (Eds.) (1995). *Children and families "at promise": Deconstructing the discourse of risk*. Albany: State University of New York Press.

Sytz, F. (1946). The unit of attention in the casework process. *Family 27*, 135–139.

Taylor, R., & Covington, J. (1993). Community structural change and fear of crime. *Social Problems 40*, 374–395.

Thoits, P. A. (1986). Social support as coping assistance. *Journal of Consulting and Clinical Psychology 54*, 416–423.

Thomas, E. J. (1978). Generating innovation in social work: The paradigm of developmental research. *Journal of Social Service Research 2*, 95–115.

Thompson, R. A. (1995). *Preventing child maltreatment through social support: A critical analysis*. Thousand Oaks, CA: Sage.

Titmuss, R. M. (1958). *Essays on the welfare state*. London: George Allen & Unwin.

Titmuss, R. M. (1968). *Commitment to welfare*. London: George Allen & Unwin.

Titmuss, R. M. (1974). *Social Policy*. London: George Allen and Unwin.

Tolsdorf, C. C. (1976). Social networks, support and coping: An exploratory study. *Family Process 15*, 407–417.

Tracy, E. M. (1990). Identifying social support resources of at-risk families. *Social Work 35*, 252–258.

Tracy, E. M. (1993). Social network mapping: An exercise for teaching about social support. *Journal of Teaching in Social Work 7*, 37–46.

Tracy, E. M. (1995). Family Preservation Services. *Encyclopedia of Social Work* (19th ed.). Washington, DC: National Association of Social Workers.

Tracy, E. M., & Abell, N. (1994). The social network map: Some further refinements on administration. *Social Work Research 18*, 56–60.

Tracy, E. M., Biegel, D., & Corvo, K. (1991). *A training program for case managers: Social network interventions with persons with severe mental disabilities*. Prepared for the Cuyahoga County Mental Health Board. Cleveland: Center for Practice Innovations, Mandel School of Applied Social Sciences, Case Western Reserve University.

Tracy, E. M., Catalano, R. C., Whittaker, J. K., & Fine, D. (1990). Methodological note: Reliability of social network data. *Social Work Research & Abstracts 26*, 33–35.

Tracy, E. M., Green, R. K., & Bremseth, M. D. (1993). *Meeting the environmental needs of abused and neglected children: Implications from a statewide survey of supportive services. Social Work Research and Abstracts, 29*(2), 21–26.

Tracy, E. M., & McDonell, J. R. (1991). Home-based work with families: The environmental context of family intervention. *Journal of Independent Social Work 5*, 93–108

Tracy, E. M., & Whittaker, J. K. (1987). The evidence base for social support interventions in child and family practice: Emerging issues for research and practice. *Children and Youth Services Review 9*, 249–270.

Tracy, E. M., & Whittaker, J. K. (1990). The Social Network Map: Assessing social support in clinical social work practice. *Families in Society 71*, 461–470.

Tracy, E. M., & Whittaker, J. K. (1991). Social network assessment and goal setting in intensive family preservation services practice. In E. M. Tracy, J. Kinney, D. Haapala, & P. Pecora (Eds.), *Intensive family preservation services: An instructional sourcebook*. Cleveland: Mandel School of Applied Social Sciences.

Tracy, E. M., Whittaker, J. K., Boylan, F., Neitman, P., & Overstreet, E. (1995). Network interventions with high-risk youth and families throughout the continuum of care. In I. M. Schwartz & P. AuClaire (Eds.), *Home-based services for troubled youth* (pp. 55–72). Lincoln: University of Nebraska Press.

Tracy, E. M., Whittaker, J. K., & Mooradian, J. K. (1990). *Training resources on social networks and social supports.* Prepared for the Social Networks Projects, Boysville of Michigan. Unpublished material available from the authors.

Tracy, E. M., Whittaker, J. K., Pugh, A., Kapp, S., & Overstreet, E. J. (1994). Social networks of primary caregivers receiving family preservation services. *Families in Society 75,* 481–489.

Trattner, W. I. (1989). *From poor law to welfare state: A history of social welfare in America* (4th ed.). New York: Free Press.

Trolander, J. A. (1987). *Professionalism and social change: From the settlement house movement to neighborhood centers, 1886 to the present.* New York: Columbia University Press.

Tuan, Y.-F. (1977). *Space and place: The perspective of experience.* Minneapolis: University of Minnesota Press.

Uehara, E. S., Sohng, S. S. L., Bending, R. L., Seyfried, S., Richey, C. A., Morelli, P., Spencer, M., Ortega, D., Keenan, L., & Kanuha, V. (1996). Towards a value-based approach to multicultural social work research. *Social Work 41,* 613–624.

Unger, D. G., & Powell, D. R. (1980). Supporting families under stress: The role of social networks. *Family Relations 29,* 566–574.

Valentine, G. (1989). The geography of women's fear. *Area 21*(4), 385–390.

Valentine, G. (1993a). Desperately seeking Susan: A geography of lesbian friendships. *Area 25,* 109–116.

Valentine, G. (1993b). (Hetero)sexing space: Lesbian perceptions and experiences of everyday spaces. *Environment and Planning D: Society and Space 11,* 395–413.

Valentine, G. (1994). Toward a geography of the lesbian community. *Women and Environments* (summer/fall), 8–10.

Valentine, G. (1995). Out and about: Geographies of lesbian landscapes. *International Journal of Urban and Regional Research 19,* 96–111.

Van Den Bergh, N. (Ed.) (1995). *Feminist practice in the 21st century.* Washington, DC: National Association of Social Workers.

Vandenberg, J. (1993). Integration of individualized child mental health services into the system of care for children and adolescents. Children's mental health administration [Special issue]. *Administration and Policy in Mental Health 20,* 247–257.

Vaux, A. (1985). Variations in social support associated with gender, ethnicity and age. *Journal of Social Issues 41,* 89–110.

Vaux, A., Burda, P., & Stewart, D. (1986). Orientation toward utilization of support resources. *Journal of Community Psychology 11,* 159–170.

Vosler, N. R. (1990). Assessing family access to basic resources: An essential component of social work practice. *Social Work 35,* 434–441.

Wahler, R. G. (1980). The insular mother: Her problem in parent treatment. *Journal of Applied Behavior Analysis 13,* 207–219.

Wahler, R. G., Leske, G., & Rogers, E. S. (1979). The insular family: A deviance support system for oppositional children. In L. A. Hamerlynck (Ed.), *Behavioral systems for the developmentally disabled. I. School and family environments* (pp. 102–127). New York: Bruner/Mazel.

Wahler, R. G. (1990). Some perceptual functions of social networks in coercive mother-child interactions. Social support in social and clinical psychology. *Journal of Social and Clinical Psychology 9 [Special issue]*, 43–53.

Wakefield, J. K. (1996a). Does social work need the eco-systems perspective? Part I: Is the perspective clinically useful? *Social Service Review 70*, 1–32.

Wakefield, J. K. (1996b). Does social work need the eco-systems perspective? Part II: Does the perspective save social work from incoherence? *Social Service Review 70*, 183–213.

Walker, P. (1995). Community based is not community: The social geography of disability. In S. J. Taylor, R. Bogdan, & Z. M. Lutfiyya (Eds.), *The variety of community experience: Qualitative studies of family and community life* (pp. 175–192). Baltimore: Paul Brookes.

Wandersman, A., & Florin, P. (Eds.) (1990). Citizen participation, voluntary organizations and community development: Insights for empowerment through research. *American Journal of Community Psychology 18* [Special section].

Ward, R. A., LaGory, M., & Sherman, S. R. (1988). *The environment for aging: Interpersonal, social and spatial contexts.* Tuscaloosa: University of Alabama Press.

Warren, R. B., & Warren, D. I. (1977). *The neighborhood organizer's handbook.* Notre Dame, IN: University of Notre Dame Press.

Webb, N. B. (1996). *Social work practice with children.* New York: Guilford.

Webb, A., & Wistrow, G. (1987). *Social work, social care, and social planning: The personal social services since Seebohm.* London: Longman.

Weick, A., Rapp, C., Sullivan, W. P., & Kisthardt, W. (1989). A strengths perspective for social work practice. *Social Work 34*, 350–354.

Weick, A., & Saleebey, D. (1995). *A postmodern approach to social work practice.* The 1995 Richard Lodge Memorial Lecture, Adelphi University School of Social Work, New York.

Weil, M. (1996). Community building: Building community practice. *Social Work 41*, 481–501.

Weinstein, C. S., & David, T. G. (1987). *Spaces for children: The built environment and child development.* New York: Plenum.

Weisman, L. K. (1992). *Discrimination by design: A feminist critique of the man-made environment.* Urbana: University of Illinois Press.

Weiss, H. B. (1985). "Preface." In Family Resource Coalition, *Programs to strengthen families* (pp. 1–6). Chicago: Family Resource Coalition.

Weissbourd, B. (1990). Family resource and support programs: Changes and challenges in human services. *Prevention in Human Services 99*, 69–85.

Wells, K., & Whittington, D. (1990). Prior services used by youth referred to mental health facilities: A closer look. *Children and Youth Services Review 12*, 243–256.

Wells, K., Wyatt, E., & Hobfall, S. (1991). Factors associated with adaptation of youths discharged from residential treatment. *Children and Youth Services Review 13*, 199–217.

Werner, E. E. (1989). High-risk children in young adulthood: A longitudinal study from birth to 32 years. *American Journal of Orthopsychiatry 59*, 72–81.

Werner, E. E. (1995). Resilience in development. *Current Directions in Psychological Science 4*, 81–85.

Werner, E. E., Bierman, J., & French, F. (1971). *The children of Kauai*. Honolulu: University of Hawaii Press.

Werner, E. E., & Smith, R. S. (1977). *Kauai's children come of age*. Honolulu: University of Hawaii Press.

Werner, E. E., & Smith, R. S. (1982). *Vulnerable but invincible: A longitudinal study of resilient children and youth*. New York: McGraw-Hill.

Werner, E. E., & Smith, R. S. (1992). *Overcoming the odds: high-risk children from birth to adulthood*. Ithaca, NY: Cornell University Press.

White, M., & Epston, D. (1990). *Narrative means to therapeutic ends*. New York: Norton.

Whitmore, E. (1991). Evaluation and empowerment: It's the process that counts. *Networking Bulletin, Cornell Empowerment Project 2*, 1–7.

Whittaker, J. K. (1974). *Social treatment: An approach to interpersonal helping*. Hawthorne, NY: Aldine de Gruyter.

Whittaker, J. K. ([1979] 1997). *Caring for troubled children*. Hawthorne, NY: Aldine de Gruyter.

Whittaker, J. K., & Garbarino, J. (Eds.) (1983). *Social support networks: Informal helping in the human services*. Hawthorne, NY: Aldine de Gruyter.

Whittaker, J. K., Kinney, J., Tracy, E., M., & Booth, C. (Eds.) (1990). *Reaching high risk families: Intensive family preservation services in human services*. Hawthorne, NY: Aldine de Gruyter.

Whittaker, J. K., & Pfeiffer, S. (1994). Research priorities for residential group child care. Special Issue: A research agenda for child welfare. *Child Welfare 73*, 583–601.

Whittaker, J. K., Schinke, S. P., & Gilchrist, L. D. (1986). The ecological paradigm in child, youth, and family services: Implications for policy and practice. *Social Service Review 60*, 483–503.

Whittaker, J. K., & Tracy, E. M. (1989). *Social treatment: An introduction to interpersonal helping in social work practice* (2nd ed.). Hawthorne, NY: Aldine de Gruyter.

Whittaker, J. K., & Tracy, E. M. (1990). Social network intervention in intensive family-based preventive services. *Prevention in the Human Services 9*, 175–192.

Whittaker, J. K., Tracy, E. M., & Marckworth, M. (1989). *Family Support Project: Identifying informal support resources for high risk families*. Seattle: University of Washington, School of Social Work.

Whittaker, J. K., Tracy, E. M., Overstreet, E., Mooradian, J., & Kapp, S. (1994). Intervention design for practice: Enhancing social support for high risk youth and families. In J. Rothman & E. J. Thomas (Eds.), *Intervention research: Designing and developing human service interventions* (pp. 195–212). New York: Haworth.

Williams, J. B. W., Karls, J. M., & Wandrei, K. (1989). The person-in-environment (PIE) system for describing problems of social functioning. *Hospital and Community Psychiatry 40*, 1125–1127.

Wilson, W. J. (1980). *The declining significance of race: Blacks and changing American institutions* (2nd ed.). Chicago: University of Chicago Press.

Wilson, W. J. (1987). *The truly disadvantaged: The inner city, the underclass and public policy.* Chicago: University of Chicago Press.

Wilson, W. J. (1996). *When work disappears: The world of the new urban poor.* New York: Knopf.

Wolfe, M. (1992). Invisible women in invisible places: Lesbians, lesbian bars and the social production of people/environment relationships. *Architecture and Behavior 18,* 111–221.

Wolfe, M., & Rivlin, L. G. (1987). The institutions in children's lives. In C. S. Weinstein & T. G. David (Eds.), *Spaces for children: The built environment and child development* (pp. 89–114). New York: Plenum.

Wolfensberger, W. (1972). *Normalization.* New York: National Institute on Mental Retardation.

Woodward, L. E. (1960). Increasing social work effectiveness in meeting mental health needs. *Social Work 5,* 59–69.

Wyman, P. A., Cowen, E. L., Work, W. C., Raoof, A., et al. (1992). Interviews with children who experienced major life stress: Family and child attributes that predict resilient outcomes. *Journal of the American Academy of Child and Adolescent Psychiatry 31*(5), 904–910.

York, S., & Itzhaky, H. (1991). How can we measure the effects of client participation on the effectiveness of social work intervention? *British Journal of Social Work 21,* 647–661.

Yourdin, E. (1989). *Modern structured analysis.* Englewood Cliffs, NJ: Yourdon.

Zalenski, J. (1994). A new/old practice to care for children: New Zealand's family decision making model. *Prevention Report* (spring), 11–14.

Zastrow, C. (1995). *The practice of social work* (5th ed.). Pacific Grove, CA: Brooks/Cole.

Zimbalist, S. E. (1970). Mobilization for Youth: The search for a new social work. *Social Work 15,* 123–128.

Zimet, G., Dahlem, N., Zimet, S., & Farkey, G. (1988). The Multidimensional Scale of Perceived Social Support. *Journal of Personality Assessment 52,* 30–41.

Zimmerman, M. A., & Rappaport, J. (1988). Citizen participation, perceived control, and psychological empowerment. *American Journal of Community Psychology 16,* 725–750.

Zimmerman, M. A., & Zahniser, J. H. (1991). Refinements of sphere-specific measures of perceived control: Development of a Sociopolitical Control Scale. *Journal of Community Psychology 19,* 189–204.

Author Index

Abbott, A. D., 30
Abell, N., 116, 173–174
Aber, J. L., 73
Adams, P., 208–209
Adler, S., 183, 185
Agnew, J., 63
Agus (or Angus?), J. H., 170, 172
Allen, L., 73
Altman, I., 85, 180, 189–190
Ammons, P. W., 155
Andrews, Scott, 188
Antonovsky, Aaron, 6, 66, 192
Antonucci, T. C., 109
Arkinson, M. K., 143, 170
Atkin, B., 107–108, 170, 172
Auerswald, E. H., 43
Austin, L. M., 31
Avery, L. S., 143, 170
Ayidiya, S., 78

Bailey, D., 167
Baker, A., 78
Baldassari, C., 190
Baldwin, A. L., 82
Baldwin, C. P., 82
Baldwin, S., 209
Bamford, T., 209
Bannister, R. C., 23
Ban, P., 172
Barnard, R. E., 73
Barrera, M., 74
Barry, M. M., 79
Barsh, E. T., 146
Barthelemy, K., 78
Bartlett, H. M., 39, 41
Beardslee, W. R., 81–82
Bechtel, R. B., 58

Beckett, J. O., 108
Behrman, J. A., 123
Bell, D. J., 183, 185
Belle, D. E., 74
Bell, P. J., 184
Benard, B., 80
Bereson, B., 193
Berger, P. L., 64
Berlin, S. B., 64, 163
Berlin, R., 82
Berman-Rossi, T., 28
Bernheim, K. F., 141, 202
Best, K. M., 81
Biegel, D. E., 72, 109, 121, 143, 209
Bierman, J., 80
Billingsley, A., 72
Birt, C. J., 7
Bisno, H., 48
Black, W. G., 29
Blunt, A., 63
Boden, D., 63
Bohm, David, 58
Bondi, L., 60
Bonecutter F. J., 115
Booth, C., 76, 97
Borgatta, E. F., 125
Boyd, C., 75
Boyer, P., 23, 26, 47, 62
Boylan, F., 107
Boyte, H. C., 68–69, 184
Bradford, J., 184
Bradley, R. H., 192
Bradshaw, C., 96
Brager, G., 126
Brassard, J. A., 71
Braziel, D. G., 133
Bremseth, M. D., 133

Maguire, P., 56
Maluccio, Anthony, 3, 59, 70, 73, 105
Marckworth, M., 115
Marrow, A. J., 2
Massey, D., 63
Mast, D., 75
Masten, A. S., 80–81
Mattaini, M. A., 91, 95, 102, 106, 114, 125–126
Mehr, J., 150
Meltzer, N. J., 155
Memmott, J., 144
Merle, S., 39
Meyer, Carol H., 21, 39, 41–44, 70, 73, 91, 95, 114
Michelson, W., 180
Miler, S. D., 61
Miley, K., 54
Miley, K. K., 134
Millar, M., 30
Miller, (?), 75
Miller, H., 39
Miller, I., 28
Miller, J. Y., 79
Mills, C. Wright, 8
Minahan, A., 16
Minahan, H., 41
Mishler, E., 64
Moen, P., 193, 200
Mohai, P., 178
Moncher, F. J., 115
Monk, J., 180, 182
Mooradian, J. K., 113–114, 119
Moore, J. A., 146
Moos, R. H., 85
Moreno, J. L., 125
Morin, R. C., 116, 146
Mowbray, C. T., 149
Mullen, Dumpson, & Associates, 39
Mullen, E. J., 39
Murray, M., 178
Murty, S. A., 109

Nagda, B. A., 60, 178
Naparstek, A. J., 209

National Association of Social Workers, 134
Neitman, P., 106
Nestman, F., 158
Netting, F. E., 89, 128
Neugeboren, Bernard, 135, 204–206, 209
Niego, S., 108
Nixon, Richard, 39
Norelius, K. I., 155
Norman, E., 81
Norman, G. R., 143
Norton, D., 126
Nurius, P. S., 64, 95

O'Brien, D., 78
O'Brien, P., 157
Oja, S. N., 167
Olds, D., 73
O'Melia, B., 54
Oretega, R., 53
Oritt, E. J., 123
Overstreet, E. J., 108, 114, 129–130

Pain, R., 181
Pancoast, D., 142
Pancoast, D. L., 141–142
Pandey, J., 76
Parker, G., 81
Parker, P., 141
Parsons, R. J., 53, 151, 154
Patterson, S. L., 144
Patti, R. J., 200
Paul, L., 56
Paul, S. C., 123
Pavelsky, P. K., 148
Payne, D. N., 209
Pecora, P. J., 8, 98
Pennell, J., 116, 146, 171–172
Perkins, Frances, 27–28
Perlman, Helen Harris, 39
Pfeiffer, S., 133
Phillips, B. U., 109
Pierce, G. R., 75
Pile, S., 63
Pincus, A., 16

Subject Index

EAI, 124
Ecological systems theory, 70–73
Ecological theory, 41–43
Ecological transition, 72
Ecological validity, 14, 72, 196, 201
Ecology of human development, 3
Ecomap, 103, 125–126
Ecosystems perspective, 43–44
Education, 55–57
Elderly, 193–196
Elizabethan Poor Laws, 26
Empowerment theory and practice,
    13, 52–59
Environment (*See also* Levels of envi-
    ronment; Marginalization of
    environment)
  actual, 31
  aspects of, 96–100
  bridging person and, 41–44
  critical and constructivist views of,
    63–69
  definition of, 84–85, 93
  dimensions of, 86
  diversity of environmental experi-
    ence and, 177–180
  exosystem, 71
  institutional/organizational, 10–11,
    86, 105, 126–127
  interest in, renewed, 63–64
  macrosystem, 72
  meaning of, 64–66
  mesosystem, 71
  metaphorical, 31
  microsystem, 71
  as multidimensional concept, 3–4
  nurturing/sustaining, 126
  participatory, 69
  perceived, 10, 105, 123–124
  person-environment transactions
    and, 68–69
  physical, 10, 73–79, 86, 105,
    124–125
  "politics of place" and, 66–68
  poverty and, 47–48
  power and, 66–68
  social, 73–79, 159–163

social/political/cultural, 11, 86,
    105–106, 127–128
  toxins and hazards in, 179
Environmental assessment
  case vignettes, 128–130
  data sources for, 94–96
  definition of, 85–86
  ecomap, 103, 125–126
  environmental intervention and,
    166–168
  frameworks for, 96–108
  guidelines for, 117–121
  helping stage and, 107–108
  as knowledge foundation for
    environmentally-oriented
    practice, 85–86
  micro and macro approaches to,
    bridging, 89–90
  in person-environment practice,
    91–94
  social network map, 107–117
  in social work practice, 90–91
  strategic and multidimensional,
    10–11
  tools and methods, summarizing,
    123–128
  underdevelopment of, 89
Environmental Assessment Index
    (EAI), 124
Environmental change, 11, 137–139
Environmental competence, 190
Environmental intervention
  choice of, 164–165
  definition of, 86–88
  in Depression years, 30–37
  diversity of environmental experi-
    ence and, 158–159
  environmental assessment and,
    166–168
  environmental change and, 137–
    139
  Family Group Decision-Making
    Project, 170–172
  focus of, 3, 163–164
  Freud and the Americans and,
    28–30